THE BEST AUSTRALIAN
ESSAYS
2014

THE BEST AUSTRALIAN
ESSAYS

EDITED BY ROBERT MANNE

Black Inc.

Published by Black Inc.,
an imprint of Schwartz Publishing Pty Ltd

37–39 Langridge Street
Collingwood Vic 3066 Australia
email: enquiries@blackincbooks.com
www.blackincbooks.com

ISBN 9781863956956 (pbk)
ISBN 9781922231871 (ebook)

Printed in Australia by Griffin Press. The paper this book is printed on
is certified against the Forest Stewardship Council® Standards.
Griffin Press holds FSC chain of custody certification SGS-COC-005088.
FSC promotes environmentally responsible, socially beneficial
and economically viable management of the world's forests.

FSC
www.fsc.org
MIX
Paper from
responsible sources
FSC® C009448

Contents

CONTENTS

CONTENTS

Introduction

This is the second innings of my invitation to edit *The Best Australian Essays*. By now I have a clearer view of the task. Originally, I had thought of an *essay* as any brief piece of non-fiction prose. I no longer do. I have learnt on the job what I think an essay is by discovering what I think it is not.

An essay is not an article written for an academic journal, with its specialist audience, arcane language and scholarly apparatus of references and endnotes. Nor is it a piece of long-form journalism whose purpose is to report objectively on one or another state of affairs where the voice of the author is (or at least appears to be) erased. Although some essays might begin their life as speeches – I once heard Isaiah Berlin deliver his dazzling essay on Turgenev, 'Fathers and Children', in a baroque theatre in Oxford – an essay is not the record of the kind of speech that cuts corners and deploys rhetoric to stir the political passions of an audience. What is it, then?

For me at least, an essay is a reasonably short piece of prose in which we hear a distinctive voice attempting to recollect or illuminate or explain one or another aspect of the world. It follows from this that no essay could be jointly authored. It also follows that, with an essay, we trust that the distinctive voice we hear is truthful or authentic, even when perhaps it is not. One of the essays I most admire is George Orwell's 'Shooting an Elephant', which I read as a schoolboy. I was rather shocked when I later learned that the incident which the author recollects in the first person might have been an invention. Sometimes, as with one of my favourites in this collection, the line between the essay and the short story can be unnervingly unclear.

What, then, is an *Australian* essay? Originally, I thought the answer to this question was straightforward. An Australian essay was one written by an Australian citizen, resident or expatriate. On the job, I have come to think things are a little more complicated. Sometimes an essay written by an Australian has nothing to do with Australia, and is obviously written with a particular non-Australian audience in mind. I am reluctant to think of this kind of essay as Australian. Sometimes, on the other hand, an essay written by an outsider is so revealing about an aspect of this country that I think of it as an Australian essay.

Last year I included an essay on Australia and coal by the world's leading global-warming activist, who had paid us a fleeting visit. This year I have included an essay by an American who, disguised as an asylum seeker, journeyed from Afghanistan to Christmas Island. I have included it because, for us, the asylum-seeker issue is now so overshadowed by two decades of cultural combat that in its compassionate but cool-headed empiricism it is the kind of essay no Australian could write.

There is another dimension to this question. While some of the essays collected here have no direct connection to Australia – on Kafka, or the poetry of D.H. Lawrence, or Doris Lessing, or the television masterpiece *True Detective* – in each case they reflect the fact that they are written by an author deeply engaged in and sensitive to the intellectual life of this country. It is also important to me that the majority of the essays either directly or indirectly concern what is truly distinctive about this country's history, politics, culture, society or landscape. Although thoughts about this question were not in my mind as I made the selection, it now strikes me as obvious that an annual collection of Australian essays which is not vitally interested in the peculiar and particular quality of life in this country would be both odd and somehow disconcerting.

How does one decide what are the year's *best* essays? This is the most difficult issue of all. Some essays in this collection plunged me into thought. Some caused me to weep. Some brought tears of laughter. Some essays won me over by the power of their writers' imaginations. Some by their analytic clarity. Some by their excruciating honesty. Some by the pain of things past or present faced without flinching. Two forced their way into the collection by a single final line. I was attracted to several striking memoirs – which seems to me, as it did last year, one of the strongest forms of the contemporary essay – but not to those that seemed self-preoccupied. I was also attracted to serious essays but irritated, perhaps unduly, by the quality of earnestness. It was important to me that there was a balance not only of gender but also of age.

Inevitably, many of the essays I regarded as this year's best were written by this country's most admired writers. Two of my personal favourites, however, were written by authors almost entirely unknown to the general public. The collection moves from the private to the public world, and from the specific to the general. My hope is that through its order (concerning which I am obsessed) it will add up to at least a little more than the sum of its parts. There were very many essays I would have liked to include for which there was insufficient space. To these authors I offer apology. There is no task more likely to cause unintended offence than editing a collection of best anythings. Before writing this introduction I asked if I might see the page proofs. Only then did I realise what the word 'best' meant for me. It was an essay that one had already read several times and looked forward to reading again.

Sincere thanks are due to the in-house editor of this collection, Siân Scott-Clash; to my very good friends and collaborators in many enterprises, the estimably intelligent publisher at Black Inc., Chris Feik, and its creative and generous guiding spirit, Morry Schwartz; and above all to the authors in this collection, whose words helped restore flagging faith in this presently wayward but fundamentally decent and interesting country.

Robert Manne

The Percheron

Moreno Giovannoni

Listen to me. I am going to tell you a story about America in the days when there was poverty in San Ginese and we used to go there to make money. I will try my best to tell it well, with skilful use of words and with the addition of some feeling from my heart.

*

At the age of twenty-four my father Vitale started working for the Madera Canyon Pine Company in California as a Whistle Punk. From Whistle Punk he was promoted to Teamster. His favourite horse was a docile, intelligent giant of an animal, a French Percheron.

The Percheron waited patiently for the man to tell him when to start pulling, when to stop, when to back up. Vitale, who had been living at an Italian working men's hotel in Fresno before moving to the logging camp, spoke no English. He was lonely in California and missed his family and the life of the village so the horse was a welcome companion.

Although there was a good camaraderie between the men in the camp, and the team even included some Italians from north of Venice near the Austrian border, who were expert timber-cutters and tree-fellers, Vitale was most at home with his loyal Percheron. He was what was known then as a proper Tuscan peasant and knew the proper Tuscan peasant's work. This meant he was used to working with animals, in particular the cows back in the village that pulled the haycarts and ploughs and gave milk that was made into butter and cheese and every year gave birth to a calf which could be sold. The stable near the back door of the kitchen at his father's house always housed one or two cows and their calves.

Now that he was responsible for looking after a horse, feeding it, grooming it, making sure it was strong and healthy and happy and ready to pull the log, stop or back up, Vitale was proud. He was the Whistle Punk when he first started, as this was the work they gave to young or inexperienced men, and he was proud of his promotion to Teamster. In San Ginese only the rich people owned horses and looking after this horse made him feel rich.

He was happy that he could at least feel rich as his American adventure had not been as successful as he had hoped it would be. In seven years he had earned his own living but had not made his fortune. That would come soon but he did not know it yet. He intended to return to Italy when the time was right and marry. That too would come, but in the pine forest that day he was reflecting on his bad luck and felt disappointment and frustration.

*

The day before the incident government officials visited the logging camp and asked him and the other men a lot of questions. The officials completed a form with all his details. They asked him whether he claimed exemption from the military draft and he said he did claim it. He did not want to join the army because he wanted to look after his parents (or 'folks', as the American official wrote on the draft card). This was not the only time they had come looking for him and he was always worried that they were going to conscript him. Although he did not know this at the time, this had already happened to two brothers of his future wife, who were from a neighbouring village (Colognora, which had an ancient cherry tree his Australian grandson would climb one day). So his future brothers-in-law were drafted and sent to fight in France. What he did know was that right now there was a war in Europe and he did not want to go to the war. He managed to lie low and on a few occasions when he felt it would be safer to hide, he hid. Even his employers helped hide him, so that after the war he was able to return to Italy without serving in the army of the United States of America.

As he was reflecting on his poor American luck he was also troubled by this official visit. Thoughts of bad luck and ominous officialdom chased each other through his head and gave him no rest the night before the incident.

On that day the Percheron was reluctant to follow the man's instructions. He sensed the man was distracted. The Percheron waited to be acknowledged, for his presence to be appreciated. Just a word, a friendly tap on the shoulder. He could not work unless he sensed the partnership between him and the man. Then he realised that not only was the man distracted but that he himself was too. He could no longer read the signals coming from the man. He didn't know whether he was being asked to pull or stop or back up. Having failed to establish the working rapport he tried very hard to work without it but kept getting it wrong. And yet they had worked together for several months now. The horse loved the man and responded well to him. He sensed that the man was an experienced handler of draft animals, although the horse didn't think of himself in those terms exactly. He didn't think of himself as a draft animal. The Percheron thought of himself as himself.

Vitale knew that the only way to work with a horse was to use a psychological approach, because a man's strength cannot match that of a horse. He normally tried to anticipate the horse's likely behaviour and gently and consistently encouraged responses consistent with the needs of the work. So what happened that day was a shock to both the man and the horse. Vitale was surprised to learn that he was capable of doing such a thing, he who in his later life, as he grew to be very old, would have a reputation in the village and the surrounding district for gentleness of manner and whose son would tell stories to his grandchildren about their gentle grandfather. When the village spoke about him decades later mention was made also of his father Tista, from whom the mild manners were inherited, and how the gentle nature was in the blood of the family.

Vitale spoke to the horse and tugged and tapped the horse in the usual way, and the Percheron did not move. He called out again, louder, and shook the reins. The horse tried to back up.

Vitale lost his temper and picked up a tree branch from the floor of the pine forest and struck the horse on the side of the head.

*

Now, the eyesight of horses is designed to see well for grazing and looking out for danger at the same time, but they adjust their range of vision by lowering and raising their head. Horses are also a little colour-blind. In the pine forest the Percheron could see the green of the trees but not the browns and greys of the carpet of pine needles, could see the blue of the sky but not the white of the clouds. In what is therefore a landscape resembling a drab mosaic, objects that are still convey very little information to a horse. Nor can horses see things nearer than three feet directly in front of their faces without moving their heads.

The Percheron did not see the blow coming, although the man was quite close to him.

Maybe it was his mind churning over the bad luck, the government officials, their questions, the war. Perhaps it was his true secret nature, tired of being buried under the gentleness and kindness that would become his trademark, that for once in his life ripped its way out of his guts and into the freedom at last of the warm June air.

The horse quickly pulled back and reared up and away from the blow, tossed its head and screamed, pawed at the ground and continued screaming in pain. The scream of a horse may sometimes be referred to as a whinny or a neigh but these words may disguise the horror a horse can feel. A horse can indeed scream and it is a horrible thing to hear.

Hidden in the screams was a frantic wish for the pain to stop and a prayer that it would go away, and panic at a world that had turned upside down in an instant. The man was a stranger suddenly and a monster.

But the eyeball had popped out of its socket and was split and the horse was blind in one eye.

Vitale pulled hard and held the leather reins tight to prevent the horse from bolting. He struggled with his friend the horse and spoke to him reassuringly. He was finally acknowledging the horse's willing presence. He hid his own disgust at his own violence from himself as well as he could. When the horse had calmed down and was crying in silence and Vitale was exhausted, not only physically but also in his emotions, and barely still holding on, he removed his shirt and wrapped it around the horse's head and over the frightening eye. He took water from the drinking bucket and soaked the improvised bandage hoping the cool would soothe the pain.

With the noise of the horse some of the other men came running. Vitale understood the enormity of what he had done. He told the boss that the horse had walked into a low-hanging branch and had poked its eye out and that he had done his best to calm it down. See how he had bandaged the head? The gentle man accompanied the Percheron back to the camp in silence, one hand stroking the thick, powerful neck. The precise details of the Percheron's fate after this are not known as Vitale did not remain with the Madera Canyon Pine Company much longer.

Soon after, he left the logging camp and continued working in the vineyards around Fresno where he made his fortune.

*

I was a little boy when my father Vitale told me this story and I cried all night at the thought of the large, innocent, blind horse. My father later added a brief epilogue to the story of the blinding, and that was that the horse continued to work with one good eye. When I became a man and reflected on this I wondered whether this little addition to the story was true or whether my father made it up. I also wondered why my father would tell me the story of the Percheron, and decided that it

*was because the truth is sometimes necessary, especially to a gentle man
seeking absolution.*

*After I had emigrated to Australia and had been away sixty years and
my father was long dead, I myself having reached the age at which he
died, the time came when all that was left for me was to reflect on certain
events in my own life. It was then that I imagined that sometimes at
night, in the silence of the old house, my father Vitale, the gentle man
who lived to be eighty-nine and whom everybody loved, remembered the
Percheron and wept.*

Southerly

The Little Prince, and Other Vehicles

Rozanna Lilley

My first car was an apple-green Ford Escort. At least, that's what I like to say. Certainly, it was the first car I drove without immediately having an accident.

I was almost thirty by the time I actually got my licence. It wasn't for lack of trying. When I finished secondary school I hired an instructor. I can't recall much about him, except that his portly middle luxuriously enfolded the handbrake. Even then, I couldn't entirely blame him for my tendency to crunch the gears. One sultry afternoon in the backstreets of Darlinghurst he asked me, concerned, about my secondary school results. I reluctantly told him I had a score that could get me into any university degree. I could tell that he couldn't reconcile my academic aptitude with my driving ineptitude.

Later, when I'd got a bit older and less steady, I had another stab at driving. I was living in a share house in an inner-city suburb. I liked the terrace because it had a stable door that swung out to a brick courtyard. My room was a separate building to the side of the courtyard. I even had my own bathroom. There was a back gate as well, so it was easy to come and go. Lovers, too, could enter and exit with impunity. Mainly it was the stable door that gave these encounters a triflingly suspended sense of the romantic. On a good day, it provided a kind of quasi-rural framing to all that haystack volatility. Seeing half of something tends to be more palatable than a vista.

I shared the courtyard terrace with two young women and a man I was later to fall in love with. He occupied another room abutting the courtyard thereby gaining a ringside seat to the circus of my early twenties. Anthony watched the passing parade for about a year, giving deft nicknames, like 'Speedy Sam', to my boyfriends. Eventually he'd seen enough and decided he may as well take me in.

Tiffany had a part-time job as a chef. She worked for the underworld giant Abe Saffron. Mr Big required discreet lunches with other 'businessmen' in private dining rooms. She never said much about her kitchen preparations but I know for a fact that, at least before his lonely suicide in his ageing mother's spare bedroom, he was partial to home-cooked quiche.

Vixen was a seemingly quiet slip of a girl. She slept in the attic and sometimes had a girlfriend, rippling with muscles and illustrated with tattoos, drop by for boisterous S&M sessions. Anthony swore that Vixen was the dominatrix. Often, though, I would find her in the living room late at night, hunched around my vertical record player, tears spilling over to the maudlin refrains of 'Will You Still Love Me Tomorrow?' Once, when stoned, she climbed into my bed, claiming loneliness. That night I didn't sleep a wink.

Vixen usually drove a motorbike. But sometimes she had brief possession of a car. She wasn't the kind of person to just leave you alone with your inadequacies. So one evening she decided to teach me to drive. It was all going okay and, for a brief moment, I thought, 'Hey, this isn't so hard.' We turned a quiet corner. The road curved but somehow I needed to keep going straight. Vixen was shouting, 'Brake! Brake!' I'd never heard her raise her voice before. I'd only heard the low moans of pleasure emanating from above. I hit the accelerator instead and we ploughed through a low brick wall, gently nudging the front of a house.

The owner emerged. She was shaken and angry. We exchanged phone numbers and she noted the numberplate. Vixen and I repaired to the corner pub, for whiskey. Later I rang my dad. Back then I imagined he could fix anything. And sometimes, when I found myself in a tight corner, that was right. He drove an hour down what he called 'the big hill' from the Blue Mountains to talk to the aggrieved house owner. He offered to repair any damage himself. In these situations, he liked to use the phrase 'I'm a handyman.' After that, I didn't try driving again for quite a while.

Eventually I found myself married. In the scheme of things, Michael both preceded and followed Anthony. We met in the bar at the Sydney Opera House. I was a tour guide and he was a stage-hand. I was especially impressed that he was a divorcee. It seemed so alluringly adult. Michael claimed he couldn't drive. That wasn't really true. He always liked to pretend he was incapable, even to himself. Eventually he told me that he had been for his truck licence in New Zealand. The story was a set piece that involved hulking Maoris in lumberjack shirts, winding mountains and the risky boundary of the wooded wild. That was the good part. Then came a halting with fear sniffing around its edges. And, after that, a refusal to ever get behind the wheel again.

That's why I was, yet again, learning to drive. We'd moved from Sydney to Canberra. I was doing a PhD in anthropology. Mike got a job at the local theatre centre. My father, Merv, bought the Ford Escort for me. He liked, perhaps I should say loved, reading the ads in the *Weekly Trading Post*. Dad didn't really con-sult me about the car. Consultation wasn't part of his repertoire. One weekend he just delivered it, telling me I owed him the pur-chase price.

A decade was sandwiched somewhere between these two sets of driving lessons, peppered with part-time work, university degrees and failed relationships. My new instructor, Paul, was a Vietnam vet with a gammy leg. He was riddled with patience. He used to pick me up from the university and we would drive, for about thirty minutes once or twice a week, around the tranquil campus. Every time I saw a corner I accelerated. I just couldn't help it. We started on a manual. About thirty lessons in, and numerous near accidents later, he reluctantly told me I was only fit for an automatic. Even then, my parking was perfidious.

By this time I had a daughter. Paul advised me to try using her trike to figure out what happened to the wheels when reverse parking. I picked it up from the pathway at the side of our rented cottage. I tried manoeuvring it backwards through the irregular scatter of bricks and insolent buttersoft jonquils. I was so permanently tired that it didn't really help.

I failed my licence a couple of times. The first time I was behind a Stop sign. There was a police car crossing the intersection ahead. It seemed like an eternity that we were waiting there and I thought the examiner looked impatient. So I hit the accelerator, lurching forwards. The police car braked just in time. The examiner looked straight ahead, as though his life was one long series of disappointing appointments. In a clipped tone he commanded, 'Drive straight back to the Motor Registry.'

The second time I went for my test I was relieved to have a different examiner. He told me to turn right. With a flair for the literal, I did. It was just a pity that we weren't actually at a street yet. At least it was a parking lot and not a house.

Finally I had a female examiner. Paul had tried to coach me through my nerves. He even lied and told me I was a good driver. At that moment I felt genuinely fond of him. When I took the test the third time I explained how hard it was to have a little kid in Canberra and a husband who didn't drive and to be trying to study and pick your one-year-old daughter up in the dark from childcare and then take her home on the bus in the dead of a cold winter. She didn't say much. When it came time to reverse park she instructed me to try an opening about the size of three semi-trailers. At last I had passed my driving test.

I was so excited when I got my licence that I celebrated by going to Superbarn and buying a boot-load full of groceries. All the other drivers seemed to be dawdling, as though the toy town air had wound down their clockwork. A couple of days later I realised the speedometer measured miles not kilometres.

I paid my dad back the $800 for the Ford Escort. It wasn't easy on my scholarship with a husband who drank and smoked his way through his weekly pay packet. I gave Paul a slightly flirty thankyou card. It seemed the least I could do, given he'd seen action.

Of course that's not the whole story of my driving. My ambivalent feelings towards cars began, like most things do, in childhood. My mother rarely drove. She had little truck with the practical side of life. Like many spouses, Merv enjoyed small acts of domestic terrorism. If we were heading down a highway he might suddenly speed up. Breaking the limit, he would manoeuvre parallel to other cars, trying to egg their drivers into macho competition. I come from a family of five kids and there were always at least three of us in the back seat, sweat stuck to the vinyl, so many struggling moths. As the Valiant accelerated we would clutch the front seat, enthralled. Mum would begin screaming. Dad would start laughing. Then I'd laugh too, just to show I was on my father's side.

My father's driving was erratic. I was a teenager before I realised that he was colour-blind. Though even now I'm not sure if he was just toying with me. When we approached traffic lights he asked if they were red or green. He had a strong dislike of rules and of authority. He wasn't very interested in parking meters or sticking inside lanes. If he wanted to change direction he would just mount the concrete road divider and head the other way. Merv often remarked that he needed a truck or, at least, a four-wheel drive because most vehicles couldn't accommodate his expectations.

Childhood was punctuated by a litany of cars, each one momentarily cherished. There was the ute and the Valiant and, later, when we moved across the continent from Perth to Sydney, shedding my three stepbrothers along the way, something smaller. In caressing tones, Dad called his Morris Mini 'the little *dauphin*'. I had never heard my father speak a foreign language before. It was unnerving. He was so large and the car was so small, it was a constant surprise that he could fit inside. But Merv always was full of surprises.

Once he bought a bus. He'd been reading the *Trading Post* again. My parents' houses were littered with the detritus of Merv's sudden passions. There was a darkroom built and never used. There were four toilets, some never properly connected to the main plumbing. There was a fridge in the living room and a fridge in the laundry and a fridge in the kitchen. It is possible to be hungry anywhere. There was a potters wheel and an etching press and new sheds constructed to hold a dazzling array of tools, initially purchased with ardour and then recklessly abandoned.

But the bus stepped things up a notch. For a start, it cost more. Although my mother rarely complained about my father's unchecked impulses, she couldn't help feeling affronted by an unroadworthy vehicle, which ate substantially into their cheque account. She didn't want a bus. She knew they weren't really going anywhere. In fact, as the years passed she had become increasingly stationary. She may have longed for mobility but, as a writer, her travels were determinedly interior.

Eventually the bus was parked in the ample backyard of a friend's wife's father who lived in a fishing village down the South Coast. His name was 'Pappy' and I used to imagine him as having the insouciant manner and unpredictable charm of Popeye. Vague plans for the renovation of the bus circled through Merv's capacious mind for years. When my parents had a particularly explosive argument he sometimes threatened to live in the now rat-infested shell. But I knew that it was bluff because he could never abandon my mother. She needed him too much.

Usually when Dad tired of cars he would take them to the countryside and set fire to them. Then he would claim the insurance. When investigators phoned from the claims office, Dad spoke to them severely. His manner was poised between murderous threat and utter inscrutability. He had learned the language of intimidation in his younger years, working as a canecutter and a merchant seaman. They always paid up.

When I claimed the Ford Escort as my first car, I skipped a vehicle. Dad bought me another car when I was in my early twenties. But I never actually saw it. It was a time in my life when I didn't like visiting my parents. Partly I was exhausted with their quasi-bohemian eccentricities. Mainly I was busy growing up.

I suspect Dad actually meant to give me the car when he bought it. But I wasn't making any progress towards a licence. So he registered it in my name and then decided to use it himself. I'd forgotten all about the car until I got a call from Kings Cross police station, demanding I front up there. In the 1980s this particular station had a fearsome reputation for lawlessness. I took Anthony along for the ride. As both a rugby player and a law student, he seemed like a good travelling companion. We caught the train there and were ushered into a bare interview room. Inside I was presented with some stark facts. I had thousands of dollars in unpaid parking fines; I never attended court; unless I paid up I would be jailed.

At this point I paused. I had been raised to believe that the worst thing a person could be was 'a copper's nark'. My parents had both been Communists; they knew what it was like to be under ASIO surveillance. The law, and especially its officers, were held in familial contempt. However I didn't want to go to prison and so my self-preservation got the better of my loyalty. 'But I don't even drive,' I blurted out. 'What do you mean?' the incredulous policeman demanded. 'My father just registered the car in my name; he drives it,' I explained.

The policeman exited, leaving Anthony and me to ponder my fate. When he returned about fifteen minutes later, he looked unexpectedly furious. Taking his accustomed seat behind the grim-grey office desk, he leaned pointedly forwards, resting his weight on his formidable elbows and hissed, 'You didn't tell me you are Merv Lilley's daughter.'

A silence reverberated. I saw no option but to agree to his account of my lineage. He leaned back and cautioned: 'How often do you see your father?' 'Never,' I instantly replied. 'He's hard to pin down. I haven't seen him for ages.' The policeman sized me up. He exhaled, exhausted with the charade. 'You tell your father, next time you do see him, that one day soon we will catch him.' I nodded my assent. A few weeks later Merv did time for parking offences. He tried to talk it up but when he came out of jail he was, for a brief period, a quieter man.

My father continued driving into his nineties. At one point he bought a hearse. It was roomy and my mother could recline fully across the lustrous scarlet back seat. As Merv chauffeured her hither and thither, their journeys conjured another era of morbid glamour, or perhaps just another point along the time-line. When she had breast cancer he would ferry her, down the big hill, to hospital, parking the hearse, haphazardly, in the ambulance entry. Once the rehearsal was over, and death over-took her (despite their satirical efforts to drive mortality away), Dad travelled solo.

Occasionally he crashed a car. In his late eighties he rolled down an embankment on the way to the local gun club. Not long after his rifle was confiscated by police. They found it nestled in the mahogany wardrobe behind my mother's billowing caftans. I had hidden it there from him. But the cars remained, sprouting prodigiously in the rambling garden. His favourite was the boxy bare-boned Suzuki.

Merv was outraged when he had to sit for his licence again. The bureaucratic imperatives of old age were, he felt, an affront to his many decades on and off the road. He failed the test but appealed the decision. He was by then well known in the lower villages of the Blue Mountains. The hearse, the flamboyantly macho manner, a seemingly random tendency to recite long reams of poetry and outrageous forms of flirtation that usually bordered on something more dangerous had inevitably created infamy. The story of his successful driving licence appeal was written up in the local newspaper and Merv momentarily enjoyed basking in the tepid sunlight of gerontocratic heroism.

After Mum died, Dad lived alone for a decade. I would drive up the motorway from Sydney, inhaling the sprawling suburbs and finally crossing the familiar serpentine curve of the Nepean River. Dad had always left the talking to Mum, and it was hard for us to know what to say to each other. I busied myself unpacking weekly groceries and cleaning the chaotic kitchen. Sometimes Dad talked about the federal agents who followed him down the Great Western Highway. Or how politicians were inverting his words on the evening news. I cried silently into the soapsuds. One Sunday, grinning, he told me about an elderly lady who approached him as he sat on a bench, resting at the local shops. She made the mistake of asking if he was okay. He replied, 'Good day – for a rape.'

I only once drove my father. Merv isn't the kind of man to take kindly to being a passenger. By then I had another husband, Neil, a son and a navy blue Passat. The electronic sunroof never did keep middle age at bay.

It was the anniversary of my mother's death, and it was my habit to take flowers to her grave. We all mourn the passing of time in different temporalities. My sister is focused on lost birthdays while I memorialise Mum's final exit. Each year in August I recall how pitiful her last morphine-addled months were; the mournful linoleum expanse of the palliative care suite; her urgent and ultimately unanswerable pleas for help and the tender reliability of my father's unswerving loyalty.

One year I decided to take Dad with me to the graveside. When I picked him up from the house he was already surly with anxiety. He didn't like it when I set the agenda. With a lapse of judgement I'd bought a posy of artificial flowers. I worried that I only went to her graveside annually and that the bloom of my grief would too quickly perish. Dad looked at my offering with disdain. He had planted a Wollemi Pine on her grave; its prehistoric claims typical of Merv's monumentalisms. 'You know she hated plastic flowers,' came the snarky rebuke.

I sighed, decades of experience having taught me to never fight back, to roll the sneers and the incursions inside, tucked away in a tight spot. We travelled through some back roads, cutting across the railway line towards Springwood cemetery. Dad started yelling out, claiming I was too close to the side of the road and that we were going to have an accident. He was too used to being in the driver's seat. Then he uttered a high-pitched scream, followed by wild laughter. 'Shut the fuck up, Dorothy,' he viciously reprimanded. I was surprised to find myself driving both my mother and my father. Three is a tight squeeze – all those ghostly refrains jostling for a front seat view.

The home in the mountains, with its stately flagstone verandah bristling with the piled high detritus of Merv's spending sprees, is largely a memory now. These days there's a caretaker and a token fortnightly payment. I had to take my father from it. There were rats nesting in the microwave and scorch marks in the front room where he often slept. The burning embers from the open fireplace were a constant source of worry to the long-suffering fellow travellers next door. One day he phoned and said, uncharacteristically, 'I need help.' When I asked him what he needed help with, he replied, simply, 'Everything.' Neil and I collected him and we all drove together, one last time, down that big hill. Merv was as excited as if he were shipping out. He didn't comprehend that he was washing up back in Sydney for good.

Dad now lives in a nursing home, appropriately enough in Lilyfield, a suburb not far from me. My husband plays draughts with him each week, and always contrives to lose. When I visit Merv often remarks on Neil's perplexing inability to improve. 'Does he come here just so I can beat him?' he heckles, beaming with pleasure that he is still on top of his game. Sometimes Dad still asks after his last car, the Suzuki. I cannot bear to tell him that we sold it for scrap metal.

We sit and talk more easily now. Dad sometimes plans his escape, driving back up the motorway. 'I'd need to go there for a couple of days to make it worthwhile', he muses. 'The trouble is', he adds slyly, 'it's not easy to organise getting out of here.' When he returns to Faulconbridge he plans to water the fruit trees and cook some dampers in the ashes of the glowing fire. After that he'll make sure that at least the Suzuki is in good mechanical condition. If the battery is dead, he'll call the NRMA to start it for him again. Then he'll back it out the driveway, without, as usual, bothering to check the rear-view mirror, and drive, well, anywhere.

I'd like to spring my dad; to return him to his autonomy and to give back the gift of freedom's dignity I took away. But it's not possible.

These days I rarely drive. Walking seems easier. It's getting close to being an eccentricity and I'm amazed it's taken me half a century to find one of my own. There's a shallow groove worn in the pavement between my inner-city terrace and the cul de sac of Halcyon House. You can't find it on the satellite images provided by Google Earth. It's a secret path, with hope and need and resentment scattered slipshod across the paving stones. As I'm walking along it I dream about the treats I will give my father, small offerings to atone for his confinement. Some days it's a rice pudding. Or maybe just a good strong cup of black coffee. Once inside Merv can mostly be found in his coffined room, the window dwarfed by a camphor laurel and the giant television blaring. Dad is usually far from there, rambling barefoot through the rural Queensland of his childhood, scrambling up the heavily laden mango trees, inhaling the heady promises of youth as he surveys his kingdom.

I spent decades refusing my father's offers of a lift and internally rebuking him for his frequent kindnesses – the art easel he made for me, permanently wonky because it flew off his roof-racks; the huge bowl of trifle with mouldy strawberries he carefully conveyed to my forty-fifth birthday; the enormous hands splayed open in a gesture of gentle regret for all things past that cannot be undone.

When I was a young woman, Dad wanted us to take a road trip, to show me the dairy farm he grew up on and to introduce me to some of our relatives. In childhood I had met only a few. One was a gemologist; another sold cars. Unlike the familiar world of my mother's side, with the seeming solidity of their upper middle class homes and university degrees, these people were mercurial. They slipped through your fingers as they sprawled untidily across the continent, their get-rich-quick schemes and dilapidated boarding houses leaving only legends behind. Really Merv just wanted us to share an adventure. But I wouldn't join him. I didn't know how to tell him that certainly I was afraid of his driving but, mostly, I was afraid of him.

These days we've settled in for the last ride. Dad dictates the itinerary as we duck in and out of byways, visiting the landscapes and characters of the past. Sometimes the stories are frightening, spotlighting the darkness of rural poverty and the terrors of a physically abused boy. At other times they are tender, full of the gentle rhythms of farm life, the quick canter of the horse who carried him across the creek to school, the lucid call of his mother across the wintry paddocks.

Mostly I'm enjoying the trip. But, wherever we roam, I keep my eyes fixed firmly on the rear-view mirror, just in case that belligerent bastard is still behind the wheel.

Southerly

Waltzing the Jaguar

Caroline Baum

'Baby, would you like to come to the car wash?'

On Sunday mornings my father often invites me to join him on this errand. I always welcome the interruption to my homework, thinking we might stop on the way home to buy some chocolate. We don't do much together except argue and eat. These we do aggressively and competitively, with my mother as unwilling spectator.

The car wash is a novelty in my 1960s London childhood. Another labour-saving device, like the ones my father orders from mail-order catalogues and the fancier ones he brings back from business trips to America.

An early adopter, he installed a fax machine at home before I had seen one anywhere else. Predicted the future would belong to computers. Bought that rabbit-shaped wine opener along with other gadgets and gizmos soon abandoned for new playthings. Ingenious storage solutions, clever cleaning devices. My favourites: a spoon with a kink in its handle so you could rest it on the lip of a jam jar; a miniature silver golf-club-shaped utensil that cooled tea (of which he drank copious amounts, weak with one slice of lemon) – perfect for an impatient man always in a hurry.

Other families might go to church, but we commune at the car wash, cleansed physically if not spiritually and soothed into a more serene state by the gentle rhythmic vibrations of the machines as we progress along tracks through various stages – rinsing, sudsing, polishing. I laugh without fail when the car is pummelled, rocked slightly from side to side by the initial bursts from the water jets. I like to watch the long fringes of fabric licking at the windscreen and feel the hum through the car door as the hard bristles whirr, buffing the duco. It's like a fairground ride without the fear.

I don't remember us talking during the seven or eight minutes it takes to get through the wash, so perhaps my father is savouring the same sensations. I pretend that the noises the machines make are a terrible storm from which we are protected. We emerge back into daylight, buffed by chamois cloths to a shellac shine, as if we have undergone a ritual of purification, all the tensions that encrust the chassis of our family washed away. When the car is clean, it's possible to believe we can start again.

*

Some girls dance with their fathers at their wedding, but I did not have that kind of wedding. Instead, I waltzed with my father in the car. A Jaguar, updated with the release of each new model, but always navy with a walnut and maroon leather interior, proof that my father is a self-made success, the deserving owner of a sleek, purring prestige pedigree cat.

We are in France on our annual summer holiday in the south, a pilgrimage to temples of gastronomy carefully chosen from the Michelin guide. Everything about our family is deliberate. My father is a planner. He reads train timetables for relaxation. He is in the travel business so even our holidays feel like work. From a precocious age, I know the differences between a four-star and a three-star hotel, how to assess whether a room is adequate in size and comforts. I make friends with concierges and am an enthusiastic patron of room service. My collection of hotel miniature soaps, shampoos and unguents is second only to my collection of shells.

I am five, maybe six years old. My father sits me in his lap, puts my hands on the black ridged wheel of the Jaguar, and leads me in swooping zigzags along the cypress-lined roads of Provence in dappled sunlight, following the shimmering, swirling cadences of Strauss and other Viennese compatriots of his own childhood on an eight-track stereo cassette (the latest innovation in sound technology).

He is never playful or light-hearted except in that moment. An uncharacteristically spontaneous and carefree episode in a life that was always disciplined, timed down to the last minute and strict in its formality: I was expected to curtsey to visitors. His wardrobe said it all: racks and racks of meticulously hung silk ties, bought in Paris, organised by colour. It was my job on school days to select one to match his handmade shirts and accessorise my choice with a silk handkerchief from a glass-fronted drawer. I loved to run my hand through the weight of their heavy tongues, feeling their dense opulence.

But I feared my father, even when he was in a good mood. His hugs were too tight and nearly suffocated me. His pale British pork-sausage fingers held my hand to cross the road in a vice-like grip. His footsteps shook the landing of the upper floor of our house, his snores rattled doors. It was like sharing the house with a giant. On Sundays he would play recordings of classical music at deafening volume, conducting at his own tempi, bending my mother's knitting needles with the force of his strokes.

On departure days before just about every holiday he would erupt in a sudden temper tantrum, turning purple with apoplectic rage, slamming doors, swearing at the top of his lungs, causing my mother to barricade herself in her room until the moment it was time to head for the airport, usually in tears.

When I was disobedient or exposed in some petty lie, he beat me with a leather travelling slipper. It was as humiliating as it was painful, more so because he'd insist that after the punishment was over, I give him a kiss on the cheek.

By my teens we were openly at war and I wished he would die, leaving my mother and me alone. We were both marathon champions at feuding. He would simply refuse to speak to me for weeks at a time when I had displeased him, ignoring my presence at the dinner table, which, when there are only three of you, makes for a very tense atmosphere. I could match him sulk for sulk, leaving my mother exasperated between us, unable to broker peace, lacking the confidence to intervene and troubled by her own memories of a brutalised childhood. Conflict was our default setting and it became so familiar as to be almost comfortable.

There were rare moments of harmony. Most of them in the Jag, as my father called it – surprisingly, as he was not usually one for nicknames and rarely succumbed to verbal laziness. As a child refugee, he took great pride in mastering English till he spoke it better than most natives with a posh accent. Together with the car it made him seem like a Tory when he was in fact a passionate Labour voter.

He drove me to school every morning for twelve years, the car foggy with the haze of his chain smoking (Benson & Hedges Special Filter, my job to push the lighter in for him. Then, oh horror, I deliberately inhaled that delicious first hit of burning tobacco, which blended perfectly with the slightly faecal sweet smell of the car's leather upholstery).

In the Jag he treated me more like an adult, discussing world affairs, explaining the history of territorial disputes in the Middle East or old enmities between European nations, his grasp of history dazzling in his ability to quote from speeches, to string together dates into chains of events across centuries, to draw maps of changing and disputed borders in the air, while displaying his natural aggression as a driver, a split-second-reflex overtaker, tailgater and lane changer, intimidating other drivers with showy manoeuvres.

His driving made me feel ashamed. On the passenger side I often met the irritated or more openly angry gaze of drivers he had cut in on. Sometimes I could see their lips move as they swore at him. At times I would adopt a sorrowful pleading expression as if I were his captive begging to be rescued, but no one volunteered.

My mother was his most anxious passenger, sucking in her breath loudly and wincing when he almost grazed other vehicles. On these occasions, when he was showing off or conducting a silent row with us, I met his aggression with feigned indifference, refusing to give him the satisfaction of a reaction while my mother gripped the seatbelt with white knuckles.

But sometimes we shared the road peacefully. When I was seventeen and at summer school at a US college, we drove together from Pennsylvania to New York, finding a sustained serenity in the rhythms of Route 209 until we were stopped by a police motorcyclist and my father was fined on the spot for speeding.

'Don't tell your mother,' he said, establishing a complicity between us that endured through years of such episodes. I never betrayed him and was soon losing points on my own licence, having inherited his lead foot.

He taught me how to park in the tightest spots, reversing into position with one elegant manoeuvre ('Never buy a car without power steering,' he advised, giving the car credit for his skill), leaving a hair's breadth between the Jag and other cars, as the French do.

When he needed to park in the centre of London he would pull in to the forecourt of a hotel where he knew the doorman, hand over a fiver and say in a genial and offhand way, 'Look after that for me, will you?' before we walked through Knightsbridge, Soho or Piccadilly on some retail errand. My mother found this embarrassingly ostentatious but I liked the efficient and lordly way he could dispose of the car without having to endure the endless circling for a meter that would run out before we had achieved our goal.

*

'Papa, what's that funny car with the bashed-in roof?' I point to a red Mercedes 280 SL. I am ten years old and the concave curve of the roof, together with the car's sleek elegance, catch my eye.

'When I grow up I am going to buy one of those,' I announce with the kind of aspirational confidence my father encourages.

'Over my dead body,' my father retorts.

'Why?'

'Because it's German.'

'So?'

I know the answer already but like to bait my father, enjoying the ensuing argument like sport.

It always boils down to the war. That is why I am not allowed to buy German pencils for school and my mother does not have any German equipment in the kitchen. And yet, my father is a mass of contradictions: he worships Karajan conducting Wagner, even taking us on a holiday pilgrimage to the holiest of holies, Bayreuth, to experience that most Germanic and Hitler-approved cultural festival.

I taunt my father throughout my adolescence with these inconsistencies, but he shrugs them off. He makes the rules, he earns the money, that's that.

'But when I am older I can do what I like,' I needle.

'You can,' acknowledges my father, nodding with equable reason before delivering his ultimatum, 'but if you do that I will disinherit you.'

He delivers the half-joke, half-threat punchline with a satisfied smile, which implies he has amassed enough wealth for this to be a significant counter-move.

*

Fourteen years later I tell my parents I am moving to Australia with my future husband.

My father's despair is limitless. He mourns as if his only child has been struck by a terminal illness. He begs, he cries, he pleads.

He has escaped the Holocaust. He has survived a fraudulent theft that left his business on the verge of ruin and rebuilt it. But this decision breaks him.

'Baby, if you stay, I will buy you a Mercedes 280 SL.'

The pathos of the bribe's appeal makes me blush on his behalf even as I write this.

*

Easter, four years ago.

My father comes home after a successful operation for bowel cancer. We attribute his disorientation to the after-effects of the general anaesthetic, as the hospital staff do. In the taxi home, his eyes are dull, like those of a cooked fish. When Felix, the concierge, welcomes him home, he says thank you without looking at who is addressing him, as if on automatic pilot, simply parroting a phrase he has been taught.

He does not seem to register that I have come from Australia to look after him, does not ask how long I am staying. It's as if I have always been there or am not there at all.

He goes straight to bed. Later, he has a little supper, and says he needs to go to the barber and will drive there the next day.

My mother and I raise our eyebrows in alarm.

'Remember, the doctor said no driving and no going up stairs for six weeks,' my mother reminds him. 'Caroline can take you.'

'She can't drive my car,' he replies firmly. He has never let me drive the Jaguar. Now it seems the same rule applies to his new car.

The Prius is just eight weeks old. After a lifetime of loyalty to the same iconic brand, my father swapped the status of gas-guzzling luxury with enviable grunt for sedate green-cred, largely at my urging. I was surprised at this sudden recognition that perhaps a fast, expensive car no longer suited his retired, more modest circumstances. He talked about the Jag with senti-mental regret, as if reminiscing about a cherished departed friend.

'Of course she can. You put her name on the insurance papers, didn't you?'

'I don't remember.'

We leave it there.

At two in the morning I am woken by a shuffling sound; it is as if a large furry animal is snuffling through undergrowth. Still disoriented by jet lag, I think it's a wombat outside a tent, before recognising the sound of my father's tread in his leather slippers, then a jiggling of keys, the zipping of a bag, the fumbling for the front door chain and bolt, the turning of a handle, the soft clunk of the door closing.

Where on earth could my father be going at this hour? I rum-mage for clothes, call the security guard downstairs and tell him to stop my father at the gate if at all possible. He says my father has already left the building.

When I get outside it is snowing, the loose, feathery kind of flakes that fall messily, as if someone in the sky has burst a doona. My father is standing by the car, fumbling for his keys in the darkness.

'Where are you going?'

'To the bank.'

'But it's two o'clock in the morning, the bank is closed.'

'I have to get to the bank urgently.'

'But it's dark, and it's snowing, and the bank is closed. Why don't we go inside, have a cup of tea and I'll drive you there when it's light? You remember you are not allowed to drive?' I say, reaching coaxingly for his arm. He brushes me away, raising what I can now see is his cane, as if defending himself from an attacker. There is a wild look in his eye, like that of a horse when it shows too much white and is about to kick.

It takes me forty minutes to persuade him to come back inside. He seems oblivious to the cold although he is only wearing pyjamas and a light dressing gown. He does not shiver, whereas I cannot stop my teeth from chattering. I make us both tea, lead my father by the hand back to bed (he has slept apart from my mother for years, snoring being the official excuse for a much deeper estrangement), lock the door and hide his keys.

In the morning it's as if the episode never happened. My father seems more alert and lucid, scans the newspaper, seems able to focus on his breakfast and announces that he will go to the barber. I remind him that he can't drive and offer to take him.

'It would be better if I drove,' he insists.

Once he is dressed we go downstairs. When we reach the car he says, 'I cannot let you drive.'

It takes half an hour to persuade him to get into the passenger seat. Once there, he settles down, gives clear, precise directions, knows where to find free parking.

'How do you like the new car?' he asks genially, back to his old self.

We discuss its silence and other special merits in the way of trainspotters or bird fanciers.

We walk to the barber, my father's brisk step and unfailing sense of direction intact.

I am the only woman there. The barber, a young Lebanese man in his thirties, greets my father, a regular customer, with courtly reverence as he goes about his lathering and shaving with a blade. I savour the atmosphere of testosterone, as generations come and go to be trimmed and clipped. My father smiles benignly into the mirror, surrendering to the trusted ministrations like a grandee favouring a servant. It must feel good to have the bristles he grew in hospital disappear, to have hot towels applied, to feel the caress of the badger-hair shaving brush and the precision of the razor expertly handled.

I think of the car wash, of these rare moments of peace that we have shared, of how cleaning is common to them. When I was a little girl and had inherited his habit of biting my nails to the quick, he used to soak my hands on Sunday mornings in soapy hot water before inspecting each finger individually, admonishing me and then slathering them with hand cream. It was probably the most peculiar ritual of our relationship and never cured me of the habit.

When my father is done, the barber helps him on with his coat. His dignity and fastidious care about his appearance have been restored, and with them a new vigour has returned, a slightly sprightlier step, a shinier eye. My father seems able to take in more of his surroundings with each passing hour; I can sense his condition improving as if mist is lifting from a landscape.

'Let's go next door, I want to show you their pastries,' says my father in the conspiratorial tone of my childhood when we would egg each other on in exploits of gluttony – I rarely won the contest of who could eat the most mountains in a block of Toblerone.

We buy meringues that look like the Alps and Florentines the size of small pizzas. The outing is a success. He does not argue about who is driving when we reach the car, compliments me on retracting the car mirrors (one of those typical extras he loves to indulge in) to handle a narrow stretch of road.

My mother is so delighted she opens a half-bottle of champagne and we all toast my father's recovery, he with a sip, we with the rest. He eats lunch and for the first time since my arrival, my mother laughs and pinches his arm affectionately, pleased to have him back.

Afterwards he goes to bed for a nap. As I tuck him in, he smiles up at me, his face lopsided and crooked. It reminds me of a photograph I have of him before he left Vienna in 1938. He must've been nine years old. The smile he gives the photographer is a mixture of charm and shyness. I see this on my father's face for a fleeting moment and then it is gone. And with it, so is my father. He will never utter a lucid sentence again.

*

'We have to sell the car,' says my mother.

We are on the number 19 bus riding home from the hospital where she has just been given the diagnosis that makes sense of the previous week's nightmare.

My father has vascular dementia. There is no cure.

We do not know how we will care for him or where. Desperate for certainty, my mother finds only one: he will not be driving again.

My parents never had a wide circle of friends; the few they were close to have mostly died. They do not socialise or entertain and retirement has not brought new people into their lives. Now what remains is a handful of my father's former colleagues and business associates. Their Christmas card list has diminished to a dozen, including Nomi, the tall Japanese owner of a prestige car showroom where my father has been a client for more than twenty years. He has sold my father each of his recent Jaguars, and now the Prius.

At home the air is leaden. Unable to focus on any useful task, I thumb through the latest edition of my father's innovation catalogue, noticing that he has marked up an invention preventing speed cameras from photographing your number plate. Incorrigible, even at eighty.

There are other people my mother could call first – one surviving member of her family, a woman friend she rarely sees but speaks to every week – but instead she calls Nomi. He agrees to take the car back.

*

After I have organised my father's care, I am not prepared for the wash of anger that pushes me under like a rogue wave out of nowhere. It is so completely unexpected, unpredictable and violent that it frightens me in its opportunistic, random attacks. I did not love my father with this kind of ferocity, so why am I lashing out so fiercely?

I call a part-time counsellor friend for advice. Grief is not her field, and she has limited time, but offers to listen if I can meet her outside her workplace.

A cafe is not private enough. 'Perhaps we could talk in the car?' she suggests.

The very space that defined so much of how my father and I related: it feels right, familiar, safe. There is comfort, too, in sitting facing forward, not having to make eye contact, but it's intimate enough to feel confessional.

Soon I am sobbing, sitting at the wheel, nose running, choking and spluttering fury. Oncoming twilight conceals my distress from passers-by.

After an hour of listening, my friend hugs me across the handbrake and I drive home, exhausted by my outburst, but also calmer, like a volcano reverting to dormancy after an eruption. The muscle memory of each gesture, braking, accelerating, indicating, offers some consolation with its mechanical repetition and achievable mastery.

I wonder if my father's muscles, atrophied as they now are, retain any patterns of the gestures of steering or changing gear now that everything else in his brain is bombed, blasted, derailed. I replay in my mind, over and over, like picking at a scab, our last drive together, the utter banality of it, the lack of portent or significance in our mundane exchanges.

If I had known we would never be able to have a normal conversation again, what would I have said?

*

When my father is diagnosed, my mother comes to a grinding halt. Like a car with a flat battery she simply refuses to start. Shock has stalled her engine. Her body smells sour: I recognise fear wafting from room to room with her like the smell of curdled yoghurt.

My father paces the ward, shouting for his briefcase. Having tormented the nurses with Chinese rope burns, he calls at midnight, shrill with distress, demanding his passport and car keys. He gets into bed with strangers, steals items from bedside cabinets, disrupts meal times, chews his bedding, tears up the newspaper, makes lewd suggestions to orderlies and escapes with an unsuspecting group of visitors. The police are called to find him.

Psychiatrists interview my father to assess the severity of his condition and determine where he should be placed. My mother and I are invited to be present. To their questions about where he lives and his interests, he delivers an uninterrupted monologue about the build-up of traffic in the neighbourhood, detailing his frustrations with lights that have no right-turn filter, causing crossroads to clog up. Cars, too many cars, fill his consciousness, together with battles with the council over parking restrictions, one-way streets, speed bumps and the absence of zebra crossings. He responds as someone literally driven mad.

Weeks after my father is institutionalised my body is traversed with aches. They begin at my ankles, travel up my legs to my buttocks and into my neck and shoulders, moving like a weather pattern from site to site, waking me at night like storms. The pain becomes more and more acute, combined with a deadening fatigue that leaves me breathless and bedridden for days. I feel as if I have battery acid in my veins.

'If I did not know better, I would think you were poisoning me,' I tell my husband. Blood tests and X-rays reveal nothing.

The pain is corrosive. I give up exercising because it makes me feel worse. I lose three or four days of the week lying prostrate, dozing. I have occasional good days when my energy returns, but the pain always comes back like a punishment, as if my body were saying, 'How dare you think you could cheat me?' Eventually a doctor agrees with my internet diagnosis of chronic fatigue combined with chronic pain – something called fibromyalgia.

'It's a dustbin diagnosis,' he says breezily, 'which means we just chuck all the symptoms into a bin that we can't explain and give it that name.'

The illness affects me for two years.

Then one day, I realise I have had five, maybe six days in a row symptom-free. I feel stronger, have more stamina, the pain is less sharp, less persistent, less frequent. I start making bolder plans, attempting half days and then full days in the city, reclaiming parts of my life.

*

I've spent the day in Sydney, back in the saddle professionally, attending meetings, going to interviews. No ambushing by a sudden rush of tears, no power surges of rage. A day of smooth, unremarkable transitions.

I drive home feeling elated: my life is back in gear.

I can't wait to tell my husband how well the day has gone, how promising some conversations have been about potential work.

I park at the top of our driveway. Those last few metres always give me a sense of satisfaction, as if I were scaling a small mountain instead of just revving the engine to get up a very steep incline. Through the drawn curtains I can see David's silhouette on the sofa, about to watch the seven o'clock news, which marks a sort of unofficial cut-off point for our working day. I know the wine is already opened. I have a small window in which to debrief him before the headlines begin. I hurry inside.

As I begin my account of the day both of us become aware of an unfamiliar sound, just on the other side of the curtains. Something scraping, with the rhythm of a ricochet, like a tin can being kicked repeatedly along a wall. Metal, tearing. Puzzled, we draw the curtains back.

Where we should see the bonnet of the car, there is a void.

A void.

Where the car—

We run outside. The car is at the bottom of the driveway at a peculiar angle, jack-knifed against a concrete retaining wall. It has come to an abrupt halt, the wing mirrors tearing away fence posts on the descent. The undercarriage has fallen out like the spilled guts of roadkill.

Neighbours, brought out by the noise, look on in disbelief as we hug and do a little dance, punching the air and laughing. The enormity of what could have happened makes us both light-headed with relief. The car has not rolled down onto the main road or gathered speed and propelled itself across the street into another house. It could have been much, much worse.

When I tell friends what happened, they nod wisely. Clearly, according to them, the episode demonstrates that I am still in shock, still dealing with the aftermath of my father's decline. For months, I buy that interpretation. I am not myself, not ready to venture into the outside world, not self-possessed enough to regain control.

But today I am not so sure. Couldn't it just be that in an absent-minded moment of eagerness to share the news of my successful day, I had forgotten one small gesture of precaution and left the handbrake off? Just how symptomatic and symbolic was that one error?

What would my father have said? Sometimes he overreacted with stinging criticism and sometimes he'd surprise me with a philosophical shrug. I can hear him making a joke of it: 'At least it was only a Holden, not a Mercedes 280 SL, baby.'

*

I delay taking the Prius back to Nomi until the day before my own departure, dreading the burial-like finality of it. I tell myself it is just another chore on a to-do list that never seems to get any shorter, no matter how many items I tick off.

When it can be put off no longer, I empty the car of the last evidence of my father's ownership and disconnect the GPS he argued with so vehemently, shouting at its implacably calm voice to 'shut up, you silly cow' whenever she urged him to 'make a U-turn where possible' after he disregarded her instructions.

Unplugging that cable feels like switching off life support.

I drive to the showroom in Chiswick, taking back roads, lingering behind the wheel, wondering how often my father used the special feature that warmed the driver's seat on winter mornings and that I now switch on for myself, to give me that cosy electric-blanket feeling of comfort. But nothing can stop me shivering as I approach my destination.

I ask for Nomi at reception. Before I know it, a tall man is standing behind me, all stillness and solemnity. He bows. There is an awkward moment before I stretch out my hand for him to shake. He takes it with his head still lowered.

'We have not met before, but of course I know all about you,' Nomi says, showing me to his desk.

'The Mercedes 280 SL, still your favourite car, yes?' he asks, attempting to lighten the mood.

'The Prius was your idea, yes? Very good choice. Your father, he like this car more than he expect after Jaguar, no?'

Choking, I can only nod.

'Perhaps he will make good recovery?'

I shake my head.

'I am very sorry,' he says, presenting me with papers to sign.

I cannot see them clearly. My eyes swim with tears, spilling down onto forms about vehicle registration.

I rest my forehead on the cool clean glass surface of the desk.

'Perhaps some tea?' asks Nomi.

I brush the tears away, shake my head in a silent 'no thank you', sign the forms and leave as quickly as I can, stumbling between new cars to the bus stop. I get on the first bus that comes, knowing it is the wrong bus, not caring, just wanting to be taken away from that place as quickly as possible.

Such a mundane chore.

It is one of the saddest days of my life.

*

When I was a little girl I had a plastic steering wheel that attached to the wall by suction. I think about whether a driving toy might help my father regain some fragment of identity, but his carers tell me no. He would only chew on such a thing and hurt his already fragile teeth. On days when we bring him down to the visitors' lounge for tea or when he is calm enough to go on an outing, he gazes at passing traffic with more animation than usual. I watch for a flicker of recognition when a Jaguar goes by, but there is none.

My Mother, My Father

A Rolf in Sheep's Clothing

Peter Conrad

'Guilty on all counts, Your Honour.' So said Rolf Harris, weeping in contrition.

He uttered those self-incriminating words and shed those remorseful tears on a television talk show in 2011, as he told the smarmily sympathetic Piers Morgan about his neglect of his wife Alwen and daughter Bindi, left behind as he frolicked round the world to further his career and amuse his fans. The solemn plea was a self-dramatising gesture and the tears may have been histrionic too, but here was unexpected evidence that the goofy Rolf – so familiar on television since the 1950s that he had become an honorary member of most British families – might be a less agreeable, more tormented character than he appeared. His daughter, he told Morgan, chastised him when she was a teenager because he was perpetually available to the passers-by who accosted him in the street but never had time for her and her mother. His closest relatives 'said they didn't know who I was. They said I was a total stranger.' He seemed to be wondering whether they were right: could he also be a stranger to himself?

Rolf was happy to plead guilty in front of a studio audience, whose applause instantly pardoned him. But in January this year, when he was charged with twelve indecent assaults on four young girls, his response was a forthright 'Not guilty', and at his trial the barrister defending him attacked his accusers, now middle-aged women, as fantasists or gold-diggers and picked apart their fuzzy memories of events that dated back to the 1970s. It was not enough to rehabilitate a man who once proudly called himself 'everyone's favourite Aussie'.

Following his initial arrest in March 2013, Rolf disappeared from view for a few months. Then in August, just before a bail hearing, he performed at a music festival in Hampshire. A roar of acclaim revived him, and gave him the courage to joke about his legal predicament. 'I would like to thank you all for my support,' he said. He then corrected the pronoun, smuttily capitalising on his slip with a reference to the cumbersome belts and adhesive pads that used to be prescribed for elderly gents troubled by hernias: 'Thanks for your support, I will always wear it.' Rolf's British public is, in more ways than one, his truss. That dependency is mutual, and his travails have alarmed and bewildered a country that used to be held together by deference and discretion and is now, after the covered-up horrors exposed by the investigation of Jimmy Savile's crimes, forced to reconsider those questionable principles.

Last year the record producer Vince Hill bolstered Rolf's reputation by calling him 'a national monument', and in her opening statement in court the prosecutor Sasha Wass described him as a 'pillar of society', so irreproachable that the BBC had persuaded the Queen to allow him to paint her; a message on a Facebook page defending him announced 'In Rolf We Trust', a paraphrase of the pious assertion 'In God We Trust' that is inscribed on every US dollar bill. But gods can let down their believers, and currencies can lose their value. Before the trial began, my accountant told me that his wife's limited-edition print of a painting by Rolf, a view of Durham Cathedral, had been demoted from its location above their fireplace and stowed in a kitchen corner. 'If there's a guilty verdict,' he said, 'it goes into the garage forever!' At Buckingham Palace, oblivion had already overtaken Rolf: after his arrest, his portrait of the Queen conveniently went missing.

*

When Rolf's agent Jan Kennedy took him on as a client during the 1970s, she remarked that, thanks to television, he had been her companion since childhood: 'I've known him all my life – but then, hasn't everyone?' Well, yes and no. If Rolf is a stranger to his own family, the rest of us have little chance of knowing who he really is. It's even uncertain *what* he is, since this one-man variety show has had so many successive careers, punctuated by timely self-reinventions.

With a diffident shrug, Rolf describes himself as a lucky amateur who happens to be 'good with people' and owes his success to geniality rather than genius. He is too modest, overlooking the force of will that has driven him all along. At school in Perth – where his parents settled after migrating from Wales in the 1920s – he was always 'being singled out as the best in the class at this, that and the other', he remembers. Yet his boisterous over-achieving was not unanimously admired. 'Nobody likes a show-off,' snarled one teacher: Australia back then was egalitarian with a vengeance. 'I was different from other kids,' Rolf has recalled, adding that his father, Crom – a quiet, withdrawn man, employed as a turbine driver at a power station, which can't have been much relief from life at home with Rolf the domestic dynamo – encouraged his eccentricity and told him to 'enjoy your difference'. That's a little implausible, since Australian parents in the 1930s seldom set out to raise crops of tall poppies. Rolf was his own creation, and his over-exuberant personality exceeded the normal requirements of social life.

At the age of ten, on a family holiday, he learnt to yodel during the drive across the Nullarbor Plain, and in Sydney terrorised his grandmother by hiding in the bathroom and ululating at her. 'I never heard that child make a pleasant sound,' said the tremulous old woman. In those days he often barked like a rabid dog, and he still inserts the occasional 'woof' into his conversation. He sings, very nasally, and plays a range of instruments, but for him music was basically an unbridled din. His wife came to tolerate his glottal shunting, snorting and gulping as the soundtrack of their shared existence. 'Rolf has always made strange noises,' she once resignedly remarked.

Performing was a logical continuation of his childish exhibitionism. His first field of endeavour was the swimming pool, where he triumphed as Australian Junior Backstroke Champion in 1946. Out of the water, he successfully auditioned for *Australia's Amateur Hour*, regaling radio audiences with the manic scatting that he called his 'virtuoso boogie-woogie'; as well, at the age of sixteen he precociously entered a painting – a self-portrait, of course – for the Archibald Prize. In a poem written for Rolf's seventieth birthday, Clive James called him 'the incarnation of / The Australian spirit, spry yet down to earth', but that tribute muffles Rolf's raucously high-spirited behaviour. In his heyday he was not so much spry as bizarre, and far from being down to earth he usually seemed to be in orbit somewhere above it, bounced about by the jolting rhythms of his wobbleboard. Level, taciturn, dun-coloured Australia could not contain this over-energised jester for long.

In 1952, Rolf sailed off to London to attend art school. On the way, he busked for the captive audience on board the ship; on arrival, he made it his personal mission to enliven the stiff, staid British. At his boarding house in Earls Court, he erupted into the breakfast room each morning, barefoot and wearing only shorts, to greet his fellow lodgers with a megaphonic reveille. 'How's it going?' he used to yell. 'C'mon, give us a big smile!' The fortress of frosty reserve did not crumble.

Rolf's unglamorous art school in South London bored him, so he strayed into cabaret and performed with his accordion in an expat den called the Down Under Club. Soon, bluffing his way into a studio, he popped up on television, where he began by nattering matily to a puppet called Fuzz. Towards the end of the 1950s came his forays into the hit parade, with the droning ballad 'Tie Me Kangaroo Down, Sport' and the outback aubade 'Sun Arise'. By the late 1960s, Saturday evenings on the BBC belonged to *The Rolf Harris Show*, and on weekday afternoons his cartoon programs made him the nation's designated child-minder. A flickering box had supplanted the hearth as the source of conviviality in British households; leering cheerily out of it, Rolf doodled caricatures or graphic puzzles, and like a latter-day Welsh bard organised singalongs that were accompanied by the didgeridoo or the jew's harp or the buzzing Stylophone or a whoop-whooping length of plywood. In addition he whistled, drummed on his face or used his tonsils as a percussion instrument, babbling rhythmically in a nonsensical coloratura that could be transcribed as 'bumph, dee, bumph, dee, chuph, chuph, bumph, bumph, bumph, brrrrrrr' or 'wunna wanna worree wa wether'.

His body functioned as a magician's bag of tricks, and for his song about Jake the Peg – reprised, to the prosecutor's astonishment, at his trial – he grew a third leg, the precursor of Sir Les Patterson's impertinent trouser snake. When the BBC allowed Rolf to stray into the commercial sector, he advertised house paint, car insurance and the benefits of drinking milk. Purportedly good with people, he seemed to be especially trustworthy with children. He therefore appeared in a video to recommend swimming lessons, splashing in a pool with some under-age playmates, and in 1985 made another educational video in which he advised a group of tiny tots against allowing adults to touch their sacrosanct bodies.

Throughout all this, Rolf's most significant achievement may be that he endeared himself to his adoptive country without toning down his larrikin act. When he arrived in London, Australians either had to pass themselves off as Brits or else – like the comedian Bill Kerr, the butt of Tony Hancock's jibes in the radio series *Hancock's Half Hour* – be treated as village idiots. Rolf's mother had coached him to smooth and round out his vowels, but he resisted her tuition; in London he was told that he sounded like 'some sort of second-rate cockney' and advised, if he wanted work on the BBC, to 'lose that atrocious accent'. When he recorded 'Tie Me Kangaroo Down, Sport' in 1957, he even had to bully the Australian back-up singers into using their own lazy drawl instead of a fake American twang: 'I don't want "tar mah kangaroo dayown, sporrrt",' he told them.

Outfacing the snobs and cultural cringers, Rolf turned his supposed disadvantage into a trademark: he succeeded, as he has declared, by being 'unashamedly Australian'. Yet this phrase, which he uses twice in his autobiography, is as revealing as his gratuitous confession of guilt to Piers Morgan. It hints that he retains the scars of early humiliations, that he is aware he hails both from the bottom of the world and, as his father sternly warned him, from the bottom class in society – at ease with the children or animals on his television shows, but less confident in the company of grown-ups.

*

'Sun arise, she bring in the morning': that is Rolf's official gospel. His song personifies the sun as a woman, 'fluttering her skirts all around', and relies on the torrid matriarch to brighten the world and dispel its gloom. Such solar good humour can be oppressive. In 2010, captioning a photograph of his geeky seventeen-year-old self, Rolf said that he resembled 'the sort of guy who'd be all over you like a rash, smiling fiercely at every opportunity', and admitted that the prospect was 'scary!'

This ebullience is not the whole truth about him: the affable Rolf has a shadow self. Over the years he has let slip anecdotes about his past, clues to a covert legacy of guilt and shame. Rolf's Aunt Pixie intimated that his father Crom had been sexually abused as a fifteen-year-old while working as a cabin boy on a boat bound from Cardiff to South America. Crom returned home after four months, now – in Rolf's words – 'absolutely hating' his own father, who had sent him off on the voyage. Rather than settling down again with his parents, he shipped out to Australia. Something is missing from a tale that Rolf admits is 'garbled', because Crom refused to discuss the unforgivable wrong his father had done him. Instead he jokingly passed on the grievance to the next generation, miming a little scene of castration during a portrait sitting: whenever Rolf reached out with his index finger to dab a section of paint or to signal some passing felicity of light, Crom waited till the digit got within close range, then chomped at it with his teeth.

Rolf's mother Marge was an ambitious woman, a gold medallist in mathematics at school in Wales and a qualified analytical chemist. Though she found little outlet for her talents in scrubby, flyblown Bassendean, she rigidly upheld genteel standards, and when playing tennis served the ball underarm because she thought it unladylike to expose her armpit. At the age of four Rolf did what he calls 'a super drawing of a man with no clothes on – he was standing there absolutely naked and urinating'. When his mother saw it, she rewarded him with a hiding. The incident forged a connection between art and indecency: Rolf had imagined what he was not allowed to look at. Even music, pure because abstract, is in his view capable of obscenity. Trying out a didgeridoo on television in 1966, he said, 'What about that for a lovely sound?' as an eructation emerged from the tube. 'It's used for luring young maidens out into the bush,' he explained, then quickly added, 'Sorry, no, forget that!'

As Rolf approached adolescence, his mother took responsibility for imparting the inflammatory forbidden knowledge to him. As he told *TV Times* in the 1970s, she decided that 'I should see her naked to let me know it was all natural', and at her suggestion 'we had baths together'. She supplemented the demonstration by buying Rolf an illustrated guide to the facts of life, then 'stayed in the room while I tried to read it'.

Since she had seemingly encouraged such intimacy, Rolf reacted in the same way when he saw her in a swimsuit she had knitted, with a fringe of tassels below the waist. In the water, the dangling strands swelled up, which prompted him to say, 'They look like pubic hairs.' Affronted, his mum belted him hard across the face. 'I was thirty years old when that happened,' he adds in his memoir. It's the most shocking sentence in the book, and it explains where his song 'I've Lost My Mummy' comes from: here a child cries inconsolably in a department store, afraid of having been abandoned, only to bawl even louder when his mother returns to collect him and gives him 'a hefty whack' as punishment for wandering off. Rolf's mother did her work only too well. In another song he attests to having lived a spotless life, at least until he met 'my two good amigos / Nick Teen and Al K Hall'. There's a coy displacement here, since drink and tobacco were never his vices.

Marriage and fatherhood came with other, built-in interdictions. In 1958 Alwen brought her pet poodle to the wedding as an honorary bridesmaid, and Rolf had difficulty dislodging it from the nuptial bed. His wife clearly needed its company and its morale-boosting devotion. Rolf much later discovered a diary she wrote in 1959 in Perth, where he was helping to set up the first local television station. Alwen, he found, felt so displaced and ignored, so nullified by the boredom of her castaway life, that she had contemplated suicide; at the time, he simply hadn't noticed. In 1964, hours after the induced birth of their daughter, he flew from London to New York to start a concert tour. When Alwen joined him shortly afterwards, bringing the baby, he failed to recognise her at the airport, and explained his distraction by pointing out that she had dyed her hair.

A subsequent episode in Rolf's autobiography, which he may now regret having made public, deals with transgressive impulses that the law warns us all to control. Bathing Bindi in their New York hotel, after having photographed Alwen as she breastfed the child, Rolf marvels at the 'minute size of everything', and lets his eyes travel from Bindi's neck to her 'delicate shoulders' and smooth tummy. Then he nears a border zone, trespasses across it, and backtracks: 'I reached her genitals and skipped that part. My brain was saying, 'Don't be ridiculous. Why are you so uptight about nudity?' I couldn't help it.' The taboo is artificial, but all the same necessary; those who defile innocence may do so because they envy it and want to share in it.

The Rolf Harris Show featured a chorus line of girls in microminiskirts and hotpants, and was nicknamed The Twinkling Crotch Show. Backstage, the shy host says, he 'tried not to watch – or be *seen* watching' the cavalcade of semi-clad young women. Throughout one season he flamboyantly flirted with 'a tall, leggy brunette called Glor, short for Gloria', who finally chastened him when they were sitting with some colleagues in a hotel lounge. After listening to a bout of his amorous drollery, she reached across, 'unzipped my fly, put her hand into my underpants, took a firm grip of my old fella and flipped it out for all to see'. What, she asked, did he intend to do about his supposed infatuation (which apparently hadn't extended to that flipped, floppy member)? Rolf turned 'seven consecutive shades of red', just as he flushed scarlet when his mother slapped him; then, in an image that begs for psychoanalytical exegesis, he wished he could 'dissolve into a grease spot and soak into the carpet'. Gloria suffered no further harassment.

A cartoon by Rolf represents grown-up sexual relations as a balance of terror, predicated on the threat of pain. In the drawing, an angry blitz of black scrawls surrounds a glaringly spotlit dental chair. A male dentist aims his drill at the gaping mouth of a prone female patient, whose teeth are as razorlike as a shark's; she defends herself by grabbing his crotch and squeezing what ought to be his testicles, though it looks as if she has fastened onto a bulbous penis. The rearing organ doesn't appear to be discouraged, but the drill is paused in midair, hesitating before it ventures into that vagina dentata. The caption to the drawing is

'We're not going to hurt one another, are we?' Cuddles, hugs and tickles, like those to which Rolf initially treated his alleged victims, are – at least in theory – exempt from such nasty adult recriminations.

In the caricatures Rolf usually adds to his autograph, his face consists of a grinning mouth sandwiched between his goggles and his goatee. His smile is evangelical, as well as something of an artwork: he often warned sulky children who cried or frowned that they were 'sculpting their faces for the future' and ruining their chances of looking benign in old age. Despite this amiability, his glasses and beard tell another story, because both, in Rolf's case, were disguises. Spectacles, as he commented when taking his own off to paint a self-portrait on television, reflect light and thereby deflect attention from the eyes of whoever you are painting; they interfere with your interrogation of another human being. As for whiskers, Rolf first experimented with them in 1949 when cast as a sailor in a musical at teacher's college in Perth. He grew them again on his way to England in 1952, protectively preparing a face with which to meet the new faces he would encounter there. His beard was a frame for his grin, and it also served, like a garden hedge, as a barricade to deter intruders. His wife preferred him with that cosy camouflage: when she first saw him clean-shaven, Alwen likened him to 'an American car with all the chrome removed' – an extraordinary image, which implied that beneath the decorative trim there was only a noisy, revved-up engine and a motorised mouth that puffed out hot air through its grille.

*

Late in the 1980s, when Rolf's act began to seem antiquated, his cover version of Led Zeppelin's 'Stairway to Heaven' updated him. 'It was very square to say you liked Rolf Harris before that,' he complacently noted. 'Suddenly it was very cool to say you liked Rolf Harris.' Musical performances at the Glastonbury Festival established him as a harmless, gormless figure of fun, immune to the irony of the ovations he was receiving from the muddy mobs of rock fans.

Rolf's original audience had grown up, so in 1994 he took on a more avuncular role and began a ten-year run on *Animal Hospital*. Like Christ, he had suffered the little children to come unto him in *Cartoon Time*; now, ministering to poorly quadrupeds, he turned into St Francis. In an episode featuring a euthanised Alsatian called Floss, audiences sniffled as a teary Rolf consoled the dog's sobbing master – 'the first time,' he later announced, 'that viewers in England had seen two adult males unashamedly crying on TV'. Once a festive, mischief-making imp, he had matured into a shrewd orchestrator of the nation's tenderest emotions. In 2001 he reverted to an earlier vocation, setting up his easel to pastiche Degas and Monet in the first series of *Rolf on Art*, a long-running show that encouraged and empowered amateur painters. As a result, the ageing Rolf joined the ranks of the Old Masters: in 2012 a Liverpool museum sold record numbers of tickets to a retrospective exhibition of his work. 'Rembrandt, Rubens and Rolf, all in the Walker Art Gallery now,' said a fawning BBC reporter.

'The world has learned from him,' Clive James declared at the end of the birthday poem he addressed to Rolf the moral mentor, 'and I likewise.' Accepting his near-priestly status, the Church of England invited Rolf to write a preface to a booklet that explained the notion of bereavement to children: 'G'day kids' was his salutation before he brought his little readers the bad news about mortality. His wife's brother suggests that Rolf may have undergone a conversion when he witnessed the healing feats of the Indian 'godman' Sathya Sai Baba (who was himself accused of sexually abusing his young male acolytes, to whom he offered his penis as a token of blessing). Short of performing miracles, Rolf said that his purpose on earth was 'to spread a little love and affection wherever I can' and 'to talk to everyone and be accessible'. Accessibility, however, is a two-way street, and in several of the incidents described by the prosecution in its case against him a child's request for an autograph allegedly led almost immediately to molestation.

In 2005 his painting of the Queen conferred respectability on Rolf, but during the sessions he did his best to be unrespectable, as if still teasing his prim mother. Rolf's music is about his body's cheeky production of sound, and painting licenses him to make an almost scatological mess. Explaining his technique, he told the Queen that when he confronts a pristine canvas his first move is to 'kill the white', dirtying it with a puddle of colour. 'Extraordinary,' she remarked with her usual equanimity. To cover up his missteps, Rolf tends to splash turpentine around, so he asked the Queen if she disliked the smell. Unfamiliar with its resinous stink, she gave a wary reply: 'Well, we'll tell, won't we, soon?' Later, flicking his brushes, he whispered to himself about the risk he was taking: 'Imagine if I sloshed paint all over the Queen!' She remained unblemished, but Rolf's banter – about domestic pets relieving themselves on the carpet, and the stench of dissected horses in the studio of the eighteenth-century equine painter George Stubbs – flirted with impropriety.

By now Rolf had attained the rank of national treasure, but rumours circulated about his octopoid gropings, and detractors who resented his ineffable good humour teamed up to vilify him on a scurrilous internet forum. One anonymous poster claimed to have seen him twist a puppy's paw on camera to make it squeal, another imagined him shooting sparrows with an air rifle in his garden beside the Thames near Windsor. A conspiracy theorist, having read *The Da Vinci Code* too often, decoded 'didgeridoos' as an anagram of 'O did God rise' and took this as proof that Rolf belonged to the occult sect of the Knights Templar. The most demented of these fantasies sent him on tour to Cambodia, where – as an 'unofficial roving ambassador of evil' – he allegedly played cricket with Pol Pot, using human skulls as balls.

Otherwise Rolf's audiences took him at face value; he alone dared to let the benign mask slip. He did so on one of his painting programs, while attempting a self-portrait in the style of van Gogh. After two hours of staring at his reflection in the mirror, he noted that his smile 'starts to crack and eventually falls off with a crash!' In its absence, the man Rolf painted is an ogre, considerably more baleful than Baron Hardup, the curmudgeon he played in the Christmas pantomime *Cinderella*. Without glasses, his eyes stare hypnotically, and a brow arches in cold appraisal; his jowls, like a mastiff's, seem to reverberate with a low and menacing growl; his mouth turns down at the corners, sourly grimacing. Here, in bright acid green and bruised purple, is a glimpse of what the prosecutor at his trial referred to as his 'dark side'. You can see why the women who testified against Rolf said they were 'terrified' or 'petrified' of him when, as adolescents, he had them in his grip.

*

In a letter written in 1997 to the father of one of his alleged victims, read out in court near the start of proceedings, Rolf quoted the naïve, intimidated teenager's description of him as 'the great television star Rolf Harris'. At the time, he saw no reason to disagree with that estimation: he was irresistible because powerful, untouchable because universally popular. But the domestic screen has recently lost the authority it once conferred on its cherished performers. Media today are interactive, with online gossip challenging the impunity that figures like Rolf once enjoyed. A website that conducts a vendetta against child abusers named him as a suspect days before the police announced that he had been questioned, and the first witness at his trial decided to make her legal complaint after seeing him at the Queen's jubilee concert in 2012: it seemed, she said, that she could not 'get away from this bloody man', who was invading her home every time she turned on the telly. She completed Rolf's humiliation by incidentally disclosing that his penis was 'very small, very very small'. The prosecutor argued that fame was Rolf's shield, but it no longer has that protective function: in the tabloids and in courts of law, diminutive old fellas can be hauled out and used in evidence against their wincing owners.

Giving evidence, Rolf's accusers and the supplementary witnesses called by the prosecution literally de-famed him. Their accounts alleging hasty, fumbling assaults in Hawaii, Darwin, Auckland, Malta, Portsmouth and Cambridge combined into the sad tale of a primal lapse, a moment when paradise was irretrievably lost: 'All the happiness was gone,' said a woman he allegedly molested when she was seven. In her summation, Sasha Wass called Rolf a 'sinister pervert', who employed his charm as a form of mesmerism and relished his demonic power over his victims. No longer disseminating sunshine, he was now portrayed as the source of all evil, responsible for the post-traumatic stress disorder, alcoholism, bulimia or aversion to tongue-kissing that had overtaken his accusers in later life. The decade he spent murmuring 'Poor little blighter' to the internees on *Animal Hospital* counted for less when set against his interest in a brusquely canine approach to courtship, exposed by a saucy postcard he sent the first complainant. On the card, a beagle imparts its life lessons, which include a recommendation that if you want sex you should beg, with the added advice that 'a cold nose in the crotch can be effective'. Twisting the knife, the addressee remarked that when he came to visit during her adolescence, 'he never greeted the family dog'.

Rolf's grovelling letter to this woman's father seems genuinely anguished, but it still hankers after the sentimental simplicities and quick fixes of his television programs. In *Rolf on Art* he advises novice painters to use oils, which allows them to wipe out a mistake 'or let it dry and paint over it'. Off the canvas, erasure is not so easy. As he tells the aggrieved parent in his letter, 'You can't go back and change things you have done in this life – I wish to God I could.' What troubles him most, however, is the damage to his self-esteem. 'As I do these animal programmes,' he writes, 'I see the unconditional love that dogs give to their owners and I wish I could learn to love myself again.' It's an obtuse, coldly self-regarding formulation. Dogs do not dote on themselves; misinterpreting animal psychology, Rolf identifies both with the adoring pet and its adored owner, which makes him his own most fervent fan. His appeal to be reprieved from self-loathing so he can love himself again reveals – somewhat crassly given the context – that narcissism is the norm for him.

Arriving at court each morning, flanked by his wan, strained daughter and his stoical wife, Rolf sported a succession of ever more iridescent ties, bright reminders of the rising sun with her fluttering skirts. Perhaps this blaze of colour proclaimed that he had done nothing wrong: as he says in his confessional letter, the affair with his friend's daughter 'progressed from a feeling of love and friendship'. He may still think, as he did when bathing Bindi, that the restrictions we impose on desire and imagination – two forces that collude inside us – are unnatural. Or there might be a more vindictive intent behind the scenarios described by the aggrieved women: were such attacks on innocence meant to console him for his own loss of it? A grey, stooped, portly Peter Pan, Rolf compulsively re-enacts a childhood that ended prematurely the first time around.

Art is an uncensored playground of fantasy, safe so long as you have a bottle of turps and plenty of rags close at hand; the problems start when art's rampant liberties extend into life. One of the most perceptive comments about Rolf was made by a conservationist who worked with him on a wildlife program in Scotland. After watching him fraternise with an armada of dolphins, the scientist said, 'If he wasn't well known, he'd be quite mad.' Like Shakespearean fools, celebrities are free to be crazy or zany, and we dispense them from the customary rules about manners and morals. But this permission is apt to be revoked abruptly when the police arrive. Is it Rolf who has double standards, or society?

The Monthly

The Breaking Point

Jessie Cole

It was the suicide of my older sister Zoe, in all her shimmering teenage glory, that pushed my father to the edge. Perhaps everyone has a breaking point. An incident or event that cannot be overcome, a moment in time that can never be erased. Most of us might get through life without encountering it, but my father was not so fortunate.

We lived far outside town, nestled in green hills, on a winding dead-end road a thousand kilometres north of Sydney. Filled with hopes for a new start, a tree-change – another world – my parents had packed up their busy city lives for the freedom of the country. My father, a psychiatrist, worked only three days a week. On days off he toiled in the garden. He began fantastical tasks and finished them in one day. Covered in sweat and dirt, with an aching back and a tired body he came in and told my mother of his progress. A Japanese garden, with a real slated pond and giant lilies, huge boulders and bamboo. An orchard with endless rows of citrus humming with bees. A rainforest, shady and ancient-seeming, strewn with fallen coloured leaves.

When I was small my father brought me special things he found in the garden. I sat steaming in the bath one evening, naked and easy, the flickering leaves of the growing forest outside whispering wordless secrets in my ears. The bathroom sat among the trees, the sliding glass doors open to the green. Coming in, dirt-speckled and sour smelling, he showed me a tiny white ball. With a delicate tug my father pulled this small sphere apart and thousands of spiders fell, sprinkling down upon me. Minuscule, they spread across the water, floating determinedly towards the edges, their legs braced against the sway of my careful movements. Hurriedly, the masses of baby spiders climbed out and along the top of the old enamel bathtub. With concentrated joy I scooped up the stragglers and flicked them gently from my fingers and out the long open doorway into the forest. I stared in wonder that so many lives had come from such a small white seamless pouch.

I understood that my father had held the power of their lives – and deaths – in his gentle hands, and felt in a subtle way that he had created them. I searched my father's face for signs of meaning, but he was unreadable and unexpectedly quiet. My mother came in from the kitchen to see what had caused my squeals, and I checked to see how deep the crease between her brows became when she saw the delicate wafting spiders.

'They're not biting ones, Mum.'

My mother's face broke into a sun-like smile. 'They're amazing.' Her words were soft, and she looked at my father with a gentle warmth. 'Where did you find them?'

He motioned out towards the garden and my parents wandered off together in search of the very spot.

My father was a man living in the moment. Before my sister died I once spotted him doing a lap of the town, ghetto blaster on his shoulder, wearing his bright yellow Esprit shirt, on an afternoon errand. Hanging around on street corners after school as a young teenager, I got a glimpse of him in the distance.

'Isn't that . . . your dad?' my tittering friends asked. When he jogged right past calling 'Hi, Possum!' it was a hard question to evade.

'But what is he doing?'

Now, I suspect he was rushing about trying to get that beloved ghetto blaster repaired, and jogging with it on his shoulder just seemed a natural time management strategy, but the yellow woman's Esprit T-shirt was harder to explain.

My father loved that shirt. 'Esprit is French for spirit!' he'd proclaim, 'S-P-I-R-I-T. You know, spirit, life, strength. That's me!'

'But why does it have to be bright yellow?'

'That's my favourite colour!'

'But it's a girl's shirt, Dad.' All I got for that objection was a slight roll of the eyes. For my father, gendered clothing was irrelevant, but in my small Australian country town a yellow woman's shirt was enough to set a man apart. Add a ghetto blaster and a zappy jog, and the word 'lunatic' easily sprang to mind. There are advantages to growing up in a family with a high tolerance for eccentricity. Boundaries are loose, undefined. Odd fashion choices are celebrated, experimental artworks championed and socially inappropriate expressions of authenticity never shunned or derided.

But what happens when your crazy parent turns out to be . . . well, crazy?

After my sister's death my family was in tatters. We were like fish swallowing air. Silence enveloped us. But in time my father's muted grief turned wild and the tangled threads of his control snagged and tore apart. My mother and I woke one morning to find he had partitioned off the kitchen with a hinged ad hoc wooden screen to which he nailed all his favourite books. 'Jess, Jess. Look, what do you think? Great, hey?'

I slid towards the table, trying to sit down among the books. 'I'm not sure about the John Cowper Powys. Your mum's always hated that book. Boring, she said. Fucking boring.' My mother tried not to look at the newly constructed shrine. There was meaning in it somewhere, this fictional crucifixion, but my mother and I were frightened, and we huddled together in a quiet fist of unnamed communion over breakfast.

Drawing of the author as a child; artwork by the author's father, 1983

'Jess, what about you? You haven't read any Kafka. You've got to, baby! I've nailed this one up here. All these books, they're between me and her. Your sister. Zoe. She'll know. She'll know even if you guys don't. Don't tell me Kafka's fucking boring! Jess, your mum does like Kafka, even if she's not willing to admit it here. Tell her! Zoe will know. So what do you guys think? How do you like it? The end of the hammer broke off last night otherwise I'd add those ones too.' My father held the broken hammer in his hand, motioning to the piles of books still on the table – 'Some Mishima, *The Leopard*.'

'You've taken up half the kitchen. There isn't enough space to sit.' My mother's voice was quavering, falling away at the edges.

'What? What are you talking about? Just move those books over and sit down. You have to complain about everything. God, Jess, your mother is such a fucking complainer. I scattered the ashes last night. Out in the garden, it was great, just me and her. I could feel her. She was with me.'

'You scattered Zoe's ashes? Where?'

'Out there in the garden.' He gestured behind him. 'It's a great spot. You'll love it.'

My mother stood up, her mouth pressed together in a tight line.

'Oh what, you have a problem with that too?' My father's face was red, his lips jutting forward. Wrapping her sarong tightly around herself, my mother replied quietly, 'What about us? You can't do things like that without talking about it.'

'Fuck! She's my daughter. I know where she should be. You're such a control freak. You want to control everything.'

'You're not the only one who's hurting.'

'All right! But I'm not taking the books down. Zoe knows. She knows what it's all about.'

'You can't do this, it's crazy.' My mother's voice was quiet.

'What, now I'm fucking crazy?' Leaving no space for reply, my father's words streamed out, relentless and loud. My mother gazed longingly at the green garden sea, as though willing the trees to come inside and rescue her.

I slipped into the garden and searched the fallen leaves for some sign of the soft grey dust. It lay in little clumps, meagre and exposed, underneath a tree that looked no different to the others. Gathering some up, I hid my sister's ashes in a little painted wooden box among my jewellery, and avoiding the kitchen and the shrine of books, walked out to the driveway and the hissing doors of the school bus.

Always a punctual man, my father began to run late for work, and in the office he made phone call upon phone call until his patients, milling about in the waiting room, looked away from each other's startled eyes. He bought a small rickety house, on impulse, in my one-street country town, with a cheque that he wrote out to friends at three o'clock in the morning, drunk, and he did not tell my mother. He dreamed of building an elaborate marble-floored Italian restaurant in his tiny new house and he drew up the designs and called the architects. He called the bank manager and the builders. He called old friends and acquaintances. His secretary phoned my mother, her voice low and disturbed.

'I'm worried about him. He looks terrible, like he hasn't slept in days. I can't get him off the phone.'

In the evening he rang home to say he'd be there soon but he didn't arrive. He disappeared and my mother's long skirts swayed as she paced, the crease between her brows a savage line. She thought of accidents and car wrecks and he did not phone and he did not phone. He had vanished into the nearest city, and it took my mother all the next day to track him down. In the consumer complex of that other world he spent and spent, his credit cards bloating.

'My daughter, everyone thinks she's dead. But she's not, she's come back! She's come back to me,' he told a stunned woman at the checkout. 'She was just on holiday. A protracted holiday!'

On the way home he took twelve hours to complete the two-hour drive, stopping along the way to make more purchases. He bought a new cane furniture suite, a brand spanking leather lounge and more and more presents for my mother, which he claimed post-acquisition were all tax deductible and therefore half price. When he finally arrived home he still didn't tell my mother about the house he had purchased, and the hefty house-sized cheque. Erratic and wired, my father talked and talked, in endless flooding words. My mother's lips tightened and she rang his old doctor friends for help and advice.

'He doesn't sleep. He doesn't eat. I think he's having some sort of episode.'

'He's just starting to feel better.'

'No, he's acting crazy. It's beyond that.'

'I saw him the other day at Jim's. He was in high spirits. Life of the party. Back to his old self.'

'No, this is not normal. He is out of control.'

The next morning, my father's day off, the handyman came to spray the orchard with white oil, but my father made him sit down and watch music videos.

'See how when Clapton comes on stage, Neil Young shifts over? They can't stand each other. You can see by the way Clapton holds his head. I've got it figured, man. You can see it, right?'

'Well, I don't know . . . but I guess I should get to work.'

'No, no, man. Just watch this bit. It's fucking great. You can see that Dylan doesn't even want Willie Nelson there. I mean, it's Dylan's concert, right? You can see this exchange. Backstage, I can tell you what happened. I can tell just from this one look. There, that bit, did you catch it? See how Dylan kind of smiles right there? Here, I'll rewind it for you.'

He had developed detailed theories about what the videos meant, and he sat and stood and sat and stood and talked to the handyman until finally it was dark and the bemused man escaped into the night.

Back at work, he came home late from the office, arms gesticulating with a frenzied flourish, and declared he had something amazing to tell my mother. Waiting while he made phone call after phone call, exhausted and bewildered, she went to bed.

By the weekend he had converted to astrology. Accosting me at breakfast, he dragged me out to the verandah. Sitting across from me with a notepad, my father asked endless questions and jotted down my replies.

Star signs. I was startled by this latest obsession but I sat with him and talked. It felt to me that this morning was the first time my father had heard me speak since Zoe died. He was vibrant, his arms sweeping out in lavish emphasis, and I tentatively smiled.

From the verandah I could see my mother lingering in the garden, wandering from tree to tree, touching the leaves gently as though searching for sustenance. She peered up at us, eyes narrowed, and then left to get supplies from the local shop. When she was gone, my father stood up, smacking his pen against the page.

'Thanks, Jess, you've told me everything I need to know. I'm working on something special here.'

'Right, okay?' I was uncertain.

'I'll be back later to tell you what I've found.'

My father went to his room and when he returned he cornered me in the kitchen. 'I've discovered something amazing, Jess. Zoe didn't leave me. She didn't fucking leave me. I've got this patient, a beautiful girl, you'd love her. You'll meet her soon. She's fourteen, and I know that she's really Zoe. She's Zoe reincarnated.'

Standing over me, my father began to cry, a deep collapsing sob. 'She's not dead, Jess. I knew she'd never leave me. I worked it out from all the things you told me, from what you said about the star signs.' Voice wavering, he wiped his tears roughly from his cheeks with the heels of his palms.

'But Dad, she's fourteen, how could she be Zoe? She was born way before Zoe died.'

'It's partial reincarnation, one of my patients told me about it. This guy knows about heaps of fucking stuff. I've done a lot of talking with him. Lots of fucking talking.'

'Dad, that's crazy.'

'You don't believe me?'

'No. You're acting crazy.'

'You want to know something else?'

'No.'

'See this picture.'

My father held up a *Time* magazine with a picture of a black-skinned man with glasses. 'Do you know who this is?'

'No.'

'It's Arthur Ashe.'

'Who?'

'Arthur Ashe, he's a tennis player who died of AIDS a few years back.'

'So?'

'Do you see anything unusual about this photo?'

'No.'

'That's me. I'm Arthur Ashe. I can tell by the shape of the glasses.'

'But he only died a few years ago, right? Come on, Dad, how is that possible? Who were you before?'

'I'm me, baby, but it's partial, you know?'

Needing to be away from him, I fought tears. 'Dad, you've lost the plot. You've totally lost the plot.'

'Fuck, you sound just like your fucking mother! Both of you so fucking critical.'

I stole away to my room and waited for my mother to come home. She arrived at the same time as the furniture van, with the fancy new lounge suite. My father asked the delivery man to stay for dinner and regaled him with tales of his newly acquired astrological knowledge. After dinner he invited the man to stay the night and then, in a flurry of movement, headed out to a party at a friend's house. We watched him go, exhaling in a communal surge of relief. This friend was a psychiatrist and a colleague, and surely something would be done. We talked shyly to the furniture delivery man, and showed him to the spare room.

Late that night the mother of the fourteen-year-old patient rang. 'Look, I'm worried about your husband. He came to my house, he just dropped by. He says he thinks your daughter has returned. He sounds crazy. I don't think it's right, I mean, he's her doctor. It's not safe. He says he wants to take her away somewhere. She's just a kid, you know?'

After my mother hung up the phone, she searched and searched until finally she found the cheque book and the house-sized cheque.

I escaped the silent fear of the house to spend the night with friends. In their bright company I drank and drank, aiming for that engulfing darkness, and found myself instead crouched in the garden, shivering and lost. My older sister Zoe, vibrant and fierce – delicate of soul and wild of heart – had disappeared from our lives, but every day the event of her death expanded, as the person she was gradually diminished. Her suicide – my father's breaking point – pulling us all to pieces. Drunk in the garden, I mourned the loss of her and the brokenness of my father.

My friends searched for me in the leafy night. Bending down, they gently pushed the hair from my face. They took me to bed, tucking the covers tightly around me and turning out the light. I lay in the darkness, my head pounding and my stomach raw, and eventually slipped off into that quiet black place.

In the morning a friend woke me gently to come to the phone.

My mother had called and it was urgent. 'Jess?'

'Yeah, Mum, what's wrong?' My throat felt razored, my voice shrill.

'Jess, it's your dad. He went missing. They lost him at the party.'

'What?'

'He disappeared and they couldn't find him.'

'Where is he? What happened?' My head throbbed loudly in my ears, and I pushed my fingers hard against my forehead.

'He's at the police station. The police picked him up.' Her voice reverberated on the other end of the line. I was afraid to speak, afraid to find out why. The silence stretched between us. 'Jess?'

'Yeah. What did he do?'

'Are you okay?'

'Yeah, I'm all right. Tell me.'

'He broke into someone's house and put some music on. He turned it up really loud and the police came. He was naked and muddy, I mean, he'd smeared himself with something.'

'Is he okay? I mean, is he hurt?'

'I think he cut himself a bit with the glass. You know, from the window when he broke in. But it's not serious.'

'Mum, what's going to happen?'

'He's not going to be charged, I don't think. It was clear that he's not well. He's going to be picked up and taken to the Richmond Clinic.'

'The Richmond Clinic? Where all his patients go?'

'Yeah.'

The phone shook in my hand, and I felt my lips turning downwards in a flickering involuntary grimace. Fighting tears, I clenched my teeth together until they scraped loudly in my ears.

'I have to go over and bring him some stuff, some books and pyjamas. I can't pick you up. Can you stay there today?' My mother sounded tired and tight. I could feel her anxiety through the white cold plastic of the phone. 'Jess, I'll ring you when I get back, okay?'

When my father broke into the stranger's house he carved mandalas into his palms with the glass from a shattered mirror, he smeared himself with sewage and ate a packet of cigarettes. Grief had unravelled his control. He was wild and savage and lost. The sorrow that had engulfed our home since Zoe's death had finally spilled into his outside life in a torrent of mad despair. He was hospitalised but he soon came out, and then he was hospitalised again. He talked of axes and Aphrodite and splitting skulls, and his old doctor friends called from Sydney and whispered to my mother down the end of the line.

'Do you have any guns there? Get rid of the axes. Get rid of anything weapon-like.'

And when the raving was over and the muted sadness returned, it was somehow our fault and he could not forgive us. He was bitter and angry and uncomprehending, and we could not forgive him. He began to talk of my mother as that woman, and when she left the house for any reason she would return to the roaring sound of a chainsaw as he cut down another of her beloved trees.

Watching my father's slide into madness was terrifying. What we had known as eccentricity suddenly became much more than that. How could we tell what was his illness and what was him? He had always been spontaneous and unpredictable: unafraid of the unknown, testing the boundaries. What were the bounds of normal? Who made those rules, and who enforced them? My family were constantly on watch, but what signs were we watching for?

Raging against the dying of the light, my father was in and out of the psychiatric ward from then on until his death a few years later. And no, the causes were not natural. He had reached his breaking point and tumbled into the abyss.

And now, still nestled in those green hills, nearly eighteen years later, I watch myself in the same way. Walking through life warily, the line between destruction and perfection so fine as to be perilous. What is my breaking point, and will my life take me there? If the line between sane and crazy is fine enough to step over, how can I know when I've taken that step? And who, apart from me, is patrolling the perimeters?

In light of what happened to my dad, that yellow Esprit shirt has taken on a whole new meaning. I keep it hidden deep in my closet, the material so soft and worn it almost comes away in my fingers. Somehow, despite everything, it has come to represent all that is wondrous about living so close to the edge. Being in the moment, being open to the world, being full of spirit and life. Being deeply and utterly yourself.

Meanjin

The Medicine

Karen Hitchcock

It's months before the world will hold its collective breath because a handful of congressmen don't want the United States to provide health insurance for the 47 million of its citizens who don't have it. I'm in the Deep South, having a beer with a senator's chief of staff, and he's trying to explain to me why Obamacare is such a bad thing. It's something to do with the deficit, with taxes and small business, and I'm not following, not even when he shows me a pretty pie chart on his laptop. I'm embarrassed at his effort and at my failure, and I keep wanting to say, 'Stop, save your breath, you're trying to convince a nobody.'

I spend my days downtown in a university hospital known for its innovations, for practising 'accountable care'. Instead of doctors and nurses and patients, they have teams and 'feedbacks' and outcomes. It's the way of the future; they want to apply it back home, where we apparently have an unsustainable system. Enter the lobby and you could be in a five-star hotel: polished solid timber and deep leather armchairs, every surface designed to be easy on the eye.

The handover from the night staff to the day staff takes place in the tearoom on the medical ward. It looks the same as an Australian tearoom, except the mugs are all neatly stacked and there's no threatening notice above the sink about how your mother doesn't work here so you'd better wash your own mug. There are a lot of whiteboards for a tearoom, and they're covered in flow charts and motivational affirmations, written by the clinicians who've all morphed into managers. There's a cork noticeboard with a T-shirt pinned up at the armpits. It's black with green text: *Help Trent Get New Lungs.* A flyer next to the T-shirt explains that Trent is nineteen, has cystic fibrosis and is trying to raise $50,000 to pay for his lung transplant. *Buy a T-shirt for ten bucks! Help me in my quest!*

The night was a tough one, but the staff aren't allowed to use negative words, not even 'busy'. Instead they smile like adverts and say the shift was 'active' and 'challenging'. Before the staff can get out of there, they have to formulate a team-building goal of the day for one of the whiteboards. They come up with *Execute the day with joy* and *Work together*, but settle on *Spread the cheer.*

We gather in the corridor ahead of the ward round. One of the doctors takes a call and announces, 'She's on her way.' Who, I ask? 'The social worker. We can't start without her.' Social workers in Australia never join our ward rounds. They have barely enough time as it is to organise all the respite and residential care, family meetings, emergency funding and home help.

The social worker arrives, and we crowd in the doorway of the first patient. He's recovering from a bout of pneumonia, and the doctor thinks he needs a few weeks in rehabilitation to get him strong enough to return home. The social worker steps forward with her clipboard: 'Unfortunately, Mr D.'s insurance doesn't cover rehab.' The doctor turns back to the patient: 'Unfortunately, your insurance doesn't cover rehab and so you'll have to go home directly. Be careful, take it slowly, see your family doctor in a week.' Mr D. nods. We move on.

The next patient is ready for discharge. The social worker asks the doctor to change drug X to drug Y as the insurance company won't pay for drug X. The doctor changes X to Y. The next patient, a pensioner, is informed that he needs two more days of in-patient antibiotics for his infected prostate. He pleads to go home: 'Doctor, please, it's costing me $250 a day in co-payments. I can't afford this.' The doctor says he's sorry. The social worker says nothing.

After work, I drive around downtown. Dozens of young fit black men mill outside soup kitchens and in car parks, their portable bedding close by. I see a woman and baby wrapped in a quilt, lying under a scraggy tree beside a mess of men and clothes and boxes. I haven't eaten all day and suddenly feel faint. I order a shake at a deserted diner. It is unimaginably delicious: chocolate ice cream made just soft enough to move through a fat straw.

I join the gridlock back to the suburbs; the streets grow quieter, greener, wider. I attend a party in a beautiful house. We are mostly doctors, drinking wine, eating steak. Our children roam the streets, clutching cups of homemade lemonade. I get to talking with one doc. To whom is he accountable, actually? How does he negotiate the health insurance minefield? What happens if the patient can't pay? He looks over my shoulder. 'Oh, we don't get involved with that side of things . . . The hospital interviews them. They work something out.' *Interviews* them? About what? 'You know, helps them calculate their assets . . .' I stare at him. He looks annoyed and says, 'Do *your* patients have to wait twelve months for their hip replacements, like they do in the UK?' I raise my glass: 'God save the Queen.' He smiles a winning smile. 'Well, Americans sure wouldn't put up with *that*!'

I couldn't wait to get back to our overcrowded hospitals that stink of hot chips, where bad things are called bad names and you can swear freely in the tearooms. Where you're a patient, not a customer, so the lack of a fatal car crash is the only thing standing between you and a new set of lungs. You may have to wait months in pain for your new hip and then share a room with three snorers, but you'll get the drugs the government lets me prescribe you, and if you can't walk post-op you'll have physical therapy someplace ugly, and if despite all that you can no longer leave your house, the social worker will hook you up with Meals on Wheels. Spread the cheer.

*

The first time I see Irena, we are two doctors down and have a full waiting room. I call her name, four times. Finally she stands up: ninety-four years old, 125 centimetres tall.

The clinic is for elderly patients with multiple chronic problems: failing heart, kidneys and lungs, dissolving bones and aching joints, bone marrow that's drying up. In the name of efficiency, these patients cannot ask to see the same doctor at each appointment; they have to make do with whoever picks them up from the pile. They are old and complex and getting expensive – we wouldn't want to spoil them. There is a desk between us, and I am supposed to type notes directly into the computer as they talk, as if I am a travel agent. Of course, most patients are deaf, so we spend the consultation shouting at each other. Apparently, a doctor who knows you and in whom you might trust is less important than that god Efficiency. I have the highest respect for rules I agree with, so I make an unofficial arrangement with the nurse coordinators and start to see regularly my own cohort of patients. Irena becomes one of mine.

Though deaf, Irena whispers. I look at her: cataract, arthritis, stains on her cardigan, false teeth that are too big for her gums so they move up and down independently of her lips when she speaks. I get inefficient: I leave the desk and sit next to her so I can hear. Her English is halting, slow as calligraphy. I ask her if next time she wants me to arrange a Russian interpreter. She looks at me and raises an eyebrow: 'You don't like my English?' I ask her how she has been since she last came to the clinic. She says what she says every time thereafter: 'I am ninety-four, doctor. I am old.' She always pauses here and raises a finger before her punchline: 'But I am not dead yet.' Then she laughs.

I sit beside her to feel her pulse or listen to her lungs, and she tells me snippets that over months become grand narratives. In Stalin's Russia, her husband was taken to a labour camp for running his own business as a tailor. They wouldn't let him take his violin. For a year, this tiny woman travelled to the camp every week and demanded they give it to him. She wrote letters. To Stalin. They relented. Her husband played so beautifully he was granted an unofficial reward: though it was against the rules, Irena could stay in the camp for a week.

Once patients enter a nursing home, they are no longer eligible to attend this clinic. It's another world, and all the rules change. I know Irena is on her way there when I sit next to her doing something clinical and she whispers in her ancient staccato: 'Doctor. This week. I dirtied myself. Two times.'

The black heart of a health system based solely on utilitarian economics is the unspoken truth that once a citizen ceases to be productive their care ceases to be cost-effective. If you are old and sick and reliant on the state, you are a dead woman. As a Russian Jew born in 1919, Irena had been a dead woman many times before – in 1941, for instance, until her father, whom she never saw again, intervened in her fate, saying, 'You must be far away by morning.'

When Irena doesn't turn up to two appointments in a row, I realise she's been moved to a home. I am sad and increasingly troubled by questions about the camp that only she can answer. Did her husband have his own room? What was in it? Was there a window? Was the bed comfortable? What did they eat? Was she happy? I start to feel panicked when I think of her. What was it like in there?

I call the nursing home and ask them to ask Irena if I might visit. She says to come tomorrow. The next day, I step into one of the taxis lined up in front of the hospital and ask the driver to take me to the nursing home. The taxi driver looks from my face to my hospital ID and back to my face; then he drives me 300 metres around the corner.

Irena's room has a narrow bed, a wardrobe, a bar fridge and a single armchair. I sit on her walking frame and ask how she is. She is old, but not dead yet. We laugh at this. She tells me she fell and thought she was being taken to hospital but instead found herself in this room. Someone brings one cup of tea and a dark brown biscuit and smiles at me over Irena's head. Irena dips her finger into the plastic cup, says 'cold' and pushes it away. When I stand up to leave, she opens her fridge. It is full of brown biscuits, piled into the door shelves and drawers. She insists that I take some and wraps a handful in a napkin. She puts the parcel in my hands: 'Will you come again?'

I push out into the sun and stride back to the hospital. The young rule the world; we stomp around doling out mean rations to the old, the machinery of our secure, able bodies purring to us the myth that we will live forever. And one by one my patients retreat to these small rooms and then slip away. Soon they will all be gone. And then it will be your turn and mine to sit in cells and drink the weak tea they hand out at eleven and two, hoarding biscuits in our fridges. Not dead, yet.

*

Before I started studying medicine, my grandmother was diagnosed with idiopathic pulmonary fibrosis. I had no idea what that was. 'Scarring of the lungs,' she said. When I announced my plan to become a doctor, she was ecstatic with pride. She'd tell anyone who listened. Like the person scanning our groceries at the supermarket. She'd look at him, then at me, then back at him, and I'd know it was coming. 'This is my granddaughter.' He'd look up, his face all like, *And?* She'd lean in and say, 'She's going to be a doctor.' I'd roll my eyes and go, 'Nan, jeez . . .'

When I visited, the first thing she'd say to me as I walked in the door was 'Stop. Stand over there. Now turn around.' I'd roll my eyes. 'I just want to look at you,' she'd say. 'Now come here, and bring that comb.' She'd been a hairdresser. My hair didn't often live up to her standards.

In second year I bought my first stethoscope. When Nan said, 'Stand over there,' I said, 'Wait!' I pulled it from my backpack, looped it around my neck and turned around. You should have seen her face.

By the time I was in third year, she was eighty-one and permanently attached to a tube that went from her nostrils to an oxygen concentrator. The tube was long enough for her to move all around the house. When we went out, she took a small oxygen cylinder on a trolley. She said, 'My lungs are "diseased" – what a terrible word . . . listen to them if you wish.' I pressed my stethoscope against her soft, pink skin, and caught my breath. By then I knew what the sounds meant. During her afternoon naps, I'd get into bed next to her with my textbook and she'd quietly watch me from her side of the twenty or so pillows.

One time she said, 'I have a really bad pain here on my right side.' 'What's it like?' I asked. 'When did it start? Does anything make it go away? Turn around.' I gently pressed the spot and she winced. 'I think you've broken a rib.' We looked at each other with our eyes open wide. Her doctor sent her for an X-ray, held it up to the light and said, 'You've broken a rib.' She beamed at him. 'I know. My granddaughter already told me.'

Just before my fourth-year clinical exams, she fell in the bathroom one night and lay on the cold tiles until morning. At the hospital they said she'd had a heart attack and things looked bad. She was too weak to drink. She gripped my hand, hard as steel, and whispered, 'I don't want to die yet.' The physician said, 'We should perhaps consider palliation . . .' I begged him, 'Please keep trying.'

In hospital she told me halting, dreamy stories about how her husband developed a brain tumour in the 1950s. They knew it was a brain tumour because he was fixing his car one day and his right arm rose straight above his head all by itself. They stood there by the car, both staring at his risen arm as if it were a stranger. After the operation, she cared for him at home. The doctor taught her how to inject morphine.

One evening Nan's IV drip blocked and a junior doctor came to find a site for a new one. I don't know what the drip was for – fluids, diuretics or antibiotics. He said to me authoritatively, 'You realise this is futile, to torture her like this?' I tried to explain – that, for her, being in hospital and the pain of a thin needle was worth the chance for a little more life – but it came out as a stutter. I just stood there under his accusatory stare, gripped with deep shame. He told me to wait in the corridor. I heard him croon to my nan as she winced with each of his failed attempts: 'I'm sorry, you poor thing. This is cruel. We know it's unfair.' There was silence for a moment. 'Let's try the cubital fossa,' he said to the nurse.

When they were done, they walked out and past me without a word. I went back in, pressed my cheek against her cool forehead and said I was sorry. She whispered, 'Don't worry. I'm okay.'

She came home for a few months. She couldn't get herself to the shops anymore and was in a lot of pain from her breaking bones. 'What do you do all day?' I asked her. 'I remember,' she said, smiling mightily. 'I play in my memories.' She was happy to be alive. But slowly her breathing deteriorated, her fingers turned purple and then she couldn't get out of bed. She couldn't think about anything except her next breath, and it was never quite enough. We talked about it. I called the palliative care service and they admitted her to the hospice, where she was given drugs to relieve the torture of slowly drowning. I'd bring a book to the ward and climb into bed with her. She'd rest her head on my shoulder and close her eyes.

There is a push for palliative care 'pathways', for treating the old in their nursing homes, for withholding treatment that is 'futile'. We seek ways to make things in the last months and years neat and pre-determined and (dare I say it) cost-effective. But no algorithm or flow chart can accommodate the messy intricacies of dying. Who decides what life is worth living? We cannot know in advance what we will find tolerable. If you had asked my grandmother if she would have been happy to live housebound, attached to an oxygen machine, even a year before it happened, she would have said no thank you. She would have chosen death. The resident attending to my grandmother's IV drip was filled with a sense of moral righteousness. He was disgusted by the attempt to pump life back into a damaged and dying old body; he couldn't believe she would choose that, or should even be offered the choice. It was failure of empathy disguised as empathy. A failure of imagination.

*

Researchers relate 'decision fatigue' in executives to the degradation of sound judgement and to poor impulse control after hours. Nearing the end of a weekend of dealing with a ward full of sick patients, and faced with a particularly challenging case, I recognise I have it by my own sudden irritability and my desire to decide *anything*, for a bit of relief. Rather than start saying stupid things in an authoritative tone and driving a Maserati I don't own 200 kilometres an hour down some freeway, I tell my registrar I'll be back in fifteen minutes and walk to my office.

Each year, medical errors cause hundreds of patient deaths in Australia. Decision-making processes are therefore interesting to educators and researchers seeking to reduce avoidable harm. You see your GP and your blood pressure is elevated: whether you will be prescribed a drug or not depends on your 'risk profile' – whether you smoke, have diabetes, have cardiovascular disease – and also on your doctor's threshold for prescribing. The doctor will hopefully include you in the decision-making process, but he or she still needs to recommend a particular course of action and tell you why. The drug must be chosen from one of dozens on the market. Each decision is made through a mix of scientific methodology, pattern recognition, probability and personal opinion.

National consensus guidelines offer basic treatment algorithms for all the common diseases. If a patient has a chronic lung disease, you can check these guidelines and prescribe what is considered to be best current practice. There are websites with 'consumer decision-making tools' where patients can type in their own data and get a computer-generated recommendation. There are also equations and scoring systems, far too many to remember, so we carry them around in apps. The Wells score determines the likelihood that a breathless patient has a blood clot in their lung; the CHA_2DS_2-VASc score guides the prescription of anti-coagulants by determining the risk of stroke from a fibrillating heart; the Child-Pugh score (based on tests for blood albumin, bilirubin and clotting, fluid in the abdomen and degree of brain malfunction) is used to work out how long a patient with a failing liver has to live. Should a drug be prescribed for osteoporosis? Type in the patient's data and get an answer. There are protocols in hospital for the treatment of disasters like heart attacks, catastrophic haemorrhage and community-acquired pneumonia. These are designed to guide decision-making and reduce human error, and are helpful if the patient's body follows protocol. But if I followed the guidelines for all of the diseases afflicting my typical elderly patient, she would be on twenty-one medications and I would be killing her.

Hippocrates said that it is more important to know what kind of patient the disease has than what kind of disease the patient has. You'd think the body would be more straightforward; we don't have that many organs and only five of them are vital. Sometimes you just don't know exactly what to do: you study the form, consult your mates and the major online encyclopaedias, take an educated gamble, then sit back and watch the race, sweating bullets. Maybe that's why some people hate doctors, those culpable, imperfect decision-making machines.

As a trainee you pass the difficult decisions to the boss, with relief. But now I am the boss, and I have a young patient with pneumonia and two litres of bacteria-filled pus collecting outside his lungs, making him septic and delirious. The treatment is intravenous antibiotics and surgical drainage. But the patient's liver is failing after a decade of serious drinking; it no longer makes clotting factors, so his blood is thin and he may bleed to death if the surgeons cut into his chest. His heart is straining;

his brain is faltering in a bath of blood-borne toxins. He will likely die without the operation. He will likely die with the operation.

The patient laughs and pulls his blanket over his head when I outline his options. His only living relative tells us to do what we think is best. The surgeons say it's my call. So do the infectious-diseases physician and the gastroenterologist. The anaesthetist says he'll intubate him but estimates that he has a seventy per cent chance of death. My team of junior doctors look at me expectantly, trusting that I have the answer. There is no protocol, no app that can share the responsibility.

All day I have that feeling you get when you take a step and think you'll hit pavement but your foot falls unexpectedly into a gutter. No sooner have I convinced myself that it would be futile to put him through surgery than I think, 'Well, why *not* put him through the surgery? What have we got to lose?' Even Hippocrates knew that 'when the entire lung is inflamed . . . he will live for two or three days'.

He could die on the table, but then again he might wake up with a clean chest cavity and say thanks. According to his Child-Pugh score, he could last three more years. You can do a lot in three years.

My other patients, with simpler combinations of pneumonia, dehydration, intoxication, and heart and kidney failure, recede in their crisp white beds. Their treatments are settled; all they need for today is time and medicine.

I tell my registrar I'll be back, go to my office, and pick up a book about a journalist and a doctor who may or may not be a murderer. I never wanted to be a lawyer, because laws are just made-up rules. I never wanted to be a gambler, because I don't believe in luck. I drink a glass of water and walk back to the ward. I take the patient's file – that poor sick man – and write a summary, each of his vital organs listed and followed by its narrative of failure. It is useful, to see the facts reduced to a story in a format that approaches an equation that ends with a decision.

The Monthly

Wolf Like Me

Antonia Hayes

The bruises came first. They were scattered about the soft skin of my stomach and thighs; my body was a galaxy of haematoma constellations. Sometimes they would worry me, bruises that appeared overnight when I had no memory of any physical trauma. Mostly I ignored them. My clusters of purple stars only bothered me on the grounds of vanity, like when I wanted to wear a short skirt or bare my midriff in a bikini. Some of my boyfriends even liked my bruises, running stray fingers over my black and blue body, asking where they came from and if they hurt. Once I was told they were sexy. Perhaps there's something charming about being the sort of delicate girl who literally bruises easily.

There were other symptoms too: crippling fatigue, rashes, joint pain, food intolerances, swollen lymph nodes, a constant battle with anaemia no matter how many iron tablets I swallowed or how many rare steaks I ate. Once or twice I'd had memory blackouts – for no apparent reason I didn't know what happened the night before, and how I'd made it back to my bed. There was that strange case of acute pancreatitis; an inflamed seventy-two hours of sharp, intense pain that my doctor couldn't explain or understand. My body had given us hints, but symptoms are never symptoms when you're not looking for a cause.

My inevitable downfall was the sun, the trigger of an intense flare of illness. My friend Bella and I had gone on a holiday to the beach, where we sat on the hot sand all day and read Doris Lessing, and lay out on cheap inflatable lilos tied to a buoy, floating under the Mediterranean sun. We jumped off rugged clay cliffs into the sea, sipped on pineapple-flavoured cocktails, laughed and danced to Europop. After a week our skin was dusky and our hair fell in saltwater waves. But I came home with a fever, aching limbs, and a violet shock of bruises. One leg was indigo and covered in welts. In the days following the holiday, my body was so heavy that I couldn't get out of bed for almost a week, and so sore that, incapable of standing up, I vomited in my sheets and lay in a pool of my own sick for several hours until I could move.

When I made it to see the doctor, he couldn't explain what had happened to me, why I was sick. There were tests and endless amounts of blood work – prodding, poking and jabbing – and the crook of my elbow became accustomed to the pierce of cold metal. He took vial after vial of my blood, hoping that somewhere in my cells was a clue to the mystery of my illness. The first round of tests sent to the pathologist were inconclusive. The next results prompted one of those urgent phone calls: 'I have some bad news for you, you need to come to my office right away.' The sort of news you can't be told over the phone.

I remember sitting in the light-blue vinyl chair, my handbag on my lap and my hands in a ball, as the doctor told me what he'd found. My platelet count was upsettingly low and my white blood cell count was frighteningly high. He showed me a sheet of paper with columns and numbers in rows that I didn't understand. Bar charts and histograms. My results were well outside the normal range. I tried to picture my blood, like a bright red pool with too many white lifesaver rings set afloat to rescue the drowning.

'What does it mean?' I asked, scanning over my platelets and cells.

'I need to test your bone marrow,' the doctor said.

'How come?' I shifted my weight in the vinyl seat.

He didn't look me in the eye. 'To make sure you don't have leukaemia.'

We had to act quickly. My appointment to have the bone marrow aspiration was forty-eight hours later, and for the next two days I was emotionally paralysed, watching videos on YouTube of tragic photo montage tributes to children and adults who'd died of leukaemia, soundtracked to sad but ultimately uplifting Sarah McLachlan songs. I read case studies of chemotherapy gone wrong and started to research holistic alternatives. The survival rate in adults diagnosed with leukaemia was fifty per cent. At twenty-six I'd never considered my own mortality before, but suddenly I had to think about a universe where the chances I might die were the same as the flip of a coin. Maybe I had cancer. What would happen to my unrealised dreams, what would happen to my very young son? Before then, those questions had only ever been rhetorical. I bought a Do-It-Yourself Will Kit online and listed my beneficiaries and the disposition of my estate. There wasn't much to give away and bequeath: I left my books to my dad, and my son to my mum.

I shuffled into the pathology lab in an open-backed hospital-green robe, and was told to lie on my stomach. As they gave me a local anaesthetic, I caught a glimpse of the needle the doctor was going to inject. Bone marrow aspiration needles are thick like a nail and as long as a forearm. On my hip there's a shiny scar where the needle went into my skin, piercing through the bone – my posterior iliac crest. The scar is a perfect circle: the precise shape of the needle's hollow form. When the needle went in, I bit the inside of my mouth so forcefully that I drew blood. I heard my pelvis break open.

Looking at my own bone marrow was an out-of-body experience – the spongy pink fluid is a secret that your bones are meant to keep from you. I thought of my mother making veal *osso bucco* and how as a child I'd refused to eat the viscous marrow wobbling inside the hollow of the bone. The doctor had drawn 20 mL, yielding approximately 300 µL of my marrow. Soon the cellular elements of my blood would be able to complete the story. I was left with another huge bruise.

It wasn't leukaemia. In my relief I wasn't able to process the bad news that came with the good. I was just so excited that I didn't have cancer. Suddenly my alternate universe with tragic photo montages and acoustic power ballads dissolved and I could see myself alive in the future again. I wanted to rip up my will, start reimagining my twilight years, and drink lots of champagne. But the pathologists had found something else in my marrow: a clinically significant number of anti-nuclear antibodies. The tests weren't over; they'd really only just begun. I was referred to a clinical immunologist, a haematologist and a rheumatologist. It took months for a conclusive diagnosis.

I had systemic lupus erythematosus. I still do. I always will.

An autoimmune disease, lupus causes the body's immune system to mistakenly attack healthy tissue. It's the ultimate miscommunication between cell and cell: my heart speaks a different language to my blood; my liver is a stranger to my lungs. There is no cure. *Lupus* is Latin for 'wolf', apparently because it 'devours' the affected part. My wolf will eat me, organ by organ, because it thinks my perfectly healthy body is a disease it needs to fight. On its hell-bent path of destruction, my wolf will damage my tissues slowly with each passing day. My wolf is already devouring my heart. Several years ago I thought I was in cardiac arrest – I clutched my chest and couldn't breathe, my body mimicking the symptoms of a heart attack. It was acute pericarditis, inflammation of the sac around the heart. The pericardium holds the heart in place and helps it work properly. Now mine is damaged and vulnerable. Because of this, chances are high it could happen again. Maybe I will feel literal heartbreak.

*

These are all things that I rarely admit to myself. The rebel inside likes to pretend that I don't have lupus. It wants to binge drink tequila and eat badly, chain smoke and stay up all night. Lie out in the sun and expose my skin to the sharp warmth of ultraviolet rays. It wants to skimp on sleep, not drink enough water, and never have to consider the consequences of neglecting my diet, exercise and required rest. I've had to learn the hard way that skipping my medication or missing a night's sleep will just make things worse. That I am photosensitive – sitting in the sun will aggravate my condition and put me out of action. That I have a chronic illness that waxes and wanes like the moon but is always cycling through a series of different shapes and changing light. Once I think I've learnt my body's idiosyncrasies, it surprises me again. It's the symbiotic relationship between physical and mental health that I've found most difficult to swallow.

That the pain I feel in my bones will often precipitate an unexplained pain inside my head.

Yet I'm careful not to be the girl who cries wolf. My wolf is a secret, locked inside a cage. Most people I know, apart from my closest friends and family, don't even know that I have lupus. Fluctuations in my body's inflammation levels mean my face can look different from one day to the next, but I'm probably the only one who notices. I don't look sick. My illness is invisible. When people ask me how I am, how I'm feeling today, I always tell them I'm fine. Better to be stoic about the joint pain that makes me cry in the shower, or pretend that my lymph nodes are a normal size, or that my hair isn't falling out by the handful, than allow other people to glimpse my weaknesses and vulnerabilities. Sympathy and pity aren't parties I want to attend, let alone be the guest of honour.

Although I try not to be fatalistic about it, systemic lupus erythematosus was written into my genes. In the spaces between history and heredity, I had a predisposition. The disease occurs nine times more often in women than in men. It is more common in women of childbearing age, and also those of Asian or African descent. And while the genetic patterns for inheriting lupus are complex, I do have a family history.

My great-aunt Rosie died from lupus when I was eight years old. She was my grandfather's youngest sister and I only remember her being sick, her face and fingers swollen from the steroids that she had to take. She was pale and quiet, and had to excuse herself from my seventh birthday party to have a sleep. The following year she was dead: her wolf ate her alive. I have no recollection of my great-aunt being the woman who loved to run along beaches that other relatives told me she was. In the photographs of Rosie before her diagnosis, before her organs began to fail, her smile is wide and her eyes are bright. That woman is a stranger to me, and I wonder if my children or grandchildren will one day stare at old photographs of my face, unable to recognise my smile or my eyes. Rosie was fifty-six when she died and sometimes I wake up in a panic, terrified that maybe I only have twenty-five years left.

It was only through considering my own mortality that I became concerned with ways I could leave my own mark. Chasing immortality is the side effect of looking death in the face. The beginnings of my quest to live forever started with what I put – and often didn't put – into my mouth. Fasting, elimination diets, raw vegetables, no gluten, no lactose, no meat; I have tried every dietary program that any naturopath has put in front of me, assuring me that it will be my cure. Once I didn't eat for fourteen days straight, drinking only water, because it was going to flush out my toxins and clear my guts; the gastrointestinal tract is a prominent part of the immune system. After a fortnight I was slimmer with sparkling eyes but also grumpy and weak. Colonic irrigation was another obsession that I thought might end my problems, but it proved uncomfortable and expensive. To this day I still try every diet that claims it will improve my longevity because frankly, I am still scared.

Not long after I was diagnosed, I met my friend Sam for a drink. Under his jacket he was wearing a T-shirt with the screen-printed face of Dr House. Below Hugh Laurie's face, the T-shirt said *It's Not Lupus*. When Sam took his jacket off I laughed uncomfortably at the shirt.

'Do you watch *House*?' he asked.

I shook my head. 'Not really.'

Sam looked down at his shirt. 'Whenever they're trying to diagnose a patient on the show, the younger doctors always suggest lupus. And Hugh Laurie always scowls, "It's not lupus!" and it never is. It's a running joke in each episode.'

'I have lupus.' I smiled to try to soften the potential severity of this.

Sam laughed. 'It's never lupus.'

I laughed with him. 'I seriously do have it, though. I was diagnosed about two years ago.'

'Oh.'

A week or so later I received a package in the post. Inside was my own T-shirt with Hugh Laurie's face, but it said, *Finally It's Lupus*. The night in the bar when I'd admitted to Sam that I had lupus, his reaction had been unexpected. There was no 'I'm so sorry' or curious 'So, how do you live with it, day to day?' platitude. Sam told me to use my lupus. He told me to write it. He told me to make it a story and explore it, and make it my thing, my point of difference. It was advice that didn't sit well with me at the time. Writing about lupus and turning disease into words, into stories, seemed really cheap.

But my quest for immortality had developed an unexpected kink: I was writing hundreds of thousands of words. Driven by my manic need to leave a mark, I documented everything. I kept diaries. I enrolled in a novel-writing course and wrote a manuscript. I wrote stories and essays and articles and poems, but I wouldn't admit the impetus for my obsessive need to write was that I was scared I was going to die. That I was afraid of the big bad wolf. That he was going to huff and puff and blow my house in, and all the straw, sticks and bricks weren't going to stop him. I had the bruises to prove it.

I am not special because I'm going to die. We all will. But my wolf is devouring my fear.

Meanjin

Sex and Cancer: A History in Three Parts

Luke Ryan

I

Despite being the foundational function of the human species, nobody talks about sex when you're diagnosed with cancer. There's a sense that sex is simple recreation, or distraction, and now that you've got real problems the whole unseemly business can just be pushed to the back burner for a while. Tell anyone that you had sex while in the midst of chemotherapy and they gape at you slack-jawed, as if astounded that a human being going through that kind of physical punishment could still be capable of a feat of such endurance. I get the feeling most people assume that when you have cancer, all your non-vomiting time is spent staring out a hospital window and considering the prospect of your own demise.

However, doctors do talk to you about your reproductive future, which, as a twenty-two-year-old, was something I thought I was a good decade away from having to discuss with anybody. Mum, in particular, was not someone I ever thought I'd have to involve in my masturbatory schedule.

When I was sick at the age of eleven, we weren't considering the reproductive repercussions of my chemotherapy regimen. I was still on the soprano side of puberty and besides a vague footnote to the effect that a year's worth of chemotherapy could, on occasion, produce long-term infertility, we didn't think twice about it. There wouldn't have been sperm to extract even if we'd wanted to. Sex in all its permutations just wasn't on the agenda.

Back then the closest I had come to sex was at the age of four, when Mum walked in on me during bath time to find me trying to get my penis up the tap. If you roll the logistics of this task around in your head for a second, you realise there are a very limited number of positions into which you can fold yourself that will allow you to place your penis inside a bath tap. Well, there's only one really: the Linda-Blair-descending-a-staircase-while-possessed-by-the-devil. Although I have no memory of the incident, or what I could possibly have been trying to achieve, let it never be said that I was not an ambitious and/or demonically possessed youngster.

My only other piece of X-rated exposure came two years later, when I walked in on Mum and Dad having sex, an event that, by contrast, I remember all too vividly. It's an incident notable not so much for the fact of catching my parents mid-coitus, but more for the fact that I then went to school the next day and told every single person there that I, and I quote, 'saw my Dad sexing my mother's bottom'. The reason we have a direct quote is because my classmate Dan went home and told his mother and she decided to let Mum know that I was going around school telling people that I had seen my parents having anal sex. In defence of my mother's honour, I was still using the word 'bagina' at the time so may not have been entirely up to date with the workings of the female anatomy. (This occurred a day after I made my first and only entry in yet another of my failed journals, Mum and Dad having confiscated this one when they found that my remarks for Saturday 4 July 1992 consisted of: *I walked in on Mum and Dad having sex haha! M15+ Whoops!* Evidently, seven-year-old Luke was difficult to impress.)

By 1997 I had only the vaguest idea that girls were important and that it would probably be good to have sex with one before I died. Fortunately, it was a topic we never needed to contemplate. Four years later I read a news story about a fifteen-year-old boy dying of cancer who had convinced his nurses to source him a prostitute and I wondered if my nurses would have done the same for me. Not that I would have had much idea what to do when she arrived – I was playing a lot of Uno when I was in hospital – but I still felt that seeing a real-life, non-Mum woman naked needed to be on my bucket list.

When I was twenty-two, though, things were rather different. In the intervening years I'd gone through puberty, grown an extra layer of hair, put a condom on a banana and even seen a few real-life, non-Mum women naked. I also now had sperm. Lots and lots of sperm. As a general rule, chemotherapy works by annihilating the fastest-replicating cells in the body, so sperm stands in the frontline of the assault. On this basis, my oncologist recommended that I freeze a sample of my sperm before I started treatment. Just to ensure that the grade-A genetic stock that had produced two separate tumours in twenty-two years could be passed on to future generations. He may not have used those exact words.

Mum was at the oncologist's with me when this discussion came up, and a couple of days later I arrived in the kitchen to see her busy with the family diary.

'Lukey, I've booked the appointment.'

'What appointment?'

'You know. The appointment.' Silence. 'Where you produce a sample of yourself.'

'Oh.'

A beat.

She grinned mischievously and said, 'I bet you're looking forward to that.'

It would have been a lazy thirty-five degrees outside as I drove to my 'appointment', an erotic temperature if ever there was one. It took me a couple of loops of the hospital to discover the down-at-heel wing to which they had relegated what a doctor friend of mine referred to as 'Jizz Palace'. I made my way up to Level 3, went down to the end of a drab, brown-carpeted corridor, turned right into another corridor, this one covered in tarnished 1960s lino and lit by dying fluorescents, and kept going until I finally arrived at an unassuming door that read, in euphemistic fashion: *Keogh Institute for Medical Research*. I knocked.

I was the first person I knew of that had ever needed to provide a sperm sample, so my understanding of the process came solely from seeing people donate sperm in frat-boy comedies. Suffice to say, in reality there are far fewer wise-cracking African-American nurses than the movies would have you believe. I opened the door on to a lab plucked straight from a low-budget 1960s sci-fi film, populated by two dorky uncle types who glanced up from microscopes that they were using to, I presume, examine sperm. They grinned unsettlingly, and rolled their chairs towards me. I tried to work out how best to tell two complete strangers that I had come to ejaculate on their premises.

'Uh. Hi. My name's Luke . . .'

'Ah, Luke. You're freezing some of your sperm today?'

'. . . Yes.'

'Excellent. Well, here's your cup.' He handed me a tiny cup. It resembled a medical-grade shot glass. 'Head next door. You'll find some magazines in there if you need them. We have some DVDs too, if you'd like?'

I didn't think I could bear browsing their porn collection while they watched, so I demurred.

'Well, if you change your mind, let us know.'

'Will do.' I was pretty confident that I wouldn't be breaking off mid-wank to ask them for more material.

'Now, we need you to catch at least sixty per cent of the sample in the cup, so make sure you're careful.'

'Um. Okay.'

'And when you're finished producing the sample come back and we'll pop it in the freezer for you.' While their enthusiastic smiles suggested an admirable degree of passion for their chosen line of work, the last thing I needed right then was the thought of them both mentally cheering me on from the next room.

'Thanks. I'll, uh, be back soon.'

'No rush. Take your time!'

I met their eyes, trying to gauge if this was a joke. It wasn't. Tiny cup in hand, I walked next door and entered the masturbatorium. This was, essentially, a glorified disabled toilet. To my left there was a table laden with an extensive array of two-decade-old porn. Next to the table there was an actual toilet, largely unadorned. In the back left corner sat a chair, done up in that ever-so-erotic, puce-coloured hospital pleather. Then, in the other corner stood a weird semi-recliner, which was essentially a puce-coloured seatback, laid at a forty-five-degree angle, with no seat and two armrests. Despite contemplating it for over twenty seconds, I still couldn't work out how or why anyone would choose to masturbate in that position. Had they received complaints? Were there folk out there who couldn't ejaculate unless they were forming a perfect triangle with the floor and the wall? And how on earth were you supposed to ensure you caught sixty per cent of your sample in that tiny cup if you were using your free hand to keep yourself upright? The mind boggled.

Plucking a weathered 1983 copy of *Playboy* from the stack, I set to. There's something inescapably weird about having to masturbate out of utility. As masturbation is probably the most useless activity you indulge in on any given day, being provided a definite reason to ejaculate sucks a lot of the already limited magic out of the experience. Also, knowing that there are two strange men waiting not five metres away to receive a cup full of your semen is less than ideal. I flicked open to June's 'Playmate of the Month', Jessica, who was reclining, nude, on a faux-revival chaise longue, like some kind of permed, well-to-do sea lion. I closed my eyes, and thought of England.

When I was finished I headed back into the lab, feeling suitably chastened.

'All done?' They beamed at me as if expecting me to compliment their public-hospital-themed self-love dungeon.

'Yep.'

'Did everything go okay? Did you catch all of the sample?'

'Yep.'

My need to escape was overwhelming. A jar of my semen sat between us on the table. It is very difficult to converse with someone while your own ejaculate sits there, staring at you accusingly. They made me sign a couple of forms. I mumbled a goodbye. I noticed they didn't try to shake my hand.

I drove home, a bit dejected, and walked into the kitchen. Mum was having lunch. She looked up at me. 'So,' she said cheerily, 'how was it?'

II

A few weeks after my trip to the sperm bank, I started dating a girl named Lucy. Dating is the sort of activity that, by its very nature, tends to be forward thinking. The moment at which something transitions from idle sex and into a full-blown relationship is usually the moment at which you begin to imagine a year, two years into the future and still see that person lying in your bed each morning. The problem with dating while you have cancer is that half the time when you look a year or two into the future, *you're* not lying in your bed anymore. Your life at that moment is more concerned with avoiding endings than searching for new beginnings.

Still, at the age of twenty-two, sex tends to be a driving force of your existence in the same way that oxygen is a pretty bang-up way to stay alive. Simply sidelining the issue because of a piffling concern like a life-threatening illness ain't going to fly. And when the sum total of your daily obligations is a fifteen-minute visit to the radiotherapy clinic (with weekends off) and all your friends have jobs and university degrees to attend to, well, having a girlfriend becomes a really useful way of passing the time.

So, I started seeing Lucy. She was a few years older than me, pale-skinned, with punkily dyed, asymmetrical hair. Her eyes had a kind, almost sad cast to them, although I later discovered this was because of the permanent watering caused by her heavy, just-this-side-of-clinical-blindness contact lenses. She was tomboyish in attitude and fashion, a girl of quiet self-possession whose wry smile gave off the impression of being in on a joke that you haven't quite worked out yet. On the first date I took her to see a band called Explosions in the Sky, and at the end of the night she kissed me in the car. For the second date we watched a film at an outdoor cinema and drank a six-pack of Peroni. I told her Peroni reminded me of summer. Lucy said they tasted like sex. It wasn't a come-on, but the way she said it made her sound devastatingly assured. We went home together. She understood enough not to ask about my illness. I think she recognised a man looking for escape when she saw him.

We got along fine, but I think from the moment we started dating we were both afflicted by the sense that we were counting down the days until it was time to break up. I was preoccupied with my health and had plans to leave the state as soon as I could. She was in the middle of a university degree and had locked herself into Perth for the foreseeable future. Nonetheless, we settled into a cosy pattern: wake up late in the morning, eat breakfast, I'd drive her to university, go to my radiotherapy appointment, and we'd meet up again that night and drink and talk until late. For me it was these small routines, these dispatches from a less complicated life, that left me feeling the most together.

At the end of May 2008, a couple of weeks before I finished my final round of chemo, she sat me down.

'Luke, this has been, um . . . great, but I think maybe we should leave it here.'

Having in my mind already departed for Melbourne, sans her, my relief must have been palpable.

'Yeah. That sounds about right. It has been . . . um . . . great.'

We were awkward, but sincere. It *had* been great, but it was done. It was hard to know what else to say. We kissed to fill the gap and both blinked back tears.

There was silence for a minute, then:

'Anyway, I think this might be me done with boys for a while.'

'Oh. You mean . . .?'

'Yeah.'

'Right.'

Looking back at the amount of *The L Word* we'd been watching, I feel like the warning signs were definitely there. I couldn't really blame her for trying it out with me, though. I was perhaps the most short-term-relationship participant you were ever going to find. One way or the other I was going to be out of the way in a few months. And, personally, at a time in my life when it was easy to feel transient, I'm just glad to have had such a decisive impact.

III

Recently I discovered that my sperm had taken the chemotherapy rather more personally than I had. Whereas most men might expect to produce something in the order of 40 to 60 million sperm with every ejaculation, I am apparently coughing out around 100,000. Of those fifty per cent are dead on arrival, leaving me with a grand total of 50,000 troops to hurl against the impregnation barricades. In my head I imagine my testicles as a post-apocalyptic wasteland where the remaining population has emerged from their subterranean bunker to discover that, yes, they really are the last people left on earth. As they stand there in uncomfortable silence, surveying the wreckage of their civilisa-tion, a single tumbleweed rolls by.

You never realise quite how far below the average age of illness you are than when you're forced to consider your reproductive prospects. The chances of me getting anybody pregnant au naturel are vanishingly remote, but I still didn't have much of a reaction when they told me. Nothing about the announcement felt real. If anything, the knowledge that chance pregnancy was the next best thing to an impossibility came as somewhat of a relief. 'Infertility? Oh, that's fine, doctor. Last night I had a dream where I was a dad and I woke up screaming.' Much better to consign that whole messy process to a controlled, deliberate future of injections and IVF and pure, unfrozen sperm.

I told Mum about the results one night as we sat drinking red wine in her kitchen. The rushed, awkward conversation of five years previously seemed an eon away. Now sex was just another topic in a lifetime of conversation.

'Well, good we got in there early then,' she said, a wry smile spreading across her face. 'How do you feel about it?'

'I think I'm fine. I'm finding it pretty hard to actually take it all that seriously. The idea of having kids is still so . . .' I trailed off, searching for the right word.

'Distant?'

'Hypothetical.'

She laughed. 'You sound like your father. We didn't have Liam until I was thirty-three and even then I almost had to blackmail Gerry into it. But, you know, five years later it was his idea to have you. It felt like the easiest decision in the world back then.' She sipped her wine and her eyes grew bright. 'Twenty-eight years later and it still does.'

A Funny Thing Happened on the Way to Chemo

Dreams of Her Real Self

Helen Garner

It was always clear to me what would happen when my parents died.

Dad would pitch forward without warning into the grave he had dug with his knife and fork. The struggle that had shaped and distorted my character would be over. I would be elated to see the back of him. Then I would torture myself with guilt for the rest of my life.

Free of his domineering presence, my mother would creep out from under her stone. She would show herself at last. At last I would know her. Shyly she would befriend her five remaining children, maybe even come to live with one of us. She would take up her golf clubs again, pull on her flowery bathing cap and swim in the surf, simmer her modest vegetable soups, knit cardigans in quiet stripes with a lot of grey. In a few years she would fade, weaken and slip away. Surely, about her, I would feel only a mild sorrow that would pass in the manner that nature intended.

She went first.

In her early eighties Dad dragged her to the last of the scores of dwellings he had imposed on her during their long marriage, a seventh-floor apartment in central Melbourne that in a fit of Schadenfreude he had bought from a member of her family whose finances had hit the wall. Isolated up there, with a view of St Patrick's Cathedral and Parliament House, she sank into a stunned, resentful gloom shot through with flashes of bitter sarcasm. She would point at a gin and tonic on the table and say, in a grim, warning tone, 'Mark my words. In a minute that ice is going to melt. Then the glass will overflow, and there'll be a *hell* of a mess to clean up.' She slumped into depression, then drifted away into dementia. She wandered at night. She fell and fractured a bone. Her body withered. In a nursing home she became savage, bestial. She snarled at us and lashed out with her claws. Lost to herself and to us, she died at last, by means of something I can only call chemical mercy. My youngest sister and I, strained and silent, chanced to be the only ones at her bedside when she exhaled her last hoarse breath.

People we had hardly seen since childhood, friends she had left behind in obedience to Dad's driven restlessness, came to her funeral. They spoke of her with tender faces.

After she died, we persuaded our father to sell his flat and buy the shabby little house next door to me. He was too proud to be looked after and he didn't like my cooking. But for two years he flourished. He zoomed to the neighbourhood cafes on a motorised scooter. He came to hear a blues band at the Elwood RSL. He began to keep company with a woman he had fancied before he married Mum, a stylish widow from Geelong who was not afraid to take it right up to him. He had to ask his daughters for advice on his love-life. He liked a spontaneous drive to the country to look at the crops. In the car we were always laughing.

One scorching summer morning, at breakfast time, he told me he hadn't been able to get his breath in the shower. I buckled his sandals onto him and called an ambulance. On Hoddle Street his heart stopped. The paramedics got it going and swept into St Vincent's emergency. The family rushed in. He was ninety-one: the doctors decided to take him off the ventilator. We stood around him in a tearful circle. They whisked out the tube. He took a huge shuddering gasp, and began to breathe strongly. The doctors and nurses joined in our shout of laughter. The stubborn old bull would never die. He was admitted to a private room on the seventh floor. That evening the others went down to the street for a meal and I stayed with him. He was unconscious, breathing without help in a steady rhythm. A nurse came in to check on him. While she bent over him to smooth the sheet under his chin, I moved away from the bed and turned to look out the window of the high, west-facing room. The sun was going down in a blaze over the Exhibition Gardens. He breathed in. He breathed out. He was silent. I said, 'He's gone.' The nurse, surprised, felt for his pulse. 'Yes. He's gone.' She left the room. I blessed him. I sat with him quietly for ten minutes, on a chair near the window. Then I started texting the others to come back.

My father's mother died, in Hopetoun, when he was two. He had a sternly loving stepmother, but there was always something of the abandoned child about him. He was as entitled and as quick to anger as a toddler. He was jealous, impatient, rivalrous, scornful, suspicious. He could not trust anyone. He could not keep friends; by the end of his life, he had none. He was middle class, a wool merchant, with money but no education. He never read a book. One of my husbands, put through Dad's insulting third degree about whether he was 'living off' me, said he was a peasant. Yet with strangers he had great charm. 'I thank you, sir, from the bottom of my heart.' He had an unerring ear for music, though he never sang except ironically. He was a good ballroom dancer. He could shape a story. He liked to laugh. 'I've never *seen* such a deflated manager.' On Mum's headstone it seemed right to mention the word *love*. For his, we could not find a short phrase to encapsulate his contradictions, our exhausting struggles. We ended up with *Our father, a boy from the Mallee*. People who had not known him were startled by the bluntness of the epitaph. But to me, at least, it evokes a landscape of complex meaning, forlorn, sometimes beautiful: a desert that now and then bloomed.

I set out to write about my mother, but already I am talking about my father.

He is easy to write about. He was a vivid, obstreperous character whose jolting behaviour was a spectacle, an endurance test that united his children in opposition to him. Things he did or failed to do gave rise to hundreds of stories that we still share and embellish.

To write about her at length, coherently, is almost beyond me.

He blocked my view of her, as he blocked her horizon. I can think about her only at oblique angles and in brief bursts, in no particular order.

When my daughter was a teenager she had a dog, a poodle-cross called Polly. Polly fell down the crack between two of my marriages. She trudged again and again across inner Melbourne to my ex-husband's house, and died a lonely painful death, by misadventure, in a suburban backyard. She was an anxious creature, timid and appeasing, who provoked in me an overwhelming impatience. She would lie at my feet, tilting her head on this angle and that, striving for eye contact. The more she begged for it, the less I could give.

In just such a way, over many years, I refused my mother eye contact. She longed for it. I withheld it. I lacerate myself with this memory, with the connection I can't expunge between lost mother and lost dog.

When, in the street, I see a mother walking with her grown-up daughter, I can hardly bear to witness the mother's pride, the softening of her face, her incredulous joy at being granted her daughter's company; and the iron discipline she imposes on herself, to muffle and conceal this joy.

Elizabeth Jolley wrote that 'the strong feeling of love which goes from the parent to the child does not seem part of the child which can be given back to the parent'. But last spring, at a big and brilliant community show to celebrate the reopening of Melbourne's concert hall, a clever conductor divided the audience and taught us to sing in parts. A thousand euphoric strangers sang, in time and in tune, a slow-modulating melody. In the row in front of me sat an old woman and her daughter. Too absorbed in singing even to glance at each other, they reached, they gripped hands, they did not let go until the song was done.

A few years before she entered her final decline, my mother and I went together to hear a famous string trio. We arrived early, took our front-row seats high in the gallery, and looked down at the stage. It was bare, except for three chairs. My mother said,

'Looks a bit sad, doesn't it.' Surprised, as if at a witticism, I swung to face her. She raised her eyebrows and grinned at me. We both began to laugh. I was filled with respect. Whenever I remember that moment, the hopeless thing in my heart stops aching, and finds a small place to stand.

I came home from university armed with the Baroque. Bach and Vivaldi, their stringent impersonality, made my mother's favourite records sound overemotional and corny. Now, if I turn on the car radio and hear Tchaikovsky or Brahms, I find tears running down my cheeks. Perhaps that's where I can find her, take her hand and walk with her: across the fields and through the splendid forests of the Romantic piano concertos she loved.

She was not confident, or quick. She did not sense the right moment to speak. She did not know how to gain and hold attention. When she told a story, she felt a need to establish enormous quantities of irrelevant background information. She took so long to get to the point that her listeners would tune out and start talking about something else. Family shorthand for this, behind her back, was 'And then I breathed.'

Shows of affection were not done in our family. We could not even hug without an ironic shoulder pat. Expressions of emotion were frowned upon. 'You great cake. Pick up your lip before you trip over it.' I saw her, as an old woman, have to muster the courage to hold out her arms for someone else's baby. Perhaps this is why she never knew that her grandchildren were fond of her. She was shy with them. Once she said to me, in her timid, patient way, 'I don't think they like me much.'

Only last week, though, there floated into my awareness, from a cache of treasures Dad had left behind, a passionately misspelt little tribute that their nine-year-old granddaughter, my niece, had written when Mum was dying. It is accompanied by a drawing: a roast chicken on a rug and far in the background two figures, one large and one small, walking away hand in hand. 'Me, Grandpa and her went on picnics in the sun, just near her house in Kew. The sun was bright and the food was delicious, mostly chicken and potatoes and sometimes delicious sandwiches. Then

we would go back home and read or watch telly. But what I liked
was often we would go into her room and look in the cupboards
and see all theese speicial things of hers some belonging to her
six children one of which is my mum. I love all six of them and
give them my best dreams of Grandma, dreams of her real self,
the self with no evil diaseases, the strongest part of her body and
everyone should know its still here.'

I think my mother was afraid of me. I went to university, the first
of her children to move beyond her ability to contain, or help.
In 1972 I was fired from the Education Department for answer-
ing my students' questions about sex. There were cartoons for
and against me in the newspapers. She showed me a letter of
protest she had laboriously written to the editor of the *Age*. The
letter revealed that she had not understood the irony of the cartoons. The one she most hated was the one that most strongly
defended me. I tried to explain this gently, but I knew she was
humiliated.

I was the eldest of six children. They kept coming. I must have
been taught to change a nappy, fill a bottle, wheel a pram, rock
an infant to sleep. Yet I cannot remember there ever being a baby
in the house.

The clean, modest architecture of Victorian baby health centres
has always comforted me.

When my daughter was born, I was estranged from my father. He
had tried to prevent me from marrying my first husband, thus
mortally offending his decent and generous parents. My mother
had defied him and come to our wedding, at which one bottle of
champagne sufficed for the entire company. But at the time of our
baby's birth she was unable to break through his veto. She did not
come to the hospital. I don't remember hoping that she would, or
being upset that she didn't. Years later my youngest sister told me
she recalled, as a very small girl, sitting in the car outside my
house with our father, waiting for Mum to come out. So she must
have fought her way past him. I have no memory of her visit.

Towards the end of Mum's life, when she was already becoming vague and fearful but was not yet demented, my widowed sister Marie was often angry with her, scornful and harsh in a way that made me flinch. The grief of her widowhood had stirred up some old rage in her that I did not understand. One day Mum asked my sister to drive her down to the Mornington Peninsula, to visit our aunt. She obliged. Next time I saw Mum, she told me, without complaint and in a puzzled tone, that when my sister had delivered her home after that outing, she had brusquely put her hand out for petrol money.

Last year I went to the Australian War Memorial in Canberra. I had expected dusty old weapons and dioramas of heroism. Instead, I found a curatorial work of inspired brilliance and grandeur, and a chapter of my mother's life that I had never before bothered to fit into the history of the twentieth century. At the desk I told the attendant the name of my uncle Noel, Mum's favourite younger brother, who was killed in the Second World War. To us she rarely spoke of him. Dad, a wool trader, was in a reserved occupation; was the war a touchy subject? But when Dad was very old, he told me that Mum had been devastated by her brother's death. She never got over it; he was 'like her twin'.

The man at the war museum turned to a computer, pressed a few keys, and handed me two sheets of paper. Flight-Sergeant. Aerial Gunner RAAF. Cause of death: Flying Battle. Lancaster crashed at Hollenstein, Germany, while returning from a raid over Brunswick on 12–13 August 1944, killing all crew members. At last I registered the dates. I had to sit down. He must have been barely twenty. When my mother got the news that his plane had crashed, I would have been a toddler of eighteen months, and my sister an infant, five weeks old. How could she have mothered us, staggering under such a blow? In her old age Mum said to me, 'Marie was a very thin and *hungry* baby – always crying and wanting more.'

Once, while my mother was staying a weekend with me, a man I was having an affair with came to see me. He behaved sweetly towards her, questioned her about her life. He asked about her childhood and her family. How had the news of her brother's death in the war come to her: by phone, or was there a letter?

She seemed astonished that someone should be interested in her. When he left, she turned to me and said, '*He's* nice.' 'He's the love of my life, Mum,' I burst out, shocking myself, 'but he's married.' I suppose I thought she would disapprove. But she cried, 'Oh!' She leapt off her chair and threw her arms around me. She said, 'Just wait.'

From what life experience, from what instinct she drew this spontaneous advice I have no idea.

She got on well with all the men in my life, and they liked her. She continued to have warm feelings for them, and they for her, years after they and I had wrecked everything and gone our separate ways.

For my work, on tram stops, in planes, in courts, I'm not afraid to question any stranger. But I never sat my mother down and pressed her about the past, about her life before me, before our father.

One evening she and Dad and I came out of a restaurant. The street was empty of traffic for a mile in each direction. I stepped confidently off the kerb but she seized the tail of my jacket and pulled me back. 'We'll cross at the lights. I'm a very. Law-abiding. Person.'

My mother was good at sewing. When I was five or so she made me a pair of pyjamas on her Singer machine. I refused to wear them because they had frills on the bottom. She pleaded with me. She told me that if I wore the pyjamas, fairies would come and they would like me because of the frills. I did not care about the fairies. Even at that age I sensed the guilty power my refusal gave me.

It seemed to me, as a child, that our mother was hopeless at giving birthday parties. The cakes she made weren't right. The decorations and games somehow missed the mark. Other kids' mothers knew how to do a party right but Mum didn't. Instead of her plain cupcakes with icing, I secretly thought, she should have made those cakes with whipped cream and little tilted wings on top that other girls' mothers presented. It was a very strong sense I had, that there was something she did not get. All my adult life I despised myself for my disloyalty. It did not comfort me to learn that all children felt their mothers to be socially lacking in some crucial way. But one day when she was old and we were talking about motherhood, she said with a casual little laugh, 'I was never any good at giving kids' parties. I somehow never had the knack.'

She used to wear hats that pained me. Shy little round beige felt hats with narrow brims. Perhaps one was green. And she stood with her feet close together, in sensible shoes.

Oh, if only she would walk in here now.

She must have been only in her late thirties when she developed a gum disease and had to have all her teeth extracted. If she had gone to a Melbourne dentist, instead of remaining loyal to the doddery old fellow who treated our family in Geelong, a less drastic treatment might have been found. Not only did he pull out all her teeth, he whacked the false ones in over her bleeding gums. She came home and sat by the fire, hunched in her dressing gown, eyes down, holding a hanky to her mouth. We did not know how to comfort her. We tiptoed around her, whispering, going about our business. Thirty years later, at home on my own one night, I saw on SBS a movie called *Germany, Pale Mother* in which a woman in wartime had all her teeth removed as a cure for her neurasthenic state. I sat breathless on the couch while the dentist in his white coat yanked out her teeth and dropped them one by one with a clang into a metal dish.

My sax-playing sister, a professional, came over last winter with her ukulele and a Johnny Cash CD. She sings in the eighty-voice Melbourne Mass Gospel Choir, but is highly sceptical of all things religious. She wanted me to listen to 'Wayfaring Stranger'. All I knew was that it is an old song of weariness, of sin; of the longing to cross over Jordan.

'Come on,' she said. 'It's only got a couple of chords. We can learn it in five minutes.'

I got my uke down off the shelf. We tuned up. Yes, it was easy, the music part.

'Listen to that harmonium-playing,' she said. 'It's exemplary.'

But the lyrics.

I know dark clouds will gather round me,
I know my way is hard and steep.
But beauteous fields arise before me,
Where God's redeemed their vigils keep.
I'm going there to see my mother.
She said she'd meet me when I come.
I'm just going over Jordan.
I'm just going over home.

I said nothing, just worked at getting the strum right. That night, after she'd left, I played along with Johnny Cash for a long time. I could hardly get the words out, but his voice, weary and cracked, gave the song a majesty that still welcomed the humble chords of a ukulele.

My mother was a natural athlete: neat, small and graceful. I was hopeless at sport of any kind. All I wanted to do was read and write. At fourteen I got my first typewriter, my grandmother's reconditioned Smith Corona portable. Mum asked me to type out the results of the Point Lonsdale Golf Club ladies' tournament, to be reported in the *Geelong Advertiser*. Perhaps she was trying to interest me in what she cared about, or was simply looking for something we could do together. At the time I took it at face value: my first typing job. We toiled together at the kitchen table after tea. She dictated, and I clattered away at my beautiful oil-scented machine, on the quarto paper of which we had bought a ream at Griffiths Bookstore. She did not lose her temper at my mistakes. I felt important and useful. We were pleased with each other when the job was done. Two mornings later we stood shoulder to shoulder, looking down proudly at the newspaper's inky columns.

I must have been about twelve when the insight came to me that my mother's entire life was divided into compartments. None of them was any longer than the number of hours between one meal and the next. She was on a short leash. I don't recall thinking that this would be *my* fate, or resolving to avoid it. All I remember is the picture of her life, and the speechless desolation that filled me.

> Mrs Thatcher has told one of her interviewers that she had nothing to say to her mother after she reached the age of fifteen. Such a sad, blunt confession it seems, and yet not a few of us could make it. The world moves on so fast, and we lose all chance of being the women our mothers were; we lose all understanding of what shaped them.
>
> — HILARY MANTEL

The quietly mighty Japanese film director Yasujiro Ozu tells story after story of adult children breaking away from their parents. His characters rarely cry or raise their voices. Their emotions are expressed in tiny signs and changes of position. A father looks down at his glass. A mother folds her hands, or draws a handkerchief from her sleeve. These subtle movements call up in me surges of excruciating sympathy for my parents, for the hurt, helpless, angry love they must have felt as they watched me smash my way out of their protection.

In Dad's house I found a little photo of him and Mum in their twenties, sitting on the front step of their first house. Between them lay a long-eared black dog, a spaniel. Dad said his name was Ned. I did not remember our ever having had a pet. I asked if the dog had died before I was born. 'Ah no. I had to get rid of him. Mum wouldn't let him inside. Because of her *brand-new mushroom-pink carpet*.' He laughed, and shrugged. 'I put an ad in the paper. A lady came round and took him. She tied his lead to the carrier of her bike and pedalled away. I thought he might have looked back, but he never even turned his head.'

A crime novelist spoke at a conference about the unsuitability of his usual sardonic tone for the war story he was trying to write, 'about young men with their stomachs torn open who cry all night for their mothers and then die'. An old man told me, after he had had open-heart surgery, that he and a whole ward full of other men his age woke in the dark from hideous nightmares, screaming for their mothers. I have never read or heard of a woman in extremis who called for her mother. It is not possible for me to imagine such a thing. Still, I did hear about a woman of my age who had died in a distant part of the country. Her parents did not go to her funeral. Shocked by this, I asked my mother, 'Would you go to my funeral, if I died far away?' She uttered a sharp pant of disbelief. 'If you died in the Arctic *Circle* I'd make m' way there.'

On my pantry shelf stands a tall storage jar that I salvaged from Dad's kitchen when we sold his house. It survived the successive demolitions of my mother's households and, I suspect, of her mind. She has labelled it, in her large, clear hand: *Sultanas*. Then she has crossed out *Sultanas* and replaced it with *Currants*. Then she has crossed out *Currants* and restored *Sultanas*. The jar, when I found it, was empty.

Her ghost is in my body. I have her long narrow feet with low arches. I have her hollow bones, her hysterectomy, her fading eyebrows, her fine grey-brown hair that resists all attempts at drama. My movements are hers when, on a summer morning, I close up the house against the coming scorcher, or in the evening whisk the dry clothes off the line in weightless armfuls that conceal my face.

In the intermission at *Shane Warne: The Musical* two smiling strangers approached me. The man introduced himself and his wife. Aside from our parents' funerals, I had not seen him since we were children.

'I knew you straight away,' he said, 'from the other side of the room. You stand exactly like your mother.'

In my forties, when I lived in Chippendale, I used to walk to work across the big gardens of Sydney University. I walked fast, thinking my thoughts. One morning a young woman passed me, going the other way. She was wearing an op shop blouse from the 1940s, striped, with shoulder pads and tiny pearl buttons. At the sight of it a bolt of ecstasy went through me, an atavistic bliss so powerful that its roots could only have been in early childhood. I wrote my mother a letter. Did she ever have a stripy blouse, rather floppy, when I was little?

A week later came a curly-edged black-and-white photo. The date pencilled on the back was 1943. A woman in her early twenties stands in a bare backyard, squinting in an unposed way that raises her cheeks and bares her teeth. Her hair is permed and pinned in a Victory Roll. On her flexed left arm sits a wide-browed, unsmiling baby. The child's right cheek and left hand lean against the stripes of the woman's rayon blouse.

The war is not yet over. Her brother is alive. I am six months old. I am still an only child. She is carrying me in her arms. She is strong enough to bear my weight with ease. I trust her. She is my mother, and I am content to rest my head upon her breast.

My Mother, My Father

The Old Australia? Oratava Avenue, 1940

Sybille Smith

In 1940 we moved to Oratava Avenue in West Pennant Hills. Oratava Avenue was nearly a mile long, with three sharp bends. No streets led out of it. It ended at a barbed wire fence enclosing a forestry reserve – a dead end. In the reserve, dense undergrowth and huge trees with tattered flaps of hanging bark created a gloom in which the constant call of bellbirds seemed like momentary chinks of light.

Oratava Avenue was scored out of a gentle green slope, so that on one side there was a high grassy bank and on the other a fall to the level of the next paddocks, with an almost continuous buttress of blackberry bushes bearing enough dusty, tight little berries for everyone to get billies full in the summer. It was 'a dirt road', just about wide enough for two cars to pass, though this was rarely put to the test as only one family, Stones the plumbers, drove a car. Scanlens had a car but it was 'on bricks for the duration', one of many phrases which seemed simply a classification, without particular reference to a war. The milkman came in a high sulky with wooden wheels early in the morning and ladled milk into the tin billy hung over the middle picket of the gate. The baker came later, in a lower sulky with rubber tyres. Where the houses were close together he walked from one to the next with a big shallow basket of white loaves and the horse followed slowly, stopping to wrench up tufts of grass at the side of the road.

Each house was close to the road on five barbed-wire-fenced acres, the smallest subdivision allowed in this area, which was called The Green Belt, intended to stem the spread of the grey city and the red-brick suburbs. There were five houses on our side, the low side, and six on the other. Being a dead end, it was more like a village than a street. Everybody knew most of what there was to know about everybody else, and had opinions to cover what they didn't know. The people at the top end knew the most, as they saw all the comings and goings, and the people at the bottom end seemed to have the strongest opinions – Mr Davis on the high side, who was very religious and said 'in the name of the Lord' at the end of every sentence, and Mr Mitchell on the low side, who said 'bloody' a couple of times in every sentence. One day Mr Davis was calling his little son, who refused to come because he was frightened of a goose on the path. Mr Davis said, 'Daniel, come to your father in the name of the Lord.' Mr Mitchell said, 'Hit the bloody goose over the head with a shovel and he'll bloody well come.'

We could not have seemed stranger if we had landed from another planet. Officially we were Enemy Aliens, having to report to the police once a week and not allowed to own a radio. In actuality we were treated with amused or detached interest and matter-of-fact helpfulness, respect of equals for something different but not therefore worse, or better. My father came from a family which for over two hundred years had farmed land in what was then Silesia. His English was good and he was immediately absorbed into the intricacies and stratifications of local interaction. He was instinctively matter-of-fact or appreciative, confident or deprecating as the context required, could wait and listen and come in just at the right moment with a remark or casual suggestion – a sense for tone and timing which, if not innate, is more difficult to acquire than the entire grammar of a foreign language. He was known to everybody as 'Joe' (his name was Josef Gottwald) and occasionally referred to as 'Doc', as if his doctorate had become a decontextualised but casually preserved memento. My mother's doctorate disappeared completely and she became Mrs Cottswold, accepted and liked not because she blended into the local scene but for her openness, humour and unselfconscious eagerness to learn. 'Sister, you got my bloody sympathy,' said Mr Mitchell when he was teaching her to milk the cow. He said it to the cow.

My grandmother, whose English had plateaued at the level of orders to porters, neither fitted nor adapted, but by her considerable force of personality and authoritative custodianship of the standards of another place and time, established herself as local representative of an unknown but unquestionable Culture. She had trained as a pianist and graduated as dux of the Vienna conservatorium, receiving the prize of a baby grand piano donated annually by the piano manufacturing firm Bösendorfer. This piano now stood in, in fact filled, the main room of the weatherboard cottage. She was known as Madame Frolitsh (her name was Else Fröhlich) and she gave piano lessons and occasional recitals for the Red Cross and the Presbyterian church fund. She played for four and often six hours a day, and her music was a physical part of the environment of Oratava Avenue, where passers-by were accustomed to walking through an area of music, impetuous but precise gusts of Chopin polonaises and Schubert impromptus, just as they were accustomed to walking through an area of shade at the Stones' gate or to being courteously approached by the two Airedales who always lay outside Harrington's. 'I never minded hearing Madame play her piano,' Mr Davis said to me many years later, and that phrasing captures the uneffusive and solidly grounded tolerance of Oratava Avenue.

There were no street numbers. You lived Up The Road or Down The Road. Our house was the third on the left, weatherboard with a corrugated iron roof. A short path overhung by old bushes of yellow ivy roses and yellow buddleia sloped to the front door, which, like most front doors in Oratava Avenue, had no lock. It opened into a verandah enclosed in diagonal lattice, which was where I slept, and that opened into a living room which contained the piano and two sofas, on which my parents slept. On the two walls that formed a corner behind the piano were two matching black-framed prints, one a life-size head of Bach looking magisterial in an elaborately tiered wig and one of Beethoven looking tormented with writhing hair. Over the fireplace was an oil painting in an ornate gilt frame, a boy returning home at sunset with a cart pulled by two white oxen and met outside the thatched farmhouse by a small flock of welcoming geese.

Under it on the mantelpiece was a plaster kookaburra on a tree stump that I won at the hoopla stall at the Castle Hill gymkhana. The door to my grandmother's room was on one side, and, opposite, a door into the kitchen. Part of the kitchen had been screened off to form a bathroom.

The back door opened out of the kitchen, and quite a long way along a muddy path was the lavatory. A huge monstera deliciosa partly blocked the path, and whenever it was going to rain a glistening lime-green frog sat on the leaves and croaked reverberatingly. We named him Knorp, as that was what his croak sounded like to ears attuned to German. The huge leaning sewage-collection truck came once a week, late at night. A man who looked like a monk, because he wore a chaff bag slit down one seam to form a peaked hood and cape, carried the can on his hessian shoulder from the lavatory up the path and around the side of the house.

The house had a cat living in it. She had faded grey fur with irregular yellowish patches, like sunlight through a dusty window. Since she had much more experience of humans than we had of cats, she took charge of our relationship and she made it clear that it was to be a purely functional one. She didn't want to be stroked. She came in the morning for a saucer of milk and at dusk for a plate of scraps, and those were the only times we saw her. We called her, noncommittally, Pussy. One morning she arrived with a tiny blue-grey dandelion puff of a kitten prancing and skipping and stalking behind her.

We were instantly captivated. This was fortunate, since Jiminy Cricket, as I long-windedly named the kitten, was the first of many, many litters. We learned to recognise the signs that Pussy was close to giving birth and prepared a box padded with chaff bags. She would inspect it with pleased interest, vanish and have her kittens on a skirt that had slipped off its hanger in the back of the wardrobe. We would move them to the box. She would lie back, pushing her paws into the padding and purring deeply, her golden eyes, in which the pupils floated small as caraway seeds, brimming with contentment and languorous trust. Half an hour later the box was empty. We might see her disappearing with the last kitten hanging like a little wet sock from her mouth. She would take them to a spot out of human reach – under a vine on the roof of the laundry, or in a crevice under the stacked bran bags in the feed shed – and rear them there. Sometimes we could hear their slatey little squeaks but we would not see them until she brought them back when they were five weeks old.

This happened two or three times a year. Spaying, which was called getting a cat Fixed Up, was not considered an option. In fact, it was a feature of life in Oratava Avenue in the '40s that there were no options. There was just What You Did, No Two Ways About It. What you did with kittens was to drown the females in a bucket before they had their eyes open. The familiarity of 'in a bucket' domesticated the notion of holding a newborn creature in cold water until it died, and the timeframe contained the humane suggestion that the kittens, as long as their eyes were shut, wouldn't notice what was happening. None of us was capable either of telling the sex of a newborn kitten or of drowning it. At the end of a year we had seven cats and it occurred to my mother that it might be possible to find them other homes. She constructed guidelines out of convenient scraps of hearsay – all ginger cats are male; there's no such thing as a female tabby; black cats are always tomcats (and so are most black and white ones). Under these reckless assertions she wove a loopholed safety net of secondary considerations – female cats don't make a smell; female cats are better mousers; female cats don't go off fighting. I would be sent out with an irresistible five-week-old kitten in a shoebox and the appropriate guarantee. We found homes for generations of cats and had thirteen of our own.

Long paddocks sloped down behind the house. A little creek fringed with maidenhair fern ran through the bottom paddock. It was amazing that so much land, which seemed to be something like air that everybody shared, could be owned. My father borrowed Mr Mitchell's draughthorse and plough. The blade sliced through the lumpy clods to show slick gleaming black with an oily rainbow shimmer. He planted rows of sweet corn interspersed with lines of valencia orange trees, and three almond trees.

My parents bought a cow called Pansy, the most beautiful cow anyone had ever seen. Her coat had patches of clearly mapped colour, continents of chocolate brown in oceans of white. Her horns were exquisitely curved and tapered, her eyes huge, dark and reflecting, with long, though sparse, lashes. Her muzzle was bluntly rounded like the toe of a gumboot, with a slimy sheen punctured by occasional bristles. Her tongue was pointed and so long that it could reach into her nostrils. She had to be milked twice a day. In the evenings I had to drive her up from the bottom paddock, walking behind her undulating rump and hearing the creaking sound she made at every step. She would surge into the milking shed, put her head in the trough and blow into her mash before settling down to steady, abstracted munching. At the thin metallic sound of the milk hitting the bucket the cats would assemble near the kerosene lantern, sitting with their tails wound neatly around their paws.

In the pebbly pale clay on the left of the house my father dug out an air-raid shelter, and all the windows had to be blacked out by having sheets of newspaper stuck to the panes. At night it was country darkness, black and solid. Nobody ever went out. There were no cars, no buses, nowhere to go. The only time I went out at night was when the horses got into the rows of sweet corn. They would eat the fresh young stalks and their stomachs would swell up as tight as drums – and would burst, it was said, unless they were walked continuously until their stomachs subsided. That took at least two hours, and – leaving my father in a fury, saying, 'Serves them right if they burst' – my mother and I would walk up and down and up and down the road with the reluctant dragging horses, poking their stomachs after every lap in the hope that they were subsiding, hearing only the soft clop of the hooves on the dust in the pitch dark.

The first horse I had was Tommy, a beautiful cream-coloured pony with a black mane and tail. He had never been properly broken in, and though he loved people it irritated him to have them on his back. Thelma Bignell from Down The Road came to teach me to ride. She had long rows of blue, red and yellow felt ribbons won at gymkhanas with her horse, Golden Prince. She despised the name Tommy and said he should be called Arab Prince as he had quite a lot of Arab in him. You could tell that a horse had Arab in him if his nose would fit in a peach tin, and Tommy's elegant narrow nose clearly could. She said that you had to learn to ride bareback, controlling the horse with your knees. Within minutes Tommy would start pigrooting and toss me off. He would come up to me and whuffle gently and nudge me with his apricot-textured muzzle, and Thelma would yell, 'Get back on! You've got to get straight back on!' and then it would happen all over again.

Thelma Bignell lived with her mother Down The Road on the high side. Patty Scanlen lived with her mother opposite. Up The Road, Winifred McCourt, who ran the kindergarten at Thompson's Corner, lived with her mother, and Miss Harrington lived with her mother diagonally opposite. There were a few older men, like Mr Mitchell, and schoolboys, but there were no young men. That didn't strike me as strange – everything was equally strange, and became equally normal – but I realise now that a whole generation of men was missing, and must have gone to the war. Bill Johnson, the headmaster's son who sometimes helped in class, was about fifteen. He was tall and his voice was deep, and if he spoke to you it was as if the sun was shining into your eyes and you had to look down and wait for things to make sense. The Big Boys, who were eleven or twelve, were in Mr Johnson's class, and most then left school to help their mothers with feeding chooks and weeding nursery gardens. Sometimes at the annual church fete, at the end of the day when land and sky separated and the sky was still light and the ground became smoky with dusk, the girls would tease and torment the boys until they grabbed a piece of ice from the refreshment tent and chased the girls squealing around the darkening lawn and put the ice down the back of their dresses.

The Presbyterian church at Thompson's Corner was a small red-brick building with a stubby little tower. Sunday school was in a room at the back. We sat at tables with our backs to the window, which looked across dark bands of bushland and bands of hazy distance, right to the cloudy storm blue of the Blue Mountains, sixty miles away. We had wool and needles to knit squares in plain stitch, which, we were told, were for scarves for Our Boys and face washers for The Missions, equally mysterious recipients. Mrs Mooney, the carpenter's wife, was the teacher. Her main theme was the necessity of obedience to God, and she illustrated it with local events to give us a personal frame of reference – 'There was a wicked man who tried to hurt Mr Mooney so God punished him and a horse kicked him and broke his leg.'

A local German family, the Marks, who had a poultry farm, gave my parents a blue cattle dog called Fipsy. She was a middle-aged overweight dog who walked as if her feet hurt, always panting, always cheerful, the tip of her lowered tail always wagging. One morning she couldn't get up. When we tried to stand her up, her legs collapsed under her. Everyone had advice. It's a tick, a poison bait, a snake, a kick from a horse – whatever it is, she'll only get worse. No point calling the vet, he'll tell you the same thing and charge you for it. Only thing to do is put her out of her misery. No two ways about it. All she wants is a knock on the head with the back of an axe – got one down the shed, have you? For six weeks we fed her and changed the sacks under her. One night we were woken by urgent barking. We went to the shed and found Fipsy standing up, barking with joyful excitement. She could walk normally.

On weekdays a loose group of children trailed up the road. Geoffrey and Amy Fleming from the last house on the high side picked up Errol Scanlen opposite, then Arthur Davis, then Elaine Stone and then me. I was not picked up, like the others, by a process of natural adhesion but officially handed over. The children turned towards my mother, faces glowing with zealous helpfulness and the pride of responsibility. Once the convoy moved on, picking up Fay and Bruce Wilson and then straggling the half-mile to school, this glow faded and I felt at best an oddity but more often a monstrosity. This was not because of any particular unkindness, simply from a throbbing sense of being ineradicably different, and not sufficiently in command of that difference to inhabit it as an alternative position. Walking to school together was just What You Did, No Two Ways About It, without affinity or alternative, and the interactions within the group were as random as the rolling of marbles in a box, and as impossible to master. We wandered along, scuffing up dust, throwing stones at telegraph poles, pulling up sourgrass stems to suck, with occasional eruptions of 'Oowah! I'm gunna tell on you!' or 'He's your boyfren!' if a girl happened to stray within a certain radius of a boy. Occasionally we drifted to a halt at a ruined straw castle of golden manure left by the milkman's horse two hours earlier, and watched with appalled admiration as one of the boys accepted the dare to eat a piece.

There was no school uniform. We wore clothes that were too big or too small, depending on the stage of growing into or out of them that you were at, faded but starched and ironed to the texture of aluminium. Down to my scabbed knees I looked like the other children, but my feet belonged in a different world. My parents, so adaptable on major issues, on minor ones retained European convictions not open to modification. One was that shoes had to be made of leather so that your feet could breathe. Leather was unknown in Oratava Avenue as a material for children's wear, being reserved for work boots and blacksmiths' aprons. My shoes were stiff and slippery and noisy, the sign and instrument of a footfall that could never merge with that of the others. And on rainy days, when the others took off their sand-shoes and wedged them in their armpits to keep them dry, I dragged carthorse hooves of leather shoes encased in galoshes.

West Pennant Hills Primary School was a small L-shaped brick building painted ochre. The headmaster's house joined onto the back of the school, and on Friday afternoons we were allowed into his garden to pick mulberry leaves for our silkworms. Behind the school was a flagpole and a bell post. The school day started at nine o'clock, when Mr Johnson came out and rang the bell. We formed two lines, one of girls and one of boys, and watched while the union jack moved jerkily up the pole. Once the flag was up we started swinging our arms and, when the momentum reached us, raising our knees to march into school, singing 'Onward, Christian Soldiers'.

There were two schoolrooms. Mr Johnson taught fourth, fifth and sixth class in one room and Miss Pollard taught first, second and third in the other. The classes were separated into rows of double desks, with seats and lids of heavy dark wood. The teacher's desk was on a low platform and had a huge pencil sharpener crouched on one side. The room was painted brown to shoulder height and then lettuce-green, and there were three beautiful high windows, each divided into twelve panes, which let in slants of high, white light in which you could see the slow circling and drifting of chalk dust.

Miss Pollard was serious, kind, strict and fair. She made you feel that it was important, and possible, to learn. While you were in the classroom it was unimaginable that you could be thinking of anything but the task she set you. While one class had a lesson the other two rows practised what they had just been taught – reading, writing, arithmetic. We did sums and learned tables, not only of numbers but rods, poles and perches and pecks and bushels, quantities as remote as Latin declensions. We copied the exquisite letters Miss Pollard wrote on the blackboard. Her letters sloped slightly to the right, the upstrokes fragile and lacily transparent, the downstrokes creamily white. To know letters and be able to join some to make a word which was in your head and would be recognised by anyone who saw it seemed an amazing and mysterious achievement. Once Miss Pollard asked if anyone knew a poem. I said I did, having made one up about a mouse who lived in a house and ate cheese and sometimes peas. After I had recited a couple of lines Miss Pollard asked me if I had written it myself and told me to sit down. I was mortified and mystified – what difference did it make, and how could she possibly tell?

Thorby's Grocery, at Thompson's Corner, was the largest building in West Pennant Hills and the centre of everything that happened. It was on a crest from which you could look over the whole countryside as far as the hump of the Harbour Bridge. The shop window had pyramids of jam tins with glossy fruit on the labels, which we cut out and pasted on the brown paper covers of our exercise books, and jars of Bushell's chicory essence and stacks of Velvet soap and diagonal rows of metal fruitfly sprayguns and soap dispensers, little wire-netting cages on handles into which you put leftover scraps of soap to shake to a lather in the washing-up water. Inside there was a wide dark wooden counter, and behind it dark wooden shelves and pigeonholes right to the dark wooden ceiling. It was shadowy, the light seeming to hover around the edges of things rather than to reveal them clearly, and this dimness corresponded to a pervading smell in which the earth crusted potatoes in a hessian sack, the crumbly round of cheese on the counter, the cut beaded surface of a pumpkin blended. On the right was the Post Office counter with a portrait of King George VI in plain khaki uniform, and next to it was the lolly counter, with big jars of rainbow balls and pink musk sticks and beautiful boiled lollies glowing like jewels. (Actually, I had never seen jewels and would have been more likely, when I did see them, to think they glowed like boiled lollies.) Food was rationed, and for every purchase a row of coupons was deftly snipped from the ration booklet. Hardly anything came in packets. Things were scooped from sacks and deep drawers with a metal scoop, and Mrs Thorby, head tilted back a little to see over the top of her glasses, would delicately shake the final ounce of sugar or rice or split peas into the brown paper bag on the scales. The meticulous weighing, the accurate cutting of the coupons, the whole sense of a presiding propriety in the person of Mrs Thorby, gave the business of shopping a sense of admission to a world of self-respecting appropriateness. 'I'd like a nice piece of pumpkin, please, Mrs Thorby,' was all you needed to say to get exactly the right amount.

The aim of my life was to be like everybody else in Oratava Avenue, an aim I was ill-equipped to achieve. In my head there was a constant tumult of excitement, apprehension, joy, hatred, devotion, misery, fury, guilt and gratitude. As far as I could see, nobody in Oratava Avenue felt any of these things. Any reference to personal feelings was sealed off by phrases like, 'I wouldn't like to say.' 'Least said, soonest mended.' The most personal expression of strong emotion you were likely to encounter was, 'It's not the heat I mind, it's the humidity.' Interaction with other children took place on the vertiginous rim between inclusion and exclusion. I watched constantly for signs to show what was meant, like a deaf person lip-reading.

When you start remembering and recounting, all the memories stitch together in uniform distinct little shapes, like quilting pieces cut out of the different fabrics of those days and weeks and years, and given definition and coherence which were totally lacking in the experience itself. It is hard to remember the unpatterned fabric of recurrent days. The waking to a dark morning with rain trampling on the corrugated iron roof and the knowledge that, beyond wish or comfort, no two ways about it, was the necessity of feeding the fowls, crouching in the rain to cut greenfeed for the afternoon with a sickle that scrunched on little particles of mud. The sensed threats and disasters, printed in newspapers flapped shut and trailing in sentences suspended when I came in. The smell of the kerosene heater and the pattern of round lights it made on the ceiling. The smell of linseed oil, painted on the horses' hooves and on the perches the fowls slept on, heads under wings, stirring murmuringly when we went down with the kerosene lantern to lock the shed for the night.

I don't remember the everyday things, things that happened every day for years and years and years. When I look back, I seem to inhabit these rooms and paddocks and streets like the figure of a stranger which appears in a photograph you take of a place that means something to you, an anonymous human presence that fixes the scale of the surroundings but is not related to your experience of them. The spaces that were mine, that enclosed my sense of my life, were like crevices and burrows in real space – tunnels through the dry paspalum in the paddocks or the stacked bran bags in the feed shed.

Under the house there was an armchair in olive scroll patterned brocade. I remembered it from our house in Vienna, where I never sat in it except on someone's knee. Now it stood behind one of the uneven brick pillars under the back of the house, where the earth had been dug away and a small area roughly cemented to store boxes of books, leather suitcases, a canvas-covered cabin trunk with a sticker saying Napoli, and the chair. I could wedge myself down between the armrests so that I couldn't be seen. Sometimes I just sat there, almost choking with the jubilation of being invisible.

In one of the boxes I found bundles of a nineteenth-century children's magazine called *Little Folk*, which had belonged to my great-grandmother. I had started to learn to 'read' German before we left Austria, in a book with big capital letters and clear explanatory pictures. Good children clustered around Father Christmas. Carefree children skated on thick ice. Happy children ran to find Easter eggs under primroses. I knew the position of each word by heart, and could navigate the page like a blind person in a familiar room. I couldn't read *Little Folk* at all. Instead of the coherent smooth outline enclosing clear spaces of colour and meaning there were black and white illustrations in nervous fine lines, full of crosshatching and ambiguity. An elegant lady stood stiffly, looking down at a small boy. Why were they there? Was she angry? Was he good? I would look ferociously at the words for a clue. It seemed outrageous that there might be something happening in the words that was not contained in the pictures, that it might be necessary to leave the sunlit clearing and go down those overgrown paths of letters. For weeks they led nowhere There were recognisable 'ands' and 'buts', 'boys' and 'dogs', but the real clues were hidden in unsayable clumps of letters – m-i-s-c-h-i-e-v-o-u-s, s-t-a-u-n-c-h-l-y, h-e-a-r-t-h-r-u-g. I remember the first time I tracked down a meaning through the letters and really read a word – it was 'galloped'. There was a sense of amazed recognition, such as you might have in a strange country meeting someone from your own town. It seemed an incredible coincidence to find a word that was familiar out here in the foreign land of print.

Reading brought an inkling of what people might really be like, in a way that learning to speak English had not done. Not that the world of *Little Folk* was any closer to life in Oratava Avenue than my own Austrian background. These children were curly-haired dimpled moppets who toasted crumpets in front of nursery fires. The big thing was that reading took you behind this unfamiliar facade to feelings and thoughts which, amazingly, were familiar. 'Dora hoped the Vicar hadn't heard her remark!' 'Tim did not wish his father to see his disappointment.' 'Marjorie could feel her heart thumping so loudly she was afraid Constable Perkins would hear it!' 'Peggy felt very alone when the door closed behind the housekeeper.' The thoughts were totally ordinary; it was the fact that people might be thinking things they did not say that came as a revelation. Learning to read made me able to imagine myself in English.

Oratava Avenue is no longer a dead end. Developers have opened new 'estates' with networks of Closes, Mews and Circuits, and roads run through to freeways and transport corridors. The only reminder of the bellbirds is a metal street sign, 'Bellbird Close'. You can drive into the forestry reserve, which is looped by one-way roads with speed humps leading to a nursery selling spindly 'natives' in plastic tubes. There are Sensory Trails with annotated specimens of fragrant, shapely or otherwise remarkable flora, and a cafe selling lattes and wraps.

Subdivision began in the '70s and 'living on acres' ceased. The five-acre blocks were cut up into quarter-acre lots. Houses covered the paddocks and nursery gardens – huge houses built right to the boundaries, gabled and turreted, Tudor and Californian and Spanish Mission in speckled chocolate or blond textured brick with triple garages and short driveways lined with tiny box hedges and white standard roses. Even the topography changed – slopes were flattened, small hills constructed. The creek disappeared which once emerged at the first bend of Oratava Avenue and wandered across Harrington's paddocks, accompanied on its winding course by arum lilies like a dwindling line of geese, to end in the maidenhair-fringed pool in our bottom paddock.

It is very easy to recast this life as idyllic, to see simplicity and moderation where there was just a lack of alternatives. We, and any of our neighbours, would instantly have abandoned our acres and our integrities to live in one of these new palaces. The small houses on the big blocks of the past were not 'tastefully' simple compared to the 'tasteless' opulence of these big houses on small blocks. In Oratava Avenue in the '40s, taste didn't exist because choice didn't exist. What you had was the same as what everybody else had, and anything 'special' – embroidered tray cloths, mulga wood pipe stands, matching pairs of oval paintings of Scottish highland scenes – was not chosen but had been handed down in the family.

This sameness in possessions corresponded to a quality of character all the more pervasive for being unspoken. I think I would call it fellow feeling – cooler than compassion, warmer than justice, and applicable to the trivialities of daily life in a way that those more ambitious ideals are not. The essence of this fellow feeling was simply that what you expected for and from yourself was not particularly different from what you expected from and for others. No two ways about it.

The Unremembered Six

Christian Ryan

Some school semester in 1969 or '70 – it was spring – a hazel-eyed boy under the influence of a particular teacher, a Mr Briggs, could feel his future floating out in front of him, uncertainly, like the insects. He thought about following the insects. The west Kent commuter town where he went to school was a place of lakes, deer, old trees and valleys. Insects were what engrossed the boy. He liked listening to Mr Briggs talk about them. So many insects, anywhere you look – what makes each of them so interesting? How is it that wherever there is a habitat, they'll find a way of living? He discovered and read a book about animal behaviour, and his curiosity grew. He sensed he could be happy in that future, that world, it made him excited, and it was an outdoors world. But a second world – and this world, the way the boy carried himself in it, was very much an interior world – was also just beginning to flicker at him. That was the spring he got picked in the school's first XI.

Cricket is a game played on a dirt pitch and grass. But it exists on the wind – the space, a kind of ether, between the ball/stroke that's just happened and those about to happen next, and the balls just bowled or about to be bowled and strokes executed or awaiting execution in all the games of cricket being played somewhere simultaneously of whatever duration, overs-span, age level, seriousness, etc., and also, most tantalising, every ball or stroke ever. Twenty-five seconds later another one comes along. But the ball/stroke that's gone doesn't actually go anywhere. The ball/ stroke hovers. Nearly always, it is hovering in a place most people cannot locate, and the people who potentially could locate it – inside their memory, imagination, in a newspaper report or book, on YouTube – are at that moment not doing so. But it is still there, somewhere. Ted Dexter once drove Tom Veivers for six during a tour game at the MCG. No footage exists. Yet a handful of the still-living recall it, and consider it maybe the finest stroke ever struck in Melbourne. One, Bill Lawry, told Jonathan Agnew last December that Dexter's drive, 'went halfway up the sightscreen, it was just flat, I was at mid-off and it could have killed me, a tremendous strike of the ball'.

The Lawry–Agnew podcast is currently google-able. Probably soon it will get dragged down, and definitely Lawry and the others who were present will someday die, and years may fly by without a single person giving a second's pause to dwell on what happened that day when Tom Veivers bowled, but even then the moment will be forever safe, forever there, this sentence's existence marginally increasing the prospect of a future kid or grown-up enjoying the sudden exhilarating feeling of that drive of Ted Dexter's popping into their head. What, though, of the ball/stroke that is unfilmed, unwritten of, untalked about, and unremembered by anyone who was there? What then?

One afternoon Chris Tavaré hit a six.

It happened in a three-day match in Newcastle, Australia, where the sky was bright and Northern New South Wales won the toss and made 163. Curator Ken Stace's pitch at the No. 1 Sports Ground was flat and good, so 163 was below-par and anticlimactic, especially as cluey judges reckoned that of all the Northern NSW line-ups ever assembled this lot had balance, experience and the best shot yet at knocking over a touring England side. They had extra incentive, too. A pre-game function was held at Newcastle City Hall and whoever did the invitation list forgot one team. The locals downed sullen beers among themselves instead that night. Late the next night, after the disaster of 163 – top score was Rick McCosker's 53, out hooking the last ball before lunch – a telephone rang at the Travelodge Motel. It was Kent calling to tell Tavaré he'd been appointed the county's new captain.

So next day, the day after his twenty-eighth birthday, walking out to bat, it is possible Tavaré felt in a place of some kind of serenity. Loose soil on the outfield, the result of recent topdressing, had disappeared after a morning's gentle mowing. Nearly 1600 spectators, paying two dollars a head, were in. Tavaré would have noticed the gasometers across the street – evocative of The Oval, London. Or did the parked cars sidled up against sections of the boundary remind him of the outground at Folkestone, Cheriton Road, scene of a 42 and a 0 he'd made two months before?

In Newcastle some people watched from their car seats. And Tavaré batted, seatbelt on. He and opening partner Graeme Fowler lasted nearly two hours together at a scoring rate of 1-point-squirt-all per over.

Batting's a chew-a-person's-insides-up ordeal. It asks that you be dominant while requiring you make yourself vulnerable – the ball, object of your downfall, rests in the bowler's hands and is outlawed from touching yours. Your goal is twofold: to survive and score runs. Routinely Tavaré made it onefold, and in this way he's in a category of not much more than one. Invincible in defence, uninterested in scoring, he was – if we apply the twofold test – a half-batsman, with the aura of an anti-batsman. Once, Tavaré spent 67 minutes on 0. Later, same innings, he spent 60 minutes on 24, first-class cricket's only batsman to have endured a pair of scoreless hours in the one innings. Adding to the burying-my-goldfish feel, he did it at HQ, the Home of Cricket, Lord's: like flatulence in the front aisle at church. I mentioned Tavaré being a one-man category – unlike the other blockers and stonewallers who clog cricket's scorebooks, and as distinct from the rearguard specialists, the human barnacles, the many vexing pissants (e.g. Geoff Boycott, who in some parallel timeless Test universe is still putting on 92 for the second wicket with Tavaré in Mumbai); unlike them, Tav, perversely, was so unrelentingly boring and so predictable in his boringness that it became not at all boring. It became – something other. This was a creepy concept to try bending your mind around, sitting on the couch, TV switched to the cricket. You could not watch. You could not look away. Your head was filled with Tavaré. And it was filled with a stack of issues and stuff totally unconnected to Tavaré. Peering at Tavaré could have the effect, unusually, of making a person feel as if they were peering in on oneself.

Naturally, only a cricket watcher whose own insides were reasonably chewed up would react that way to Tavaré. In Newcastle, Fowler was caught at short leg, David Gower came in, and he and Tavaré added 90, Tavaré's contribution being 30 – and at some point during their partnership the crowd started hooting.

'Yeah, I remember, maybe,' says Michael Hill, Northern NSW's captain that day, 'there was some hooting. But look, we played Rest of the World in 1972 and Graeme Pollock and Sunil Gavaskar added about a hundred after lunch, in even time, perfect batting, beautiful batting. They got hooted because the ball kept going along the ground. Very tough judges in Newcastle.' Also, at an indeterminate hour, possibly post-hooting, and certainly after the morning's batting was done and he'd squeezed in some side-practice, England's captain Bob Willis returned to the Travelodge to answer letters. Willis was resting this match. Gower stood in. And the captain on tour always has bags of incoming correspondence to keep up with.

There's a little-seen Patrick Eagar photo of Tavaré – different innings, same summer, a fast bowler is about to let fly. It is a rear-view landscape shot. It is, to the uninitiated, a photo not of Tavaré but of four slips and two gully fielders, crouching chevron-style not arc-style, a mildly unusual geometric formation which is why Eagar has taken it from behind. But if you are a Tavaré person it is to Tavaré your eyes cling. In the far left corner of the frame, he is waiting on the crease. Dangling exactly vertical is his bat. That's not how the textbook teaches you to do it. In the same vertical line, going up, are his weirdly long forearms, his above-the-elbow region, and the back of his helmeted head. Textbook-wise, he should be approximating a back-to-front question mark, but he's an exclamation mark minus the dot, an unbent line – with some air of impermanence, as if he has just floated into shot, and is tilting, tipping . . . Tavaré! This is what stills photography can do to the stillest batsman the game has known. It can render him so still he starts sliding backwards. I can't look at the photo without feeling unsettled and downhearted, and I don't think that's right and I don't think Eagar intended it that way. In another photo – just a grainy square in a magazine, no photo credit, badly cropped, the bat's sawn off at the top – Tavaré is essaying a drive: bare-headed, aggressive, everything's flowing, classical. And I don't know which of the photos, unless it's neither of the photos, is playing tricks.

After dealing with the ball, each ball, he would wander halfway to square-leg, head bowed. Whether he was relieved to have survived the last ball or gathering strength for the next, no one was sure, and nothing showed on his thin face. Cheekbones jutted out of the gauntness; his eyes seemed deep-set in their sockets. When people picture him now, the thing they are picturing is often that walk towards square-leg, which was not a tic he started off with but something that developed many years into his career, by which time he'd been to Oxford and completed a zoology degree.

He still thought about the insects – how, wherever there is a habitat, they'll find a way of living.

*

Perth, in the summer that straddled 1977 and '78, was a yellow-lit city of flies, highways, the Channel 9 Appealathon, sand, Hungry Jack's signs, a sort of LA of Australia running at quarter speed, where ambition is soaked up in sunscreen and washed off in the shower block afterwards, and where Tavaré came to bat at number three for the University Cricket Club. He was well loved by teammates. At least three still see and keep in touch with him.

Greg Davies – 'Square of the wicket: fantastic. Particularly on the off side. Tavs rarely let anything short get past him.'

Leigh Robinson – 'Chris was a stylish batsman. Seemed to be getting out caught behind. But he had lots of shots. Hit the ball quite hard.'

Colin Penter, captain – 'A dashing player. Very strong off the front foot. Strong cutter. Wasn't a big hooker. Still strong through the leg-side, though, off pads . . .'

He averaged 14 in October, 13 throughout November, 6.75 in February and 10 in March. In between he collected a 68 at James Oval in his only innings all January. On the last day of 1977 he made 125 at Cresswell Park, hammering the Claremont–Cottesloe bowlers in an elegant and brilliant exhibition that included a two-hour partnership of 162 runs with Greg Davies, who nonetheless can't quite place it.

*

Was it really an urge to catch up on his letter writing that drove Bob Willis back to the Newcastle Travelodge? Watching Tavaré bat can have been no easier for those who knew him than it was for us, who could only guess at him. A fortnight later Tavaré assembled 98 runs across nine hours, fifty-three minutes and two innings at the WACA, and Willis in his tour diary painted the dressing-room scene thus: 'Two of the side lying on benches, not watching the game at all, and two more intent on the television. Some were reading or playing cards.'

'I do enjoy watching Tav bat,' Willis himself would say to Mike Brearley in earlier times. Something unbearable, beautiful, pain-ful – loveable – wraps round the cricketer who plays his own way, even if it is a closed-off way. Their vulnerability is palpable. So much is on show, and at stake – nothing less than a likeness of them. If Tavaré was batting, that meant Willis's grateful bowling knees were getting some sorely needed sleep. But even for Willis this was a delicately balanced thing. The phenomenon of Tavaré setting himself at the crease, like a tree's roots expanding, freed the batsmen around him to play their strokes, or else it pressured them into having to overplay too many strokes, no one could pre-dict or tell which and it changed on an innings-to-innings basis. And yet Ian Botham would say: 'I like batting with Tav.'

Botham was next man in – 'best player England has produced since Dr WG Grace,' shouted the *Newcastle Herald*, advising its readers to flock to the ground. Immediately Botham got away with a backward sweep and a heave, which made his Ashes mira-cles of 1981 feel close. An off break came down, and he drove and edged it to slip.

Accompanying Tavaré the whole circumference of Australia was his wife Vanessa, and he was happier with her nearby, although aeroplane tickets were pricey and a player's tour fee modest. Also, she had phobias about flying – for which she required sedation – and heights as well. And this tour of Aus-tralia consisted of twenty-five flights in 127 days, from one down-town hotel to the next, most of them taller than the Newcastle Travelodge. It was hard on her, worried him. Getting to New-castle alone had involved a coach, a twenty-seater plane, then another coach. Test cricket – the seconds between those heavy-footed walks towards square-leg – was strain enough.

'Unsmiling,' remembers Bob Holland. 'Serious. Tall. He played with a straight, dead bat, or let balls go, and there was no reaction to any sledging, no annoyance, his character did not change.' Holland, joined by the captain Hill and Colts offie Steve Hatherell, was part of a Northern NSW spin trio against Tavaré. A big-breaking, back-spinning leggie, Holland played eleven Tests for Australia, and first grade till he was fifty-two, and in his life bowled to Sobers, Gavaskar, Viv, the Chappells, but never another like Tavaré. 'Can't think of another one. With first-class cricketers, when they got half an opportunity to attack, they usually did. He wasn't like that. He would wait and wait and wait.'

Holland's spin partner Hill had encountered English occupiers before: John Edrich, Geoff Boycott. Tavaré was something unique. 'But closer to Edrich than to Boycott because Boycott was much more technically perfect.'

In Newcastle, a breeze fluttered across the ground and Tavaré called for a sweater. 'Hit the fucking ball,' hollered a spectator, 'and you'll keep yourself warm.'

Alien-seeming to some Australians, this was a man who donned a headscarf, pinafore and attended the England touring squad's Christmas Day dress-up lunch as Hilda Ogden from Coronation Street. Quintessentially English was another interpretation: he did the *Telegraph* crossword, roast beef was his favourite food, and the place he best liked to play cricket was The Parks in Oxford. He mixed well with others but was early to pyjamas and bed. Not a big drinker, he'd drink a bit. Shirts, not always quite figure-fitting, were perfectly ironed. The tour social committee fined him, affectionately, for braininess. In interviews it was as if he had a cutting and brilliant riposte that would put everyone on the floor but something was holding him back from using it. And so he'd give the predictable answer in his downbeat voice. Installed in his car, future county teammate Peter Roebuck noticed, was a device to make it go exactly seventy miles per hour on motorways. Cricket wrested control away, it was cricket controlling him. How he was doing on the field – that's how and who he was. 'Sometimes tortured,' according to Willis, who he'd come to for advice, and then follow the advice. Self-preoccupation was not a problem. He'd make team-centric suggestions about field settings, training routines. Generally, though, he did not speak a lot. He liked gardening, and woodwork, and films, and home. He once said to Willis that maybe a degree of screwed-upness was crucial to both their success.

Alien-seeming – they did not think that in Perth.

Something was afoot in Newcastle.

Tavaré hit an off-drive so hard it hurt the hands of the fielder who stopped it. In the eighty-ninth over he was 85 not out and the Northern NSW bowlers reached for the new ball. Tavaré stepped forward, sort of skipping. Some shots, visiting commentator and pundit Henry Blofeld saw, showed a lovely flowing arc of the blade. To the spinners he, occasionally, danced.

Ghost rumours linger, of what journalist Alan Gibson thought he saw when Tavaré batted half a day at Leicester during the 1978 county season – 'Some of his drives reminded me of Beldam's pictures of Victor Trumper'; of a twenty-seven-ball ton at Crystal Palace's football field in the 1981 Lambert and Butler Floodlit Cup.

In Newcastle, hitting Holland to the midwicket fence brought up 100. 'Frustrating,' Holland recalls. 'Bowl six good balls and he'd play six back, so I'd try tossing one higher, it would be slightly overpitched, and he'd hit it hard and very, very classical.' In stands of 55 with Derek Randall and 37 with Ian Gould, Tavaré was the dominant partner. Vic Marks had heard him remark once or twice before: 'I'd love to be able to play like Lubo [Gower] or Gatt [Gatting]. I can't.' Now Marks and Tavaré added 47, Marks making 6 of them.

Suppose in Newcastle, Australia, he batted four seasons in one day. If, watching Tavaré, it turns out we never really knew him, is it possible to know anyone, by watching?

He moved from 123 to 131 in two balls, off-driving then on-driving Hill right and left of the sightscreen. His first 50 had taken 222 minutes, the last 50 took fifty. When, half an hour before stumps, he was bowled for 157, nearly no one who came to the ground had left, and people clapped.

Sometime between 50 and 85 a six was hit, an on-drive.

Hill remembers spilling a catch – 'a sitter, waist-high, two hands, standing in the gully where I'd fielded all my life' – when Tavaré was 34 not out and ex-Test man Gary Gilmour was bowling off a seven-pace run-up.

CHRISTIAN RYAN

Part-timer Robert Wilkinson remembers the wicket he took, Gould (though he misremembers it as Gower) 'caught at mid-wicket'.

Matthew Engel's *Guardian* report makes no mention of a six.

Wicket-keeper Kerry Thompson admits, 'Nothing about the match jumps out at me.'

Hatherell has 'virtually no memories of Tavaré'.

One photo exists of Tavaré's innings, and he is on-driving, along the grass.

Left-arm quick Timmy Towers died of cancer at thirty-six.

Holland remembers Eddie Hemmings's nine wickets and shrewd strategising ('despite the burden of a pillow under his shirt').

Mid-on fielder Greg Arms remembers Holland bowling from the southern end and Tavaré hitting from the north, towards the city, 'a couple whistling past me'.

No one remembers a six.

At the school where it all started, Sevenoaks School, that's where he is now, teaching biology, with additional responsibilities for school hockey, netball and cricket. It does not take much – being there's enough, he says – for his own school cricketing days to come roaring back fresh, and from there it is a small leap to other balls blocked, hit high, still rising, never landing.

The Nightwatchman

Doveton

Dennis Glover

If you were asked to journey back to a different time and place, when and where would you choose? For me, the child of auto and cannery workers, there's only one answer: Detroit in the early 1960s. It was when the unions were strong, wages were high, blue-collar skills were still at a premium and unextraordinary people spent their lives creating extraordinary automobiles to the soundtrack of Phil Spector's wall of sound. I'd go back to Motown.

Of course, it's impossible to go backwards in time, so blue-collar America must make do with the Detroit of today, where their children scavenge among the city's industrial ruins, stripping the lead from factory roofs to the beat of gangsta rap, like squatters stripping marble from the ruins of Rome after the triumph of the barbarians.

In 1960, thanks to its auto industries, Detroit had the highest per capita income of any city in the United States. Think of that: not New York and its bankers, but Detroit and its factory workers were the locus and symbols of global affluence. That's called democracy.

Since then the city's population has fallen by sixty-three per cent, 78,000 of its homes lie abandoned, and its murder rate is eleven times higher than New York's – mainly because the auto plants shut down, taking ninety per cent of all manufacturing jobs.

But Detroit is a long way to go just to feel depressed and possibly even get shot. There is a far easier alternative, especially if you live in Melbourne – go to the street where I grew up, in Doveton, in Melbourne's outer south-east.

Let's start in the past, using the time machine of my memories. It is 1975, I am eleven years old, I'm playing cricket in the middle of my street. The nature strips are a four, and it's a six if you can hit it over the front fence of anyone's house. There's no risk of trouble, as everyone's dad is at work.

On the offside, number twenty-eight's dad is at Perkins Engines, number thirty's dad (mine, a leading hand) is at GMH so is thirty-two's (he's a GMH line manager, and one of my dad's bosses, who caused a minor street-wide sensation when he brought home a Leyland P76). From memory, thirty-four and thirty-six were in vehicle production too, probably making trucks at International Harvester.

On the offside, twenty-three worked for Ford (it must have been in retail, as the Ford plants were far away), twenty-five was a self-employed car mechanic, and twenty-seven was an engineer called Boothroyd, the only person in our street with a degree. He who worked on the Holden design staff and was an officer in dad's Dandenong-based Army Reserve artillery battery. My best friends, two of the players in our games of street cricket, were named John (now a left-wing state Labor MP) and Jimmy (who worked his way from apprentice draughtsman to the manager of a major engineering works).

The former's dad worked as a cleaner in the same GM plant as mine, and the latter's dad ran a small garage that specialised in converting imported American cars from left to right-hand drive. Every week there would be a gleaming new Chevy, Ford or Chrysler ('as big as a whale') sitting in his drive. Cars – their design, manufacture, repair and sale – gave us our bread and butter, our political direction and our social structure. They were the art we created, and the delight of our little community, which centred on the primary school and neat strip shopping centre at the end of the street, with its kindergarten and its stop for the bus that would take our mothers to Dandenong for the weekly shopping.

I'm sure you get the picture – my little valley was green. But even after making allowances for nostalgia, here was a community built for us little people, in the age before capital cut itself free from our democratic control. In it were managers, factory workers, small business people, all living together, with their children going to school together. It all added up to a relative prosperity unknown to ordinary Australians, and perhaps ordinary people anywhere in the world until then. No wonder our dads were in the Army Reserve: this was worth fighting for. Take the vehicle plants and the canneries away and you take away more than jobs.

Little did my friends and I know we were living out the final days of a two-century industrial revolution, which we blithely assumed would go on forever. At fourteen, my father had been apprenticed into the Hilden Mill, in Lisburn, not far from Belfast, in Northern Ireland. Built in the late 1700s, the mill was one of the very first steam-powered cotton manufactories, and even in the early 1960s its massive stationary engines drove cotton spinning machinery through huge wheels and leather belts. Dad's job as a hackle pin setter was to keep the production of the factory's high-grade sewing thread running efficiently.

Industry ran in his blood. His grandfather had been a labourer at Harland and Wolff shipyards, where he smashed thousands of infamously brittle rivets into the steel hull of the *Titanic*. This all made my father a valuable commodity when he migrated to Australia in 1963, giving him his pick of available jobs – first at International Harvester and then at General Motors Holden, where he remained for most of the rest of his working life.

Something keeps drawing me back to the street. Two years ago, when Dad died, I stood outside my old house and wept, but not just for him. No more fours and sixes to hit here, the fences are long gone, and the nature strips and front yards are buried under concrete and rusting cars. Number twenty-eight has an old caravan out front, just visible behind a collection of abandoned vehicles. The thing that made me shudder, though, was my own former home, where I lived until I went to university to study history and law just after my eighteenth birthday in 1982. Today its collection of towing trucks, decaying vehicles and stacks of metal panelling are suggestive of a car wrecking business.

From craftsmen to scavengers in one generation: here was the economic progress we were told would make us all wealthier. I hope that little home scrap business is thriving, but I challenge anyone to look at a sight like my old street without wondering what has gone wrong.

My reveries in my old street that day were interrupted by a huge man in a singlet and shorts who stepped out from a driveway to pointedly take my photograph in a manner obviously intended to intimidate. I wondered why, and left, bemused.

Some six months later I guessed the reason. My neighbourhood was in the news: a drive-by shooting had punched three bullet holes in the metal shuttered windows of a house further down the street, which, with its high walls, imposing gate and security cameras, resembled a fortress. The street is now a place obviously wary of strangers, and it doesn't pay to loiter.

On my following trip just before Christmas, I went to the site of our old primary school. If you have ever read John Wyndham's classic novel *The Day of the Triffids* you would know that its best scene is the one where the protagonist travels back to London years after the apocalypse to find the once great city reclaimed by nature, with pavements choked by spreading weeds, turf growing on roofs, tree roots undermining buildings and branches poking through smashed windows. That's the primary school today, a vandalised jungle slowly disappearing under nature's onslaughts. There's a website that features haunting images of abandoned man-made structures, and if I were a better photographer I would take a photo of the school and post it there.

The school was closed a couple of years ago and replaced nearby with what is known as 'a birth to Year 9 community learning centre', which specialises in countering socio-economic disadvantage. It's sadly necessary today, but when there were jobs and when there was prosperity – when we had auto plants and canning factories – all the local children needed to succeed in life was something called a school.

You can download reports from the new learning centre's website, and they tell you that seventy per cent of the local eleven-year-olds are below the expected level in reading, and eighty-four per cent of local fifteen-year-olds are below the expected level of numeracy for their age. If we take the educational reformers' word for it and accept NAPLAN scores as accurate measures, the only conclusion to draw is that this new economy we have created is failing places like Doveton.

Many comfortable and progressive Australians think such forgotten and neglected places exist only in outback Australia. They should go to Doveton. Like many similar factories, Doveton's biggest source of employment – the GMH plant in Dandenong – closed its gates in the mid-1990s after a long decline. Dad had been laid off a little earlier, in the 'recession we had to have', and got another job the very next week – cleaning vehicles in a used car yard for lower pay, prestige and respect. My mother lost her job too, when Heinz downsized, and she never worked full-time again.

Places like Doveton contain a valuable lesson for us. They show what happens when the auto plants and the canneries shut down: you go from 1960s Motown to Piranesi's Rome in a single generation. South Australian premier Jay Wetherill tells us that the combined effects of closing Ford, Holden and possibly Toyota will be a decade-long recession along the south-eastern seaboard.

The gutsy Liberal MP Sharman Stone fears that if SPC Ardmona closes, the same fate awaits the people of Shepparton.

Who knows if they're right? I can only accept what I see with my own eyes, which is this: in Doveton our auto plant and cannery started disappearing two decades ago and my old neighbourhood still has not recovered. So, sadly, my money would be on both being correct.

In *The Road to Wigan Pier*, George Orwell said that it was a kind of duty for people in power to see the places the economy and our politicians have failed, lest we should forget they exist. But what conclusions should the powerful draw from places like Doveton?

Most obviously, that when you shut the auto plants and the canneries, the little people pay for generations.

But there is another lesson, one that provides some hope if we are willing to heed it: the need for a wider moral approach to economics, and policymaking more generally. Today we tend to see economic policy through narrow statistical prisms like 'productivity'. If we all just become more productive and give up unaffordable luxuries, the Productivity Commissioners tell us, a new Golden Age beckons.

But like a cat chasing its tail in ever decreasing circles, that Golden Age is never obtained. To the people of Doveton, the

Golden Age seems to lie only in the past. In their aggressive push to make places like Doveton more productive, all the economists have done is ensure they produce very little at all.

Essentially, Doveton's fate demonstrates that our approach to economics needs to be widened and deepened to take in the sorts of moral and aesthetic considerations that earlier policy-makers, like the ones who created Doveton, accepted implicitly. People have to be efficient, sure, but they don't have to live alongside junk yards, their schools don't have to be turned into urban jungles, and they don't have to be cleaners and gleaners.

They deserve to live in pleasing surroundings and have the chance to create objects of beauty and utility that embody crafts-manship and pride – things like cars, things like food. Creating Holdens in real life beats creating them in our dreams. Our economists need to understand this as they contemplate creating yet more Dovetons.

The Age

My Fellow Australians

Don Watson

At this time of the year, my sleep is a cavalcade of dreams. Too much family stirs the mental pot. One thing leads to another and the next minute Tony Abbott appears, sitting backwards on a bicycle and wearing an Australia Day T-shirt, a proxy for some oppressive childhood memory no doubt. He goes at a good clip along an avenue of gums and shadows, pedalling round corners without so much as a rearward glance, and still managing to talk. 'I have a resting heart rate of thirty beats per minute. To put that in perspective, a resting crocodile's is twenty-eight. Malcolm Turnbull's is seventy-six on a good day. Even John Howard never clocked less than seventy.'

He is winding up a steep hill now, through a forest, standing on the pedals – don't ask me how.

'The more regularly one drives up the pulse, the more it falls at rest. With brutal exercise I have recorded rates that are the human equivalent of an Etruscan shrew.

'To rip through the rind of comfortable existence and enter the lowest deep of pain is my pleasure. I am an endorphin addict. It is how I know myself. Without exercise – at a dinner, for instance, or reading a briefing paper – I struggle to remain convinced that I am not hibernating like a python in a cave.

'Only when I exercise do I feel truly alive; yet the more I exercise, the less alive I feel when I am not. It is the paradox of my existence.'

At that point he shoots down a fire track, and I wake and dictate all this into my smartphone. Once asleep again, I find him in a forest clearing, standing bow-legged on an old-growth tree stump and spouting to a gathering of lyrebirds. With his blue swimmers visible beneath a tattered toga, he might be the prophet Isaiah, but for some reason Thomas the Tank Engine also comes to mind.

'My fellow Australians,' he says. 'Today we celebrate Australia's remarkable progress from convict settlement to the great nation in which we live today. Surely no people on the planet have more reason to be joyous.

'How magnificent we are! What a future lies before us! What a past behind! We must remain true to our Judaeo-Christian values, and steadfast and fearless as the Anzacs. Great challenges lie ahead – the Budget challenge, the education challenge, the national broadband challenge, the arrival of their Royal Highnesses the Duke and Duchess of Cambridge and Prince George in April.

'Let us now resolve to pay any price, bear any burden, meet any hardship, to make sure we can't think of anything else while they are here.

'By all accounts Prince William is a keen adventurer like myself, and I have already invited him to join me in an ironman contest and to go a few rounds in the ring. I urge you to flock and fawn and hang your flags up and down the land. Buy the souvenirs and mags. Leave them in no doubt that the sun will never set on your affection; that you would rather die than live without them.

'The future king and queen will have scarcely left our shores when we begin the centenary of the outbreak of World War I. And, as if that were not enough excitement for one year, nine months later we have the centenary of the landing at Gallipoli. What else can one say but "Yippee"?'

The lyrebirds oblige. The forest resounds with their mimicry. And he goes on.

'Of course it goes without saying that these last two are solemn events. We should not commemorate historical episodes that saw the deaths of millions with the unbridled gaiety we bring to Australia Day, which – putting aside the destruction of an ancient civilisation and a legacy of rank injustice, suffering and despair – commemorates an event that caused the deaths of comparatively few. A couple of hundred thousand perhaps, if you count the disease and alcohol and so on, over several generations. Maybe half a million – tops.

'That is a good many more than the 60,000 Australians killed in World War I. I know. I can count. But what are we supposed to do – get out the black armbands again, and bow our heads and fill our hearts with awe and sorrow every 26 January? Not on your Nellie. That's what we do on Anzac Day.

'Yes, there is a downside to our history. In much of life there is a downside. It comes with the upside. You can see that in the example of my heart rate. Difficult things happen sometimes. Besides, many of the deaths were not deliberately inflicted: the worst we could say of most of them is that they were careless; incidental, as it were, to the colonial and national projects on which the furtherance of our Judaeo-Christian values depend. Most of them were no one's fault, really. And frankly, some of them were their own fault, partly, frankly. And unlike the Anzacs, they were defending no one's freedom or values, or the Australian way of life – unless you count their own. It's chalk and cheese – well, chalk anyway.'

*

At this point, silence descends on the gully. All birdsong stops. The leaves of the trees cease to rustle in the high breezes.

'It's all relative, you see. It's all a matter of context. It ain't necessarily so, and all that. What's important is not truth so much as . . .'

And here he hesitates, and a preternatural and nightmarish grin takes possession of his face. His eyes roll back and beads of sweat bubble on his brow. When at last the grin has gone, he exhales and mutters, 'Sorry, just stretching my glutes.' And he continues:

'There is no need to go into the micro details of history. The important thing is not to politicise these commemorations. Under my government, Christopher Pyne – a bravura example of Western civilisation and Judaeo-Christian Anzac values if ever there was one – will put a stop to the rewriting of history by postmodern, multicultural, left-wing relativists. We will decide what we know of history, and the circumstances in which we know it. We will make an end of it.'

And then I'm wakened by a possum chattering on the roof. Or so I think, but it might be one of the lyrebirds.

Good Weekend

Men of a Certain Age

Rachel Nolan

At an International Women's Day event in March this year, Prime Minister Tony Abbott, in describing the progress women have made, noted, 'It wasn't so long ago as a Sydneysider that there was a female lord mayor, a female premier, a female prime minister, [and] a female head of state in our governor-general . . .'

It should hardly have been surprising that his remarks were ridiculed. No one had done more, after all, to see that three of the four had by that time been replaced by more traditional appointments – older, private school–educated, conservative white men.

The Abbott government is the first in Australian history not just to stifle but also to reverse the progress of Australian women.

It began within days of Abbott becoming prime minister at September 2013's federal election, when he announced a nineteen-member cabinet with just one woman, the lowest level of female representation since 2001. It continued in January 2014, when a former chief of the Australian Defence Force, Peter Cosgrove, was chosen to replace Quentin Bryce, whose term as governor-general was about to expire.

In between times the tone was amplified with a slew of significant appointments weighted overwhelmingly towards older, business-oriented, climate change–denying, Sydney-based, conservative men.

Having mocked the then new prime minister Kevin Rudd for

'hitting the ground reviewing' in 2007, Abbott has commenced his tenure in much the same way. 'Independent reviews' have been commissioned across portfolios, and the choice of reviewers speaks volumes about the new government, its bedfellows and the advice it wants to hear.

Sydney businessman Tony Shepherd, sixty-nine, is chairing the National Commission of Audit. He is the immediate past president of the conservative Business Council of Australia. Sydney businessman Maurice Newman, seventy-six, chairs the Business Advisory Council. A friend of John Howard's, he is the former chair of the Australian Stock Exchange. Sydney businessman David Murray, sixty-five, chairs the financial system inquiry. He is a former CEO of the Commonwealth Bank. Sydney businessman Dick Warburton, seventy-two, chairs the review of the Renewable Energy Target. Like Murray and Newman, Warburton is an outspoken climate change sceptic, so his appointment to review one of the key planks of the government effort to combat climate change was unsurprisingly met with outrage and incredulity by environmentalists, climate scientists and renewable-energy advocates.

In social policy, Abbott's big appointment is Sydney-based charity executive Patrick McClure, sixty-three. The former head of Mission Australia, who rose to public prominence as the face of welfare corporatisation in the Howard years, now runs the welfare review. Kevin Donnelly and Ken Wiltshire are carrying out the national curriculum review. Both are long-term fixtures on the political scene who have supported not just conservative education causes but also the cause of the Liberal Party itself. Donnelly was a staffer to Kevin Andrews, now the minister for social services, some years ago.

Over in the courts, the government has again turned to trusted sources as it introduces the American practice of seeking to criminalise its political opponents. The top two contenders to become Australia's Kenneth Starr are: Ian Hanger QC, sixty-seven, who was a former colleague of Attorney-General George Brandis at the Queensland Bar and is now inquiring into the home insulation scheme, and Dyson Heydon, seventy-one, the Howard government High Court appointee now leading the royal commission into unions.

Another striking aspect of the Abbott appointments is that so many are retreads from the Howard years. Cosgrove, McClure and Heydon in particular had strong public association with Howard decisions. The Warburton connection from that time is accidental but telling nonetheless. In 2002, Warburton and Abbott both received Ernie Awards for sexist remarks. Warburton's Ernie was for the comment, made as the chair of David Jones, that 'he was unable to find a woman of sufficient talent to join the Board'. Abbott's gong, ironically, was for saying that paid maternity leave would happen 'over this government's dead body'. (The 2002 Gold Ernie went to Abbott associate George Pell, who said abortion was a bigger moral scandal than sexual abuse of young people by priests.)

The appointment of Howard-era people by the new government provides a telling insight into Abbott the PM. Notably, for a man who's been in public life since university days, Abbott hasn't enunciated a unique political philosophy or surrounded himself with a clique of fellow travellers stretching beyond the party room. Unlike Bob Hawke, Paul Keating, Howard or even Julia Gillard before him – but like Kevin Rudd – Abbott is an individual to whom the party turned, not the leader of a push.

Analyses of Abbott's political philosophy often reflect on his influences – notably B.A. Santamaria and Howard – rather than assessing any vision he has presented for the country. The immaturity of Abbott's political philosophy has been revealed when he has confronted issues beyond the narrow platform he laid out pre-election: when hard choices – the questions on which populism offers no guide – have needed to be made. The prolonged indecision around the sale of GrainCorp was the clearest example of this vagueness; the flat-footed response to manufacturing job losses is much the same. In the absence of a clear personal political philosophy, Abbott's choice of advisers becomes critical to the direction of the government.

A key difference between the Abbott government and its critics involves the question of diversity. The PM has argued loudly and repeatedly that all the appointments have been merit-based – and that their limited gene pool has been coincidence, happenstance or of secondary importance anyway. Meanwhile, the critics argue that diversity matters, not only in terms of who sits around the table but also in the perspectives they bring and the kind of advice they provide as a result.

A recent Fairfax article by Waleed Aly, commenting on the government's proposed changes to the *Racial Discrimination Act*, made a critical point about society's need to understand diversity. He argued that the issue with the *RDA* is not whether or not it's legal to racially vilify someone (the focus of the debate so far) but who determines the standard by which racism is judged. As the proposed amendment stands, the test of whether something is reasonably likely to intimidate or vilify is to be determined 'by the standards of an ordinary reasonable member of the Australian community'. Fair enough, says Aly. 'But then it adds in the most pointed way: 'not by the standards of any particular group within the Australian community.'

'Of course, only white people have the chance to be neutral because in our society only white is deemed normal; only whiteness is invisible . . . This is just the level of privilege we're dealing with.'

The 'reasonable person' envisaged by the Abbott government is not just white but also, it would seem, old, conservative and male.

*

'I think it would be folly,' Tony Abbott said back in his university days, 'to expect that women will ever dominate or even approach equal representation in a large number of areas, simply because their aptitudes, abilities and interests are different for physiological reasons.' Far from growing out of such a view, he took a similar stand twenty years later in a radio interview, rhetorically asking, 'If it's true . . . that men have more power, generally speaking, than women, is that a bad thing?'

In 2010 he suggested that the 'housewives of Australia' would reflect on the carbon price 'as they do the ironing'. And in March this year, again at the International Women's Day event, he reflected, 'the deal that [Australia] gives to women . . . is obviously pretty good', as if equality, living standards or personal freedom were not human rights but somehow the gift of society – and, by implication, the men who are running it.

The feminist response to Abbott's appointments paints the

exclusion of women as an injustice. 'When women make up more than half the population,' said sex discrimination commissioner Elizabeth Broderick, 'it's disappointing that there's only one woman in cabinet.' Liberal senator Sue Boyce and former Liberal senator Judith Troeth have also expressed their displeasure. 'Why aren't women equally as good [at running the country] as men are?' Troeth asked.

The justice argument ignores the differences between men and women. When women were first fighting for equal opportunity, consideration of these differences was considered either a distraction from the basic goal of better representation for women or an excuse to justify their ongoing exclusion. The field on gender difference has been left almost entirely to conservatives, who have used it – relentlessly – to justify inequality.

Alongside the justice argument sits a body of suggested action. From the former Victorian premier Joan Kirner with *The Women's Power Handbook* (1999) to the Facebook executive Sheryl Sandberg with the bestseller *Lean In* (2013), women have written guides to success that encourage women to be tough, act more assertively and overcome what for many is a reluctance to self-promote. The subtext is that with a bit of 'you go, girl', women can make it in a man's world.

What is rarely said about this thinking, though, is that while many women (this author included) find it quite possible to learn to play such a role, the very act of doing so, day after day and year after year, can be a dehumanising or, more truthfully, de-feminising experience. Female political candidates are told to dress differently, to wear less jewellery and colour and more sober suits; they're told to lower their voices in fear of the great turn-off, that they'll come across on the radio sounding like a girl. They're constantly told to toughen up, to not act 'emotionally'. It's well understood that tears in the office would spell disaster. Angry responses are fine, however. There's no shortage of anger in politics.

My own experience of this process, as a transport minister and later as a finance minister in Anna Bligh's Queensland state government, is that while women can do it (and indeed it's satisfying to develop a sense of authority), there can be something soul-destroying about it, too. The constant act of self-promotion sits uneasily with many women, as does the need to defend against the ego-driven players (almost always men) who are constantly point-scoring and looking to knock you off your guard.

The distinctive character traits of many women at the top serve to reinforce, not dismiss, that sense of dissonance. That the Margaret Thatchers, Angela Merkels, Julie Bishops and Peta Credlins of the world often stand out for being tougher than tough suggests not that women are on the verge of forever breaking the glass ceiling, as is often assumed, but that only those who have a level of confidence or force of opinion that is highly unusual among women can make it in what remains a man's world.

There are a million explanations – from science to self-help – for the origin of men's and women's difference. Neuroscientists interpret MRI scans to argue that men's and women's brains are wired differently – with men having connections within brain hemispheres, aiding coordination and linear thinking, while women are connected across hemispheres, aiding intuition and empathy. While this work has been seen on the one hand as confirming gender differences commonly observed throughout society, other scientists argue that, as the brain changes with behaviour, these wiring differences only reflect the sheer inescapability of social norms.

The popular spiritual author and 'guru' Eckhart Tolle describes the differences in understandably different terms: politics, he says, is driven by ego – the part of us that needs constant affirmation that we're right – but that ego tends to be a men's field, while women are driven by a deeper, more humble and more spiritual sense of self.

Whatever the origins of difference, it is fair to say that the public responds differently to women and men in leadership.

In Australia, the fact remains that the women who made it to the very top have been flung from political office, not just in defeats but in landslides (or in Julia Gillard's case a projected landslide) driven by a sense of public rage.

The former NSW premier Kristina Keneally (who took her party from fifty seats to twenty, after a sixteen per cent swing against it) and the former Tasmanian premier Lara Giddings (from ten seats to seven in a ten per cent swing) were both judged weak leaders. Giddings found it impossible to get through a profile interview that didn't canvass her desire to 'meet the right man'; Keneally fought aspersions that she was someone else's 'girl'. Both Anna Bligh (from fifty-one seats to seven, sixteen per cent swing) and Julia Gillard faced public loathing for 'betrayals' (on asset sales and carbon tax respectively).

Compare this to Bligh's and Gillard's respective successors, Campbell Newman and Tony Abbott, who performed their own post-election backflips – on public service sackings and telecommunications and education spending respectively – but were instead perceived as simply politicians predictably breaking promises.

As I touched on in a piece for the *Monthly*'s blog last year ('What It's Like To Be a Woman in Politics'), the extreme public emotional responses to Bligh and Gillard seemed unfathomable to those who knew what clear-headed, decent, reasonable people they were in a working environment.

In Sheryl Sandberg's *Lean In*, the Facebook chief operating officer cites empirical evidence that shows women are viewed as less likeable the more powerful they become. This trend, in controlled studies, does not apply to men.

In 2014, the proportion of women in Australian parliaments is actually trending down. Following this year's state elections, twenty-one per cent of Coalition MPs across state and federal parliaments are women, while Labor has more than twice that level of female representation at forty-three per cent. The fall in overall numbers of women in Australian parliaments is entirely the result of the conservative ascendancy.

When the country's first female PM has been stalked from office in a tide of sexist abuse and the perpetrators have the same power they always had, when the number of women in Australian parliaments has peaked and declined, and when the country's most infamously sexist political leader can blithely describe himself as a feminist (as Abbott did again at the International Women's Day event), the argument that if women learn the right skills they will soon justly prevail has been blown apart.

*

Perhaps, then, it's time to move on from the justice argument and acknowledge that women are different – and that their different perspectives are exactly what we need.

This question of difference was tackled recently in a *Time* magazine piece by the American banker Sallie Krawcheck, who'd run Smith Barney (a part of Citigroup) in the wake of the global financial crisis. Krawcheck recounts how she was first howled down and then lost her job after suggesting the bank partially reimburse investors for losses on unintentionally high-risk products it had sold them. While at first she didn't see the experience as a gender issue at all – understanding it instead as her failing to toe the party line – she later saw research suggesting it was quite normal for women to be more risk averse, to place higher value on client relationships and take a longer-term view. Perhaps her non-conformity was a gender issue, after all.

Australian opinion polls consistently show that men and women both view and prioritise issues differently. The ABC's Vote Compass, which saw 1.4 million Australians privately express their views ahead of the 2013 federal poll, showed for instance that women were substantially less likely than men to support higher defence spending, but that the opposite was true of university funds. Women were more likely to support higher foreign aid spending and less likely to back deficit reduction if it came at the expense of social services.

In politics, the Australian woman who has spoken most compellingly about the observed differences between men and women in positions of power is not one of the highest profile figures but Meredith Burgmann, who was a member of New South Wales's upper house from 1991 to 2007.

Burgmann says that in her years in parliament two of the key issues on which she saw men and women split along gender lines were gun control and swimming-pool fences. Her observations are compelling because they at once seem predictable – of course women will have different views on some issues – but also fly in the face of conventional thinking that would suggest that the classic 'women's issues' – those things about which women might be expected to take a distinct and united view – are abortion and childcare.

Burgmann points out that abortion splits on religious lines and childcare on ideology. Gun control, and particularly the question of unsecured guns in homes, is a matter of how women see personal security. Pool fencing is crucial because mothers know to the core of their being that a child can slip away in the blink of an eye.

Half a world away, and on a bigger stage, another political figure offers a very different take on different male and female thought processes. The International Monetary Fund's managing director Christine Lagarde has repeatedly opined that the global financial crisis was caused by too much testosterone. 'In gender-dominated environments, men have a tendency to . . . show how hairy chested they are,' she said in 2011. 'I honestly think that there should never be too much testosterone in one room.' It's not known whether a response to her comments has been sought from her immediate predecessor at the IMF, Dominique Strauss-Kahn.

As every era has perennial issues – health, education, economic growth, inequality and the like – so too are times defined by existential concerns, issues that grip the public consciousness in overarching terms. Today, there is of course the serious matter of slow growth in the long shadow of the global financial crisis, but there is also the rise of China and the age-defining threat of climate change.

Thinking people are forced to decide: either reject the well-established science of climate change, a move which essentially involves rejecting the supremacy of science in modern thought, or reflect seriously about our social and economic assumptions in order to find a way forward.

The new chief executive officer of the Australian Conservation Foundation, Kelly O'Shanassy, says she sees differences between how men and women respond to the challenge of sustainability. 'With climate change, people tend to see the issue either from a technological perspective or a social and behavioural one. Men tend to look at technology while women innately understand the different kinds of lives and different kinds of behaviours we will have to have. They see the long-term, massive social issues like health problems that will come if we don't respond to climate change.'

Australia's head-in-the-sand model of selling our resources to China and buying their cheap consumer goods is unlikely to give rise to the pioneering thinking needed to go on living sustain-ably. The environmental challenge and the rise of China are closely linked. If the rise of China is effectively the result of that nation's adoption of the Western business model, particularly of competition, science and consumerism, then we must also con-front an inescapable reality that Chinese development to West-ern standards, along with that of the rest of Asia, will add enormously to carbon emissions.

Queensland University of Technology sustainability expert Jim Gall describes the change needed as an intellectual revolu-tion akin to the Enlightenment, and he reflects a wide body of writing when he suggests feminism is a central part of it.

'It's not about women having a fair role in this model that is failing us, it's about asking what it is about the way women think that gives us a way out of this mess,' he says.

'What Abbott's trying to do is reinforce the old system, but there's no future in that . . . People might want to take shelter in this harbour for a short time but in the end we know these envi-ronmental issues are real and we know we have to change.'

As environmental campaigners, too, men and women often behave differently. 'Men sometimes get caught in the bravado of a particular campaign and can lose heart if we don't win,' Kelly O'Shanassy says, 'but women tend to stay focused on the funda-mental reason for change. They can see it and are resilient whether the immediate battle is lost or won.

'Living sustainably requires a different, more collaborative and less top-down leadership approach. Diversity is an important part of that.'

Former Queensland environment minister Kate Jones agrees. For her, women are in it for the long term, because they see the environment as a security issue. 'It's a cliché but it does become even stronger and clearer once you have kids.'

The opinions of O'Shanassy and Jones are backed by research. A major CSIRO scan of available polling data conducted in 2011 showed that across a range of polls, women were six per cent to eleven per cent more likely to believe in anthropogenic climate change and to support action. This is consistent with other data showing that, as concern about climate change declined from its 2007–08 peak, the desertion was starker among men; when it came to concern about climate change, women were more likely to stick around.

The CSIRO climate change study is not the only hard data showing Australian women take a distinctive view. A Newspoll survey published in early April showed the Abbott government's primary vote had plunged across mainland states by an average of around six per cent. The key reason for the collapse? Women's personal satisfaction with Abbott had fallen from a net satisfaction of zero (forty-one per cent positive, forty-one per cent negative) in the last polling period to a net satisfaction of minus eighteen per cent just three months down the track.

'If one thing can be blamed for the lack of a honeymoon for the Abbott government, it must be the speed with which women have turned off the PM,' observed Peter van Onselen in the *Australian*.

*

Tony Abbott recently claimed, yet again on the occasion of International Women's Day, that 'true equality is always the result of more economic opportunity'.

The comment was a scripted one, made in support of the government's controversial paid parental leave scheme. The reductionist perspective it represents, that government is essentially a matter of economic management, appears central to the Abbott government's approach. After all, its only real foreign policy wins have come on economic matters – prioritisation of growth at the G20 in February and the trade deals in Asia more recently. Its significant appointments have overwhelmingly been of conservative company directors, and now the prime minister describes gender equality as an economic matter, too.

As a minister who privatised $10 billion of assets (two ports and a railway), I'm as committed as anyone to the big, hard, serious business of economic reform. This is not, therefore, an argument that we should avoid troubling ourselves with the economy but rather an assertion that economic reform alone is not enough.

The country's challenges are far more complex than the economic problems confronted during the Hawke and Keating years or those addressed by Howard as he created what is now the model for Abbott's leadership. The Australia of 2014 is a precarious place. Its economy sails in troubled waters as manufacturing goes offshore and a post-GFC lag in confidence sets in. Its environment is threatened and its per capita emissions remain among the highest in the developed world. Its region is influenced by China, now stretching its muscle and its money through the region with soft and hard diplomacy.

Tony Abbott has a woman problem and he has an agenda problem, too. He must develop an answer clear and simple enough to convince people there's a future for jobs. He needs a consistent economic and national security response to China and a coherent position on climate change. Doing that will require diverse and complex thinking, something unlikely to come from the uniform advisers he's so far engaged.

And while it is one thing for the women of Australia to be offended by their exclusion, it is quite another for all of us to see our future endangered by a narrow band of conservative older men set on returning us to a past that can no longer exist.

The exclusion of women is the exclusion of diverse thinking. For the whole country, the price paid for the prime minister's sexism may yet turn out to be very high indeed.

The Monthly

Freedom Abbott

David Marr

In Tony Abbott's Australia, a young woman faces jail because word got out that one of his daughters was given a $60,000 scholarship to study at the Whitehouse Institute of Design. This scholarship was never advertised. Students at the college in Sydney had no idea such largesse was available. News of Frances Abbott's win provoked a two-month investigation by the New South Wales police and a charge of accessing restricted data without authorisation. Penalty: imprisonment for a maximum of two years.

How different it was all those years ago when young Tony won his Rhodes. Now that's a scholarship. The win wasn't a secret. No one faced jail when the news broke. But the young man and the prime minister have this in common: a most uncertain respect for free speech. Abbott had made his name at the University of Sydney as one of Bob Santamaria's acolytes working to silence student unions by starving them of funds. The day the Rhodes was announced, in November 1980, he told the *Sydney Morning Herald* that John Kerr, Malcolm Fraser and the uranium industry were not 'legitimate concerns' of student unions. 'In my view, vast amounts of student money are being spent on extreme causes.'

Abbott never seemed the sort of man who would go out on a limb for liberty. In parliament he made a spectacle of himself early on by suing over a silly slur in Bob Ellis's book *Goodbye Jerusalem*. He was up to his neck in the legal manoeuvring that landed Pauline Hanson in jail. He had the courage to demur when John

Howard put WorkChoices before cabinet, but there is no record of him standing up to his patron when Howard prosecuted whistleblowers; stripped NGOs of funding; whipped museums into line; widened sedition laws; imprisoned the innocent Dr Mohamed Haneef without charge; and subjected the ABC to a decade of partisan abuse. When it came to liberty, Abbott was one of the Coalition pack.

Yet one morning in August 2012 he walked into the Amora Hotel in Sydney and pledged to take up arms in the Freedom Wars. 'We are the freedom party,' he told an exuberant crowd gathered by the Institute of Public Affairs (IPA).

> We stand for the freedoms which Australians have a right to expect and which governments have a duty to uphold. We stand for freedom and will be freedom's bulwark against the encroachments of an unworthy and dishonourable government.

No Coalition leader has ever talked freedom as Abbott did that morning. The passion, the rhetoric and the undertakings he gave were new in the politics of this country. He might have been an American on the stump. Angels sang and trumpets sounded. He was promising to do more than stop the boats, axe the tax and end the waste. As prime minister, he would restore our lost freedoms. A new Abbott had appeared from nowhere to join the others who jostle for our attention. Politics Abbott is the one who rules them all. Values Abbott has his commitment to faith and a unique political past. Intellectual Abbott can turn out opinion pieces on anything from reshaping the federation to the future of marriage. But here on the stage of this big city hotel was Freedom Abbott:

> Without free speech, free debate is impossible and, without free debate, the democratic process cannot work properly nor can misgovernment and corruption be fully exposed. Freedom of speech is part of the compact between citizen and society on which democratic government rests. A threat to citizens' freedom of speech is more than an error of political judgement. It reveals a fundamental misunderstanding of the give and take between government and citizen on which a peaceful and harmonious society is based.

Two years later, I sit here writing Freedom Abbott's obituary. I'll honour the form with the story of his rise from nowhere, the hopes he raised in his brief life, his impact on the politics of the nation, and his sudden death in August in the same week the cops charged the supposed Whitehouse whistleblower. They were rough days for liberty. By the time the prime minister abandoned his crusade to gut the *Racial Discrimination Act*, promised new powers to ASIO and prepared to store our metadata for the use of intelligence agencies, Freedom Abbott was on the slab.

The death wrecked Tim Wilson's Free Speech 2014 symposium. Gathered in Sydney that week by the new human rights commissioner were figures from the Left, Right and Centre, a peace council of the factions called to explore the great prospects for liberty under an Abbott government. But the day was a wake, with the same coffee and smoked salmon that come with a funeral – and the same gloom. The attorney-general, George Brandis, found another funeral to go to at the last minute. It wasn't brave, but what could he have said to us? His libertarian rhetoric, even more lyrical than Abbott's, had just been junked by his master. The Freedom Wars seem over without a shot being fired. So much praise had been wasted, so many hopes dashed, and now so much blame is being dished out. Abbott's naïve admirers have turned on him for betraying Australia. In the aftermath of an abandoned war, the politics of liberty have shifted to a dark place.

'Dead is dead,' said Gertrude Stein. 'But dead is not done. Not over.'

*

Abbott could always talk freedom. It was a topic fit for think tanks: civilised, big-picture, fundamental but tame. He always saw the dangers. They went back to Genesis: 'In the Garden of Eden, Adam and Eve could do almost as they pleased. But freedom turned out to have its limits and its abuses, as this foundational story makes only too clear.' Cynics might argue the church had to be fought tooth and nail for liberal democracy to emerge. But Abbott has always said we have Christianity to thank for freedom and 'the presumption of innocence, universal suffrage, limited government, and religious, cultural and political pluralism'.

Among today's great defenders of 'freedom under law' he lists the crown and the papacy.

He never thought freedom owed much to the Left. Tom Paine is not among his heroes. No revolution, not even the French, is given credit for liberty's rise. Nor are unions, the labour movement and Marx. He is polite to Americans: he acknowledges the overthrow of George III matters to them, though he's sure it means nothing to us. His praise stops short of the First Amendment. He doesn't gush about the Universal Declaration of Human Rights.

For the past few centuries, freedom has spoken English. True, there were one or two upheavals along the way, but Abbott has always seen peaceful England setting the standard for liberty's rise. He doesn't turn to the great legal theorists to make this point. He quotes Tennyson's lines about 'A land of settled government, / A land of just and old renown, / Where Freedom slowly broadens down / From precedent to precedent'. This is his go-to quote when he talks freedom. He finds these lines pithy and beautiful. He loves to quote them when he's talking liberty to American think tanks. Sometimes he rolls on to the next verse, condemning another England where 'banded unions persecute / Opinions, and induce a time / When single thought is civil crime, / And individual freedom mute'.

An Oxford man is expected to dish out this sort of stuff. But an Oxford man might also have a closer look at what Tennyson is writing here: a Tory attack on the *Great Reform Act* of 1832 and the political division it provoked in England. His favourite quote on freedom is, in fact, an attack on one of the key, hard-fought victories against aristocratic power in Britain. Perhaps Abbott has no idea of this. Perhaps he's just smitten by the poetry. What's certain is his affection for the idea that liberty evolves naturally over time, dropping gently from the heavens. This is not freedom made by great upheavals or witnessed in declarations. There is nothing hard and fast about it. More than anything, it's a matter of instinct. You know it when you *feel* it.

Abbott was always worried about the need to keep a brake on freedom. It's the lesson of Adam and Eve, the teaching of his faith, and the fear that drove Santamaria's crusade all those years ago in the universities of Australia. The Santa crowd saw themselves as campaigning for order in a world where too much freedom might mean curtains for civilisation. Abbott has grown since then as a man and a politician, but in 2002, as a young minister in Howard's government, troubled by divorce and drugs, he was still lashing out at

> a highly contagious mutant strain of liberalism that can't work out when one person's freedom stops and another's starts, and which feels constrained by the ideal of freedom from discouraging (let alone preventing) self-indulgent, counter-productive and destructive behaviour. The liberal state carries within it the seeds of its own destruction if it is just liberal, if it cannot coerce or even criticise the misuse of freedom.

Abbott believed in a liberty of rules with freedom restrained and protected by the state. He doesn't celebrate free spirits except, rather touchingly, those who ride bikes: 'The bike is a freedom machine.' And he finds repugnant the idea of having a bill of rights to guarantee our liberties. He is not alone there on either side of the House of Representatives. Politicians look after themselves. Their instincts are finely honed. As Abbott told Laurie Oakes one night in 2008: 'The problem with a bill of rights is that it takes power off the elected politicians.'

Freedom Abbott was still a few years away. Politics Abbott played a part in his unexpected birth. From the US, Australian conservatives had imported the strategy of branding their opponents – 'liberals' there and 'the left' here – as enemies of freedom. This works better in the US, where there's a big constituency for the notion that controlling guns, taxing carbon and giving medicine to the poor are a frontal attack on freedom in a nation whose defining purpose is the pursuit of freedom. Here, we hanker as much for fairness as we do liberty. We don't fear government. We're not happy about paying tax but we don't see it as a fundamental assault on freedom.

But Australian commentators took up the drumbeat of Fox News, and Liberal Party leaders began, shyly at first, to present themselves as evangelists for liberty facing the hostility of the left. 'The left has embraced a new authoritarianism,' Brandis declared in April this year, in a ripping interview with the libertarian Brendan O'Neill for the website *Spiked*. 'Having abandoned the attempt to control the commanding heights of the economy, they now want to control the commanding heights of opinion, and that is even more dangerous.'

Brandis invokes the ghosts of Stalin and Pol Pot to press home his attack on the left. Those with a taste for personal abuse more developed than mine might call this line of argument insane. I call it surprising. 'How can it be,' Brandis asked a crowd at the Centre for Independent Studies in August last year, 'that at the end of a century that saw the embrace by the authoritarian Left of murder on an industrial scale as a political and ideological method, how can it be that we, on our side of politics, abandoned human rights as a cause to the Left?' His message was: 'We have to re-embrace the human rights debate. We have to remind people that we in the Liberal Party are the party of human rights.'

More than anything, the Left is charged with smothering dissident voices in the debate over global warming. They treat sceptics with disrespect. Laugh at Lord Monckton. Reserve ABC science shows for scientists. Fail to give dissenters an honoured place on the platform. The exercise of judgement – scientific and editorial – in the debate is condemned as the bullying, authoritarian, anti-free speech behaviour of the Left.

When Abbott jumped the ditch in late 2009 to join the sceptics, this became part of his thinking. So too did the American notion that small government equals freedom. He had dismissed the idea earlier that year in his memoir, *Battlelines*, but it began to shape his rhetoric. Replying to Rudd's budget in 2010, the new leader of the Opposition declared: 'The Coalition wants lower taxes, smaller government and greater freedom.'

And the leap to the sceptics drew him closer to Andrew Bolt, an eloquent News Ltd voice on the side of the Liberal Party and a scourge of plans to combat climate change. Abbott came to comfort the shattered columnist a few days after the Federal Court's mortifying judgement in the case brought by Aborigines Bolt had attacked baselessly in the *Herald Sun*. Bolt told John van Tiggelen of *Good Weekend* that his 'very influential' guest had 'dropped in to urge him to keep going on all fronts. The impromptu dinner guest told him and his wife that his TV show, merely by existing, gave heart to a good many people.'

Abbott did not defend Bolt's journalism: 'The article for which

Andrew Bolt was prosecuted under this legislation was almost certainly not his finest.' But he called for the gutting of section 18C of the *Racial Discrimination Act*, which penalises speech likely to 'offend, insult, intimidate or humiliate' on grounds of race. The court had found that Bolt ticked all four boxes. Free speech advocates, long worried that the act set the bar too low, were calling for 'offend' and 'insult' to be pruned from the section. Julia Gillard's government was hammered for defending 18C as it stood.

'This law will haunt Labor and constitute another chapter in the degeneration of its culture, a process now dangerously advanced,' declared the *Australian*'s editor-at-large, Paul Kelly. 'Indeed, it is hard to find a more perfect example of the trap of political correctness and the legal-human rights culture of legislating for good behaviour than this application of the *Racial Discrimination Act*.' He commended Abbott and Brandis for swiftly promising to fix the act. 'It signals a new cultural attack on Labor on grounds of political correctness.'

Freedom Abbott was a bastard child of the Culture Wars. He quoted Edmund Burke and John Stuart Mill, and even Voltaire, but his passion for freedom wasn't a thing of abstract philosophy. Abbott was about to do what he did so well as leader of the Opposition: blast the government with whatever was to hand.

Something else was in the air in the days of Freedom Abbott's birth. The *Australian* had received a fresh cache of documents about Bruce Wilson, the crooked former Australian Workers Union official who was once Julia Gillard's lover. Earlier attempts to smear her with Wilson's crimes had damaged Gillard badly. But she fought back hard and saw Bolt silenced, Glenn Milne dumped by the *Australian* and shock jock Michael Smith ousted from Sydney radio station 2UE. Now after a year's lull, the story had returned. It was gold for Abbott, but, inside and outside the government, News Ltd was being accused of a vicious beat-up. The *Australian* on Saturday, 4 August 2012 had the story everywhere: on page one, 'Cops wanted Gillard's ex charged'; on page two: 'Coalition wants alleged bagman investigated'; on page twenty-three, Cut and Paste: 'Fifty shades of nay, or how the real Dr No of politics keeps Labor from getting tied up'; and on the same page an editorial: 'AWU scandal questions linger'.

Two days later, Freedom Abbott materialised in the ballroom of the Amora Hotel, electrifying a crowd of 300. His rhetoric was wonderful. Again and again, he was stopped by applause. He was so forgiving about the press. No journalist could fail to be pleased by his promise to protect speech that wasn't always accurate and wasn't always fair: 'The price of free speech . . . is that offence will be given, facts will be misrepresented, and sometimes lies will be told. Truth, after all, only emerges from such a process. But thanks to free speech, error can be exposed, corruption revealed, arrogance deflated, mistakes corrected, the right upheld and truth flaunted in the face of power.'

Then his focus narrowed: 'This is not a government that argues its case. Mostly, it simply howls down its critics using the megaphone of incumbency . . . Late last year, Communications Minister Stephen Conroy accused the Sydney *Daily Telegraph* of a deliberate campaign to 'bring the government down'. The prime minister had a screaming match with former News Ltd boss John Hartigan over an article about her prior-to-entering-parliament dealings with a union official . . . The prime minister personally insisted that News Ltd in Australia had 'questions to answer' in the wake of the UK phone-hacking scandal even though she was not able to specify what these might be. It seems obvious that her real concern was not Fleet Street–style illegality but News Ltd's coverage of her government and its various broken promises, new taxes and botched program.'

News Ltd was facing a distant threat on another flank. The former Federal Court judge Ray Finkelstein had delivered his report on media regulation. Controversy had been raging for months. All the proprietors were furious, but at the Amora Hotel Abbott leapt only to the defence of News Ltd, claiming Finkelstein's proposed News Media Council 'looks like an attempt to warn off News Ltd from pursuing anti-government stories'.

Freedom Abbott drew his first breaths speaking the language of a News Ltd executive. Hardly anyone noticed at the time. Abbott's commitment to fight the Freedom Wars made the headlines. He nominated Brandis as his consigliore in the Coalition campaign for liberty. An agenda of sorts emerged: 18C would be slashed, anti-discrimination laws wound back and a 'freedom audit' conducted of all Commonwealth laws to identify those that violated traditional rights and freedoms. Asked if he had what it took to achieve these reforms, Brandis replied: 'I was born for it.'

Abbott's calls for fresh candour and vigour in public debate were pitch perfect. The week before polling day he told the *Australian*:

> Any suggestion you can have free speech as long as it doesn't hurt people's feelings is ridiculous. If we are going to be a robust democracy, if we are going to be a strong civil society, if we are going to maintain that great spirit of inquiry, which is the spark that has made our civilisation so strong, then we've got to allow people to say things that are unsayable in polite company. We've got to allow people to think things that are unthinkable in polite company and take their chances in open debate.

Australians frustrated by Canberra's old indifference to liberty could cast their vote on 7 September 2013 with reason to hope. Even on the Left there were signs of goodwill. Think tanks were cautiously delighted. But on victory night, something odd happened. I was there at the Four Seasons Hotel in Sydney in a throng of excited Liberals, drooling lobbyists and exhausted journalists. Flanked by his wife and daughters, the new prime minister declared Australia open for business. All the old mantras about boats and waste and carbon tax had a run, but there wasn't a word said about liberty. Freedom Abbott didn't show.

*

The swearing in of a cabinet was once a silent show except for the muttering of oaths. Now there are speeches. In the drawing room of Yarralumla with his cabinet duly sworn, Tony Abbott faced Quentin Bryce. He told Her Excellency: 'We hope to be judged by what we have done rather than by what we have said we would do.' Fair enough.

10 October 2013: The state and territory attorneys-general meet in Sydney without discussing shield laws. The issue was on the agenda. With the change of government it vanished. It hasn't appeared since. Efforts begun under Gillard to introduce uniform national laws to give effective protection to journalists and their sources have ceased.

25 October: Scott Morrison first utters the phrase 'on water operations' to justify the unprecedented secrecy that surrounds

the Abbott government's blockade of refugee boats. Morrison whittles away the few rights and freedoms left to those caught up in Operation Sovereign Borders.

2 December: Brandis authorises an ASIO raid on the Canberra office of Bernard Collaery, the lawyer representing East Timor in its dispute with Australia over the Timor Sea Treaty. In March this year, the International Court of Justice at The Hague orders Australia to seal the material seized and keep it from all officials involved in the dispute. The order is binding.

3 December: Abbott rages against the ABC and the 'left-wing' *Guardian* for together reporting that Australian spy agencies had targeted the phones of Indonesian President Susilo Bambang Yudhoyono and his wife. 'The ABC seemed to delight in broadcasting allegations by a traitor,' he later told Ray Hadley of the Sydney radio station 2GB. 'This gentleman Snowden, or this individual Snowden, who has betrayed his country and in the process has badly, badly damaged other countries that are friends of the United States, and of course the ABC didn't just report what he said, they took the lead in advertising what he said.'

11 December: Brandis announces terms of reference for the Australian Law Reform Commission's audit of Commonwealth laws that compromise freedom. The terms' focus is not individual liberty but 'commercial and corporate regulation; environmental regulation; and workplace relations'. Free speech barely makes the list. Brandis tells the *Australian Financial Review* he is most perturbed by the 'reversal of the onus of proof, the creation of strict liability offences, the removal of lawyer–client privilege and removal of rights against self-incrimination'. It reads like a list of everything tax evaders loathe about the law.

17 December: Brandis appoints the policy director of the IPA, Tim Wilson, to the Australian Human Rights Commission. Wilson's mission is to restore balance to a body which the attorney-general believes 'has become increasingly narrow and selective in its view of human rights' under Labor. This is code for the culture war complaint that the Left is manipulating anti-discrimination laws to impose its moral agenda on a reluctant society. The Bolt case is a particular focus of the fear that protecting blacks, gays, foreigners and cripples from discrimination is stripping the rest of us of our freedom.

29 January 2014: Abbott blasts the ABC for reporting claims that Australian military personnel have punished asylum seekers by burning their hands. 'I think it dismays Australians when the national broadcaster appears to take everyone's side but our own,' says the prime minister. 'You shouldn't leap to be critical of your own country.' News Ltd joins the attack. The ABC falters. Its managing director, Mark Scott, apologises for imprecise wording in the original report, but three days later, Fairfax's man in Indonesia, Michael Bachelard, finds asylum seeker Yousif Ibrahim Fasher: 'He says he has no doubt that what he saw at close quarters on about January 3 was three people's hands being deliberately held to a hot exhaust pipe by Australian naval personnel to punish them for protesting, and to deter others from doing one simple thing: going to the toilet too often.'

6 March: Abbott threatens to cut the ABC's budget if it doesn't cave in to Chris Kenny. The Chaser team had crudely photoshopped the head of the News Ltd pundit onto a man with his pants down mounting a labradoodle. Kenny sued for $90,000. Missing in action is Abbott's defence of lively debate where 'offence will be given, facts will be misrepresented'. He tells 2GB's Ben Fordham the ABC should settle the case or else: 'Government money should be spent sensibly and defending the indefensible is not a very good way to spend government money. Next time the ABC comes to the government looking for more money, this is the kind of thing that we would want to ask questions about.' The ABC buckles. Kenny gets an apology and cash.

13 March: Brandis decrees artists who refuse private sponsorship on political grounds may be stripped of public funding. Troubled by Transfield's links to offshore detention centres, a handful of artists had pressured the company to withdraw sponsorship from the Sydney Biennale. Brandis asks: 'If the Sydney Biennale doesn't need Transfield's money, why should they be asking for ours?' He directs the Australia Council to find a formula for deciding when public funding will be withdrawn because private sponsorship has been 'unreasonably' rejected. He does not rule out compelling arts organisations to take tobacco money. Months later, the council is still labouring over the words. However it's done, Brandis wants artists to know they will pay a price for embarrassing the government. This threatens direct political

intervention for the first time in the allocation of Australia Council funds.

24 March: Brandis tells Senator Nova Peris: 'People do have a right to be bigots, you know.' The next day, he releases draft legislation to gut sections 18C and 18D of the *Racial Discrimination Act*. Abbott backs him. The proposal – drafted by Brandis himself – would allow almost unrestrained racist abuse in the name of freedom. Ethnic community leaders lobby for the act to be left as it is. Polls swiftly show nine out of ten Australians disapprove of the changes. Three-quarters of the 4100 submissions received by Brandis's department are hostile. The department blocks their release.

23 May: Morrison strips the Refugee Council of Australia of half a million dollars allocated in the budget only ten days before. The minister explains: 'It's not my view, or the government's view, that taxpayer funding should be there for what is effectively an advocacy group.' The CEO of the council, Paul Power, calls the cuts petty and vindictive. 'This in many ways illustrates the state of the relationship between the non-government sector – particularly organisations working on asylum issues – and the government at the moment.'

1 July: Community legal centres across Australia are also forbidden to use Commonwealth money for advocacy or to campaign for law reform. During the Labor years, funding for NGOs had come with the guarantee that they were free 'to enter into public debate or criticism of the Commonwealth, its agencies, employees, servants or agents'. Under Abbott, the guarantee disappears. So do many sources of independent advice. The budgets of the National Aboriginal and Torres Strait Islander Legal Service, the Environmental Defender's Offices and the National Congress of Australia's First Peoples are slashed. Axed are the Social Inclusion Board, the National Housing Supply Council, the National Policy Commission on Indigenous Housing, the National Children and Family Roundtable, the Advisory Panel on Positive Ageing, and the committee of independent medicos advising the refugee detention network, the Immigration Health Advisory Group.

16 July: Brandis threatens laws to double the sentence for reporting 'special intelligence operations' by ASIO. Whistleblowers would not be protected, and journalists would not even need

to know the operations were 'special' to find themselves in prison for up to a decade. No public interest defence would be available. The shadow attorney-general, Mark Dreyfus, says: 'We will not tolerate legislation which exposes journalists to criminal sanction for doing their important work, work that is vital to upholding the public's right to know.'

4 August: Twenty-two-year-old student Freya Newman, a former part-time librarian at the Whitehouse Institute of Design, is charged with unauthorised access to restricted data following reports of Frances Abbott's scholarship, after complaints to the police by the institute. The chair of the institute is Liberal Party donor and friend of the prime minister Les Taylor.

5 August: Abbott announces the metadata of all Australians is to be kept by internet service providers for two years and made available to ASIO and police. That trawl will, of course, include the metadata of whistleblowers and journalists. He abandons at the same time his two-year crusade to amend the *Racial Discrimination Act*. Both moves he justifies in the light of terrorist outrages by Australian nationals in Syria. 'When it comes to counterterrorism, everyone needs to be part of 'Team Australia',' he says, 'and I have to say that the government's proposals to change 18C of the *Racial Discrimination Act* have become a complication in that respect. I don't want to do anything that puts our national unity at risk at this time, and so those proposals are now off the table.'

*

Freedom Abbott had outlived his purpose. He was useful in Opposition. That's when phony contests like the Culture Wars can wreak havoc on your opponents. But to keep the banner of freedom flying in office was always going to be hard. No Australian government has ever managed the feat. And Abbott is proving no political pioneer. Nothing done in his first year advances the cause he championed in Opposition. His rhetoric has proved threadbare. Poor old Values Abbott died on budget night when an ordinary Liberal Party agenda was served up to the nation. A couple of months later, Freedom Abbott followed him to the grave.

The IPA marked the burial with a brutal full-page ad in the *Australian*. 'Freedom of speech is an essential foundation of democracy,' said Abbott across the top of the page. Across the bottom the IPA replied: 'We agree, Prime Minister. That's why we will fight to repeal section 18C of the *Racial Discrimination Act*. Even if you won't.' John Roskam, the executive director of the IPA, spoke of a party base betrayed and Australians left 'sad, angry, disappointed and worried' by Abbott. 'If the Coalition can sacrifice freedom of speech so easily, there's nothing to stop, say, freedom of religion or the principle of equal education for girls and boys one day being treated in exactly the same way . . . under Tony Abbott, the Coalition believes freedom of speech is a threat to national unity.'

Brandis was simply humiliated.

Muslims were furious. Every ethnic community in Australia had put up their hand to protest, but Abbott had used the Muslims to cover his retreat. Tabloid pundits rammed the message home. It didn't help that depraved clowns with Australian passports were cutting off heads for the Caliphate. Bolt blamed the Jews, the Muslims and, most of all, politicians who caved in to Muslim constituents:

> Pardon? We must placate Muslim Australians by restricting our freedom to say something critical of their culture, for example, extremists being so prone to jihad? Of course other ethnic and religious groups – not least Jews – also fought to save these restrictions. But make no mistake: muzzling Australians is now seen as necessary to please migrant communities. Among Liberal backbenchers who fought Abbott's changes, none was louder than Craig Laundy, whose seat of Reid has a Muslim minority comprising 10 per cent of the vote . . . politicians are now so desperate for these blocs of ethnic votes that they sacrifice Australian values to accommodate imported ones.

Tim Wilson was left with no freedom agenda. The day Brandis was supposed to address Free Speech 2014, Wilson announced he would soon set off on a 'Rights and Responsibilities' tour of the nation to hear what we have on our minds. He will likely discover nothing new. Our worries don't change much with time: the fate of the ABC under Coalition governments; the expanding reach of intelligence agencies; heavy-handed film censorship; feeble protection for whistleblowers and journalists; punitive laws against demonstrators; attacks on freedom of association; and the old bugbear of defamation. Nothing stifles public debate in this country as much as the fear of being sued for defamation. But a smart guy like Wilson knows even before he sets out that the Human Rights Commission can't fix much on that list. Almost all our worries are matters of state law. In July, the retiring disability discrimination commissioner, Graeme Innes, told the National Press Club: 'The best way, frankly, for the attorney to provide the commission with the greater capacity to deal with the freedoms he talks about would be to put forward legislation for a charter of rights.'

That's the last thing Abbott stands for, though there is a fascinating shift underway in conservative Australia. Once despised as undemocratic, a bill of rights embedded in the constitution is beginning to be seen as a last resort to save our Way of Life. Even conservative Christians, hitherto the most implacable opponents of anything like the US First Amendment, are beginning to see their salvation might lie in such a form of words: 'Congress shall make no law respecting an establishment of religion, or prohibiting the free exercise thereof; or abridging the freedom of speech, or of the press; or the right of the people peaceably to assemble, and to petition the Government for a redress of grievances.'

And Abbott? Abandoning his freedom crusade has left him a diminished figure: not a pioneer of liberty in anyone's eyes, just a blowhard on the campaign trail. The promises of freedom join all the other broken promises. Under Abbott no laws limiting freedom have changed for the better. Movement has all been the other way. The Coalition is running on instinct. We are back where we were under Howard. Freedom counts for little in political contest in this country. The only Abbott that matters, Politics Abbott, soldiers on. He has not lost his faith in himself. Astride the grave of Freedom Abbott in early August, as he ramped up ASIO's powers and ditched his libertarian ambitions for 18C, he was still declaring: 'I'm a passionate supporter of free speech.'

The Monthly

The Last Instructions of Patrick White

J.M. Coetzee

Patrick White is, on most counts, the greatest writer Australia has produced, though the sense in which that country produced him needs at once to be qualified – he had his schooling in England, studied at Cambridge University, spent his twenties as a young man about town in London, and during World War II served with the British armed forces. What Australia did provide him with was fortune, in the form of an early inheritance – the White family were wealthy graziers – substantial enough for him to live an independent life.

The nineteenth century was the heyday of the Great Writer. In our times the concept of greatness has fallen under suspicion, especially when attached to whiteness and maleness, and Great Writers courses have largely been retired from the college curriculum. But to call Patrick White a Great Writer – specifically a Great Writer in the Romantic mould – seems right, if only because he had the typically great-writerly sense of being marked out from birth for an uncommon destiny and granted a talent – not necessarily a welcome one – that it is death to hide, that talent consisting in the power to see, intermittently, flashes of the truth behind appearances.

The life arc of the kind of artist White felt himself to be is most clearly shown forth in *Voss* (1957), the novel that made his reputation. Johann Ulrich Voss sets off with a miscellaneous band of followers on a journey of exploration into the vast Australian outback. Most of the party die, including Voss himself; but in the course of their long march Voss makes discoveries about the human spirit in extremis that, by a kind of spiritual telepathy, he transmits to the beloved he has left behind in Sydney, and through her to us.

White's sense of being special was closely tied to his homosexuality. He did not contest the verdict of the Australia of his day that homosexuality was 'deviant', but took his deviance as a blessing as much as a curse:

> I see myself not so much a homosexual as a mind possessed by the spirit of man or woman according to actual situations or [*sic*] the characters I become in my writing . . . Ambivalence has given me insights into human nature, denied, I believe, to those who are unequivocally male or female.

The award of the Nobel Prize in 1973 took many by surprise, particularly in Australia, where White was looked on as a difficult writer with a mannered, unnecessarily complex prose style. From a European perspective the award made more sense. White stood out from his Anglophone contemporaries in his familiarity with European Modernism (his Cambridge degree was in French and German). His language, and indeed his vision of the world, were indelibly marked by an early immersion in Expressionism, both literary and pictorial. His sensibility was always strongly visual. As a young man he moved among artists rather than among writers (he was an habitué of the studio of his close contemporary Francis Bacon), and often remarked that he wished he could have been a painter.

Between 1939 and 1979 White published eleven big novels. In the remaining years of his life, up to his death in 1990, he produced stories, plays, and memoirs, but no fiction on the previous grand scale. His health was declining. Since childhood he had suffered from asthma; in his last years he was flattened by severe respiratory attacks for which medical science could offer little help. His letters suggest that he doubted he had the staying power, and perhaps the will too, to bring off a substantial new work.

To an inquiry from the National Library of Australia as to his plans for the disposition of his papers, he responded: 'I can't let you have my papers because I don't keep any.' As for his manuscripts, he said, these were routinely destroyed once the book had appeared in print. 'Anything [that is] unfinished when I die is to be burnt,' he concluded. And indeed, in his will he instructed his literary executor, his agent Barbara Mobbs, to destroy whatever papers he left behind.

Mobbs disobeyed that instruction. In 2006 she committed the surviving papers, a surprisingly large cache packed in thirty-two boxes, to the NLA. Researchers, including White's biographer David Marr, have been busy with this *Nachlaß* ever since. Among the fruits of Marr's labours we now have *The Hanging Garden*, a 50,000-word fragment of a novel that White commenced early in 1981 but then, after weeks of intense and productive labour, abandoned.

Marr has high praise for this resurrected fragment: 'A masterpiece in the making,' he calls it. One can see why. Although it is only a draft, the creative intelligence behind the prose is as intense and the characterisation as deft as anywhere in White. There is no sign at all of failing powers. The fragment, constituting the first third of the novel, is largely self-contained. All that is lacking is a sense of where the action is leading, what all the preparation is preparatory to.

After the initial burst of activity White never returned to *The Hanging Garden*. It joined two other abandoned novels among the papers that Mobbs was instructed to destroy; it is not inconceivable that these too will be resurrected and offered to the public at some future date.

The world is a richer place now that we have *The Hanging Garden*. But what of Patrick White himself, who made it clear that he did not want the world to see fragments of unachieved works from his hand? What would White say of Mobbs if he could speak from beyond the grave?

Perhaps the most notorious case of an executor countermanding the instructions of the deceased is provided by Max Brod, executor of the literary estate of his close friend Franz Kafka. Kafka, himself a trained lawyer, could not have spelled out his instructions more clearly:

Dearest Max, My last request: Everything I leave behind me . . .
in the way of notebooks, manuscripts, letters, my own and

other people's, sketches and so on, is to be burned unread and
to the last page, as well as all writings of mine or notes which
either you may have or other people, from whom you are to
beg them in my name. Letters which are not handed over to
you should at least be faithfully burned by those who have
them.

Yours, Franz Kafka.

Had Brod done his duty, we would have neither *The Trial* nor *The
Castle*. As a result of his betrayal, the world is not just richer but
metamorphosed, transfigured. Does the example of Brod and
Kafka persuade us that literary executors, and perhaps executors in general, should be granted leeway to reinterpret instructions in the light of the general good?

There is an unstated prolegomenon to Kafka's letter, as there
is in most testamentary instructions of this kind: 'By the time I
am on my deathbed, and have to confront the fact that I will
never be able to resume work on the fragments in my desk
drawer, I will no longer be in a position to destroy them. Therefore I see no recourse but to ask you act on my behalf. Unable to
compel you, I can only trust you to honor my request.'

In justifying his failure to 'commit the incendiary act', Brod
named two grounds. The first was that Kafka's standards for per-
mitting his handiwork to see the light of day were unnaturally
high: 'the highest religious standards', Brod called them. The second was more down to earth: though he had clearly told Kafka
that he would not carry out his instructions, Kafka had not dismissed him as executor, therefore (Brod reasoned) in his heart
Kafka must have known the manuscripts would not be destroyed.

In law, the words of a will are meant to express the full and
final intention of the testator. Thus if the will is well constructed –
that is to say, properly worded, in accordance with the formulaic
language of testamentary tradition – then interpretation of the
will will be a fairly mechanical matter: we need nothing more
than a handbook of testamentary formulas to gain unambiguous
access to the intention of the testator. In the Anglo-American
legal system, the handbook of formulas is known as the rules of
construction, and the tradition of interpretation based on them
as the plain meaning doctrine.

The plain meaning doctrine has for a while been under siege. The essence of the critique was set forth over a century ago by the legal scholar John H. Wigmore:

> The fallacy consists in assuming that there is or ever can be *some one real* or absolute meaning. In truth, there can be only some *person's* meaning; and that person, whose meaning the law is seeking, is the writer of the document.

The unique difficulty posed by wills, one might add, is that the writer of the document, the person whose meaning the law is seeking, is by definition absent.

The relativistic approach to meaning expressed by Wigmore has the upper hand in many jurisdictions today. According to this approach, our energies should be directed in the first place to grasping the anterior intentions of the testator, and only secondarily to interpreting the written expression of those intentions in the light of precedent. Thus rules of construction no longer provide the last word; a more open attitude has come to prevail toward admitting extrinsic evidence of the testator's intentions.

In 1999 the American Law Institute, in its *Restatement of Property, Wills and Other Donative Transfers*, went so far as to declare that the language of a document (such as a will) is 'so colored by the circumstances surrounding its formulation that [other] evidence regarding the donor's intention is *always* [my emphasis] relevant'. In this respect the ALI registers a shift of emphasis not only in US law but in the entire legal tradition founded on English law.

If the language of the testamentary document is always conditioned by, and may always be supplemented by, the circumstances surrounding its formulation, what circumstances can we imagine, surrounding instructions from a writer that his papers be destroyed, that might justify ignoring those instructions?

In the case of Brod and Kafka, aside from the circumstances adduced by Brod (that the testator had unrealistic standards for publication of his work; that the testator was aware that his executor could not be relied on), there is a third and more compelling one: that the testator could have had no reliable idea of the broad significance of his work.

Public opinion is, I would guess, solidly behind executors like Brod and Mobbs who refuse to carry out their testamentary instructions on the twofold grounds that they are in a better position than the deceased to see the broad significance of the work, and that considerations of the public good should trump the expressed wishes of the deceased. What then should a writer do if he truly, finally, and absolutely wants his papers to be destroyed? In the reigning legal climate, the best answer would seem to be: do the job yourself. Furthermore, do it early, before you are physically incapable. If you delay too long, you will have to instruct someone else to act on your behalf, and that person may decide that you do not truly, finally, and absolutely mean what you say.

The Hanging Garden is the story of two European children evacuated for their safety to Australia during World War II. Young Gilbert Horsfall has been sent from London to escape the bombing. Eirene Sklavos, whose Greek father, a Communist, has died in prison, is brought to Sydney by her Australian mother, who then returns to the theatre of war. The two children find themselves boarding with Mrs Bulpit, a British-born widow.

During their first night alone at Mrs Bulpit's the children, whose ages are not given but who must be eleven or twelve, share a bedroom and, for most of the night, a bed. In Eirene there begins to grow an obsession with Gilbert in which inchoate sexual stirrings are mixed with an obscure realisation that they are not just fellow aliens in a new land but two of a kind (yet of what kind?), brought together by fate. Of Gilbert's feelings for Eirene we know less, in part because he is trapped in boyish male disdain for girls, in part (one guesses) because his realisation of her importance in his life was intended to come later, in the body of the book that never got written.

The children make Mrs Bulpit's overgrown garden, on a cliff overlooking the bay, into a refuge from the crassness and tedium of life in their new country. In a huge old fig tree they build a tree house where they can hide out and practice intimacies that have more to do with physical curiosity than sexual desire.

After a year or two of Mrs Bulpit's increasingly distracted foster care, during which news arrives that Eirene's mother has died in a bombing raid, there is a revolution in the children's lives. Mrs

Bulpit succumbs to cancer, and they are farmed out, Gilbert to a prosperous accountant, Eirene to the home of her mother's sister Mrs Lockhart, where she has to fend off the groping hands of Mr Lockhart and fight for some vestige of privacy from the loutish Lockhart boys. From Gilbert she receives a single letter, in which he hopes wistfully that he and she can stay in touch. Though she broods on memories of their time together in the garden over-hanging the sea, they have no further contact. The fragment ends in mid-1945, with victory in Europe and the prospect that the two children will be returned to their native countries.

Greece and Australia constitute the opposing poles between which Eirene moves. Having just begun to get a feel for Greek politics and her parents' position in Greek society (her father seems to have been a romantic leftist from an 'old', antimonar-chist family), she must now navigate the very different Australian system, where she will be looked down on as a 'reffo' (refugee) and suspected, because of her dark skin, of being a 'black'. At school, her precocious acquaintance with Racine and Goethe will count against her (anti-egalitarian, un-Australian).

White has a fascination much like Gustave Flaubert's with the horrors of bad taste, instances of which he records meticulously. 'I love plastic flowers, don't you?' remarks the mother of one of Eirene's classmates. 'I think they're more artistic than the real.' Mrs Bulpit, with her racial animosities and her nostalgia for 'the Old Country', her secret drinking and her stomach-turning cooking, is a social type White pins down with Dickensian preci-sion. Another type to come under scrutiny is the headmistress of an upmarket girls' school, her spectacles 'radiat[ing] the supe-rior virtues of the pure-bred Anglo-Saxon upper class', who interviews Eirene as a prospective student. Surprisingly, she accepts the little foreigner. Her motive becomes clearer when, later, she begins to caress the child suggestively.

Other minor characters are brought to life in a quick phrase or two: a teacher whose laugh 'sounds rubbery, sticky, like a tyre on a bumpy road'; a girl who, according to schoolyard gossip, 'laid down with a GI in the scrub . . . and he gave her a packet of cigarettes. She said it was immense.'

But the spiritual meanness of Australian society that White had anatomised in such earlier novels as *Riders in the Chariot*

(1961) and *The Solid Mandala* (1966) is not the real focus of his concern in *The Hanging Garden*. Even the grotesque Mrs Bulpit is allowed her relaxed moments. 'I'm not all that gone on foreigners, but she's a human being, isn't she?' she says of Eirene; generally she does her best for the two children under her care without understanding either one in the least.

Several motifs that are sounded in the fragment hang in the air with little indication about how White meant to use them. One of these is the garden of the title, which seems destined to bear some symbolic weight but in the fragment is simply a place where the children go to get away from their keeper. Another is the shrunken head brought back from the Amazon by the father of a school friend of Eirene's, which immediately enters her private world as a sacred talisman. But the most intriguing motif is the *pneuma* that Eirene remembers being spoken of on the island in the Cyclades where she spent a year with her father's family. *Pneuma*, she tells Gilbert, cannot be explained in English. The truth is, she has only the vaguest of ideas herself. *Pneuma* is in fact one of the more mysterious forces in both ancient Greek and early Christian religion. *Pneuma*, issuing from deep in the earth, is what the oracle at Delphi inhales to give her the power of prophecy. In the New Testament *pneuma* is the wind that is also the breath of God:

> The wind [*pneuma*] blows where it wishes and you hear the sound of it, but do not know where it comes from and where it is going; so it is with everyone who is born of the Spirit [*pneuma*].

Similarly, Jesus breathes on his disciples and says, 'Receive the Holy Spirit [*pneuma*].'

Like the Panageia, the all-powerful mother goddess whom Eirene also recalls from her time on the island, *pneuma* belongs to the syncretic popular religion of rural Greece, fast vanishing in our day, a religion in which archaic elements survive embedded in Orthodox Christianity. White clearly intends *pneuma* to be more than a mere marker of Eirene's Greek origins. *Pneuma*, Eirene obscurely feels, watches over Gilbert and her; White may well have intended it to foreshadow the breath or spirit that takes over the artist and speaks through him or her, and thereby hinted at what the future would hold for his two characters.

In Greece, Eirene reflects, memories are 'burnt into you'. Not so in Australia. In Australia there is no sense of mortality: 'Australians are only born to live.' At moments like these, Eirene becomes a mouthpiece for insights that do not realistically belong to an adolescent girl, however much possessed by *pneuma*. Whereas Eirene's younger sensibility is represented in a mix of narrative modes, with interior monologue predominating, the narrative of her adolescence seems to confront White with troublesome technical difficulties. He makes her keep a diary, but then seems to be unsure whether her narration is identical with what she writes in the diary or whether it is some later, more mature elaboration of what she wrote there, or whether keeping a diary is simply girlish activity that has nothing to do with how her story is told. Of course we should not forget that what we are reading in *The Hanging Garden* is only a draft (according to Marr a second draft). But failure to find a plausible voice for the maturing Eirene may well be a sign that White was losing interest in the project as a whole.

White had a deep attachment to Greece, principally through Manoly Lascaris, whom he met and fell in love with in Alexandria during the war, and with whom he came to share the rest of his life. White's 1981 memoir *Flaws in the Glass* contains a lengthy record of their travels together in Greece. For a period, he writes, he was 'in the grip of a passionate love affair, not so much with Greece as the idea of it'. At one time he and Lascaris thought of buying a house on Patmos. 'Greece is one long despairing rage in those who understand her, worse for Manoly because she is his, as Australia is worse for me because of my responsibility.' It is possible that through Gilbert (standing in for himself) and Eirene (standing in for Lascaris) he hoped, in *The Hanging Garden*, to explore more deeply feelings of despairing rage at a beloved country that has fallen into the hands of a brash, greedy, nouveau-riche class.

White explores sexual feeling between the two refugee children without false delicacy. Gilbert fights against giving in to his feelings for 'this dark snake of a girl', yet as he masturbates her image comes unsummoned, 'standing over him looking down, prissy lips pressed together . . . haunting him'. He is baffled by Eirene's power over him. 'She was nothing to him, another kid, a *girl*, a Greek . . .' Yet when, years later, he writes his first letter to her, he calls the letter 'a line from your fellow reffo', as if to concede he has accepted their common destiny.

Eirene's feelings for Gilbert are more complex, and indeed constitute the heart of the fragment. While she is still prepubertal, sexual interest in him is at war with fastidious distaste for his clumsy boy self. She has a dream in which he tears off her clothes in the school toilet and discloses not a 'flower ringed with fur' but a 'baby's wrinkle', to the jeers of the watching children. In other dreams, fragmentary memories crop up of witnessing her parents in a sexual embrace, of her mother's flirtations with other men. In these dreams she figures as the excluded other, angry, helpless, the one who wants but is unwanted.

Then as she reaches sexual maturity her feelings grow less confused. On their last night before they are separated, the two go to bed together and are intimate without having sex in the usual sense of the term. Eirene is able to feel quite motherly toward the sleeping boy. She will look back on him as 'almost part of myself, the one I have shared secrets with, the *pneuma* [which] I could not explain, but which he must understand'.

At her new school Eirene is adopted by a fashionable classmate named Trish. Trish confides that what engage her most are money and social success. What of Eirene? '*Love* I think is what I'm most interested in,' Eirene replies. Trish shrieks with laughter. 'That's not very ambitious Ireen you can have it any night of the week.' Eirene is mortified; yet even so, she is sure she is on the right track. Love, but more specifically 'transcendence', is what she is ultimately after. Whatever transcendence stands for, it seems to have no grip in the Australian landscape; yet

[I know] about it from experience almost in my cradle, anyway from stubbing my toes on Greek stones, from my face whipped by pine branches, from the smell of drying wax candles in old mouldy hill-side chapels . . . Mountain snow stained with Greek blood. And the *pneuma* floating above, like a blue cloud in a blue sky.

Intimations such as these, hinting that she is in the world to transcend the world, mark Eirene as one of White's elect, along with *Voss* and the four *Riders in the Chariot* and Waldo Brown in *The Solid Mandala* and Hurtle Duffield in *The Vivisector*: outsiders mocked by society yet doggedly occupied in their private quests for transcendence, or, as White more often calls it, the truth.

New York Review of Books

The Agony and the Ecstasy

Nicolas Rothwell

Franz Kafka woke abruptly at four a.m. on 11 August 1917. Something was wrong with his throat. There was saliva in his mouth: he couldn't swallow it, it kept welling back up. He got out of bed and lit a lamp – then he realised it was blood, clotted blood. It filled his mouth, it was thick and salty on his tongue. He rushed over to the washstand: out it poured, deep red into the white bowl, for minutes on end. He looked up from where he stood. He stared out at the street, he saw the looming silhouette of the Prague Castle in the gleam of dawn. At last the flow faltered, then stopped. He lay back down on his bed, and slept. Some while later, his housekeeper, Ruzenka, came in to wake him and make breakfast. She saw the bloodied washstand at once. '*Pane Doktore*,' she said, in Czech. 'You don't have long to go.'

In a letter describing this episode, one of his life's fulcrum events, Kafka runs through his reactions with great precision and great calm, as if those moments had marked a kind of liberation for him – and that morning serves as the hinge-point of a remarkable new biographic study by Reiner Stach, devoted not only to the author but to the surrounding circumstances of his life: a work that is at once complete and fragmentary, definitive and tentative, allusive and revelatory – in short, sublimely Kafkaesque, almost as if it had been dreamed into being by the benign ghost of the writer himself.

From the day of his first pulmonary haemorrhage, Kafka's fate was fixed. He viewed the tuberculosis that had made its home inside his lungs as a special presence, 'an illness bestowed on me'. His thought swerved more and more towards the bare bones of things. He had already written the book for which he is best known today, that punishment fantasy *The Trial* – it lay in his desk in manuscript, unknown. In September, he made a decision to travel to the tiny village of Zurau in the Bohemian countryside to convalesce. While there, he wrote a letter to his long-suffering fiancee, Felice Bauer: its words were dark as night. There were two combatants at war inside him, he declared, and their confused war raged incessantly. The blood was not coming from his lung but from a stab delivered by one of these combatants:

> And now I am going to tell you a secret that I don't even believe myself at the moment (although the darkness that falls about me in the distance at each attempt to work, or think, might possibly convince me), but really must be true: I will never be well again precisely because it is not the kind of tuberculosis that can be laid in a lounge chair and nursed back to health, but a weapon that continues to be of supreme necessity as long as I remain alive. And both cannot remain alive.

It is thought and writing of this kind that dominates the movement of Stach's narrative. Stach aims to write at Kafka's level, to push through to his subject, to be worthy of him. The upshot is two volumes that have already been widely praised as definitive, as triumphs of the biographic art – a third, dealing with Kafka's youth, was delayed in the vain hope that key archival sources would be released: it is due to be published at last, out of sequence, this year.

By chance, Stach's long, fine-grained, hyper-detailed account of Kafka's last decade appeared in the same month as a very different portrait of the writer's life: a slender sketch of his social and cultural background and the role that background plays in his best-known texts. It is the work of the distinguished Holocaust historian Saul Friedlander, who was himself brought up in pre-war Prague and has always felt a special closeness to Kafka and his words. The two books complement each other: they do much more than merely advance our appreciation of Kafka and his milieu. Previous biographies have presented him as inert, passive; these versions provide motives for his actions and his inaction, they make him flesh and blood. Stach provides us with the texture of Kafka's experiences and the events surrounding him; Friedlander reads the writings with eagle eyes, attuned to the nuances and lurking clues in every phrase. Yet both biographers, inevitably, fall short in their attempts to catch and clarify Kafka's elusive art. It is the sheer stuff of it that escapes them, the sudden jumps of insight and the transformations within it that stay concealed and veiled. Stach describes in detail the raw magma of Kafka's mid-period writing – the so-called 'octavo notebooks' of 1916–17, each about eighty pages in length – a compact size, suitable for carrying around town in his breast pocket:

> A startling and confusing sight: long, short, and very brief entries, prose and dialogue, a couple of lines of poetry, dated and undated texts, normal handwriting randomly alternating with shorthand, a scattering of headings, entire pages crossed out, word-for-word repetitions, disjointed statements, fluid transitions and long dividing lines punctuated by doodles, mysterious names, an address, drafts of letters, a checklist of errands, torn out and mixed-up pages, a random slip of paper . . . everything looking as though he had spread his papers out all over the floor while writing.

It is a jungle: drafts, feints and explorations – yet wherever the words of a tale or story emerge, they are clear, and set: 'Precisely where the perfection is beyond any doubt, the creator of these texts seems quite sure of himself. The author as creator ex nihilo.'

But those words set down, if studied closely, do at least lead back towards the life: and the life provides their fitting frame. With the deftest of touches, Stach succeeds in establishing a context for his hero – and he goes beyond the familial and professional worlds that previous biographers have seen as the sole key to Kafka's work.

His subject is a man recognisably under the influence of politics and world events: they filter into the novels and the shorter fictions in telling ways. Thus the darkest of Kafka's published stories, *In the Penal Colony*, gains new resonance when seen in the atmospherics of its time and against the backdrop of the trench warfare under way on the eastern front. In much the same way, the death of Emperor Franz Josef and the impending demise of the Austro-Hungarian Empire stand behind *An Imperial Message*, one of Kafka's shortest and most haunting tales. Chapter by chapter, detail by detail, *The Years of Insight* binds the writer and the writing together – works that had seemed beyond life, inexplicable, take on a different kind of depth.

Some preliminary conclusions can be drawn: a reassessment shimmers into view. For us, readers of these studies, the idea we have of Kafka changes: he can no longer be quite what he was made into by his first associates or by the coterie of admirers who saw the condition of modernity mirrored in his work, and paused to see little else.

The course of Kafka's literary career is well known thanks almost entirely to his closest friend and constant advocate, the ambitious Prague man of letters Max Brod. The two met while Kafka was still a student at the Charles University. He cut a striking figure: he was tall, elegantly dressed and handsome; he was also thin, reserved and pale. He was the only son of an inner-city Jewish family, assimilated, prosperous, without strong intellectual or literary leanings. At that point Brod was already on the road to making his own career in books and journalism: he drew Kafka out, encouraging him, promoting his fledgling efforts. It was Brod who placed Kafka's first stories and introduced him to the editors who would publish him; Brod who was the chief confidant and first listener to Kafka's readings of his painstakingly redrafted manuscripts; Brod, too, who eventually became Kafka's literary executor and had responsibility for presenting the posthumous work.

In this capacity, when sifting through Kafka's papers after his death, Brod came across the following lapidary note, written on the cusp of his final illness:

> Dearest Max, my final request: Everything I leave behind in the
> way of diaries, manuscripts, letters, from others and my own,
> sketches, and so forth, to be burned completely and unread, as

well as all writings and sketches you or others may have, and ask for them in my name. If people choose not to give you letters, they should at least pledge to burn them themselves.

Comprehensive instructions! Brod ignored them: that decision preserved *The Trial* and *The Castle* for the world, as well as the diaries and letters that seem increasingly to contain the molten core of Kafka's genius.

But inevitably, given Brod's position, the Kafka that was offered to the world was his version: he edited the manuscripts and tidied them up, he made himself the canonical interpreter. Brod had fled from Nazi Europe to Palestine, and the account of Kafka he perfected had a romantic tonality about it. Kafka the unknown genius tormented by the demons of the twentieth century, overwhelmed by the horrors of regimented, bureaucratic life, shadowed by anti-Semitism, alienated, haunted. Such is the Kafka Brod opted to highlight – with much justification.

There was, indeed, a prophetic tone in Kafka's work; he did dwell on the deadening effects of the modern bureaucratic state, he was keenly aware of the growing racial tensions in Czechoslovakia after the proclamation of independence in 1918; and it was true, too, that he was fascinated by Hasidism and Zionism, he learned Hebrew, he even toyed with the idea of migrating to Palestine. But Brod's Kafka was somehow Brod-like, a Kafka for a certain place, viewed from a certain perspective: all subsequent study and scholarship has been in effect a revision of this initial Kafka given to history.

Both Stach and Friedlander are revisionists in this tradition, seeking a clearer picture. Stach's work, quite overwhelming in its subtlety and scope, succeeds in this task on multiple levels: embedding Kafka in the tempo of his times, highlighting the links between Kafka's tales and the dramatics of early twentieth-century Expressionist film and theatre, placing the work firmly in the Germanic literary descent-line, bringing out the half-known story of the dying writer's last, most poignant romance. Friedlander offers an even more startling re-reading: his study is of great intensity and textual closeness; and he finds evidence that Brod suppressed little telling hints of erotic feelings for children in the diaries and manuscripts: was this, Friedlander wonders, the true root of the shame that convulsed Kafka and forms the cryptic bedrock of his literary persona? A reading of Kafka's letters suggests the depth of the psychodrama that was under way.

Here he is, writing to Brod two years before his death, his best-known works all behind him: 'Writing is a sweet and wonderful reward, but for what? In the night it became clear to me, as clear as a child's lesson book, that it is the reward for serving the devil. This descent to the dark powers, this unshackling of spirits bound by nature, these dubious embraces and whatever else may take place in the nether parts which the higher parts no longer know, when one writes one's stories in the sunshine. Perhaps there are other forms of writing, but I know only this kind; at night, when fear keeps me from sleeping, I know only this kind.' This was the tone of Kafka's internal landscape: it was to this landscape that he travelled when he sat at his writing desk. There were elements in common between his quest for the absolute and the mood of the age – but this tone of doom in the cradle of being is something new. Perhaps the most crucial of all the necessary reassessments, then, concerns the initial reception of Kafka's work and the reputation he won in his lifetime.

Stach makes clear that Kafka was far from a struggling, underappreciated author. The contrary was the case: his uniqueness was quickly recognised. At first, of course, Brod seemed to outshine him, in the sense that Brod was better connected and a more assiduous publicist, but Kafka's sparse writings were spotted and singled out as soon as they appeared in print. Robert Musil, the author of *The Man Without Qualities*, made a point of meeting Kafka and admired his work; Kurt Tucholsky praised him to the heavens; Thomas Mann realised his significance; as for Franz Werfel, who shared Kafka's background and was the greatest star of literary Vienna, he wrote Kafka a fan letter for the ages: 'Dear Kafka, you are so pure, new, independent and perfect that one ought to treat you as if you were already dead and immortal. What you have achieved in your last works has truly never existed in any literature, namely taking a well-crafted concrete story that is almost real and making it into something all-encompassing and symbolic, that speaks to a tragic dimension of mankind.'

Stories such as *Metamorphosis* or *In the Penal Colony* were so fierce, so unrelenting in their attack, they simply could not be read as standard features of the literary landscape. Kafka was on his own; he knew it; his first readers knew it too. In the years after his death, his work continued to circulate quite widely. It came into the hands of a new generation – among them the last hothouse flowers of central Europe before the shadows fell. In their various ways, Walter Benjamin, Bruno Schulz, Gershom Scholem and Elias Canetti all saw Kafka as a master beyond compare. The notoriously self-involved Canetti actually wrote a book devoted to 'Kafka's Other Trial'. This is not so much a case of influence as of priority. Kafka proved to be the pathfinder: he led the way – into a future with an expiry date.

How, then, to account for what Kafka has become in the years since? The Kafka who lived and breathed, wrote and agonised, in Prague, Berlin and a score of health resorts and clinics strewn through German-speaking Europe – that figure is no more.

He has been refashioned, he is an emblem for the times: to be precise, for post-war modernity. Just as Mozart, that irreducible genius in whose work sweet and bitter fuse impalpably, became the mascot of the eighteenth century, his heritage role bodied forth in the grotesque 'Mozartkugeln' of marzipan on sale at every street-corner confectioner in Vienna or in Salzburg today, so Kafka has been pressed into service as the imagined symbol of our age. His gaunt, consumptive face stares out from a hundred film posters. His haunted eyes incarnate alienation. His books are read as tales of the individual crushed by the bureaucratic system, he is delicacy and sensitivity, he is innocence in a world of dark and hidden forces. In short, he has been assimilated to his pallid victim-hero Joseph K. in the pages of *The Trial*.

His name has been reduced to an adjective: when we wish to designate something grotesque and malformed in the administrative strata of our societies, it is Kafkaesque – we invoke him, we look to his vision, or what has been confected as his vision of the world: he even became a noun for a while in the years of Soviet and Czechoslovak Communism, when 'Kafkarna' was the term dissidents used to describe the plots and provocations of the all-surveying, paranoia-disseminating secret police. This is quite a fate for a writer: to be loved and revered and not be understood or known.

Brod is only partly responsible for this betrayal: the creation of the Kafka image was in great part an international concoction, well-judged to buttress theories about the soulless modern state and the dark Freudian monsters lurking in the heart of man. The key to the creation of the emblem was his estrangement from the routines and the humdrum of his time and place. Kafka as universal required the erasure of Kafka the specific, the German-speaking writer, at home in busy, independent Prague. Stach, Friedlander and their like are thus engaged in a corrective exercise. Their new 'K.' has loves and foibles, he is agonised by his relationship to Judaism, he is fond of clothes and the latest movies, he is a gifted administrative figure, he is dazzling and seductive as much as still and strange.

It is the storm whipped up around the angel of history that these new assessors are writing against – in vain. How not to see Kafka in the dark gleam of retrospect? How not to end a biography as Stach ends, with a note remarking that all three of his sisters and a great part of his network of friends died in German concentration and extermination camps? This 'catastrophic blow to civilisation' left nothing of the world Kafka knew intact, his biographer concludes: 'Only his language lives.'

But alongside it, now, is a clearer picture of what he was, and what came to him in the confluence of his imagination and his life. The denouement was slow, and hard.

Kafka formed a last romantic tie, with Dora Diamant, a young woman, Polish-born: she cared for him and nursed him. Her role in his life only became evident with the publication of a memoir-narrative a decade ago.

The treatments Kafka was subjected to in the last phase of his illness were intensive. He looked back on what he had written and came almost to fear his own texts, as well he might: the title story of the collection he was proofing in his final weeks, *The Hunger Artist*, described a man who no longer wished to eat – Kafka, when he worked through its pages, was no longer able to take solid food into his mouth. He knew it. Death was looming, death, his constant subject, the natural completion of his arc in writing.

It has been easy, very easy, until now, to bring his fiction into his life, to think, with sentiment, that Kafka, just like poor, pale Joseph K., was quickly, quietly hustled from the world and silently dispatched. But here is the great corrective Stach's last volume brings: Kafka is seen most truthfully as a writer who loved life, he was an ever-shifting blur of sight and thought, he was more vivid than others because of his internal rigour, not less.

At the Kierling sanatorium near Klosterneuburg, his last weeks were lived out in a constant bout of pain. Professor Tschiassny came in on one occasion and surprised Kafka with the news his throat was looking better. Dora came into the room and found him in tears. He embraced her repeatedly and told her 'he had never wished for life and good health as much as he did now'.

Things, though, took their course: consumption consumed him; there was no escape. He was given morphine in greater and greater doses; he sent Dora away so she would not have to see him die, but his resolve failed: he called her back. She sat at his bedside and held up a bunch of wild flowers to his face. 'And Kafka, who had appeared to be unconscious, raised his head one last time.'

The Weekend Australian Review

Oh Walt, You're a Leaky Vessel

David Malouf

A good many writers of fiction have also in the course of a busy writing life produced memorable poems, George Meredith for one, Thackeray for another, and several poets have produced single novels that stand as undisputed masterpieces: one thinks immediately of Goldsmith's *The Vicar of Wakefield*, Lermontov's *A Hero of Our Time*, Mörike's novella *Mozart's Little Journey to Prague*. But few writers have an equal reputation in both fields: Goethe in Germany, Pushkin in Russia, Hugo in France; in England Hardy, maybe Kipling.

D.H. Lawrence is surely one of the few. In a frenetic publishing life, and during many moves – from England to Germany in 1912, and on to Italy; to Australia, Mexico and the United States in the 1920s, and finally to Spain and the South of France – he worked simultaneously, and always at the highest intensity, on novels, poems, travel books, criticism, reviews. There is no time after he began in 1909 when his notebooks are not filled with poems, and no time in his publishing life when he is not between novels and volumes of short stories, either preparing collections of poems or seeing them through the press.

All of this needs careful tracking. There are multiple typescripts. Postage, because of his travels, forms part of the story, and so does accident. So does interference or confiscation by the customs authorities in the cause of public decency. The fact that he was seldom at hand when the poems were being edited means that many of the publications are corrupt, and they may also differ for another reason. Because of Lawrence's subjects, and the language he uses, many of the poems were at the last moment expurgated by the publisher or withdrawn, not always after consultation with Lawrence (again the matter of distance) and not always with his consent. All this is thoroughly dealt with in this new Cambridge Edition in two volumes: one for the poems and Lawrence's prefaces to the various collections (this is the first complete and corrected edition of the poems); a second for the vast critical apparatus such an undertaking involves, the variant versions, notes on each poem and on the publication of each book and its reception – even a note on pounds, shillings and pence.

The result is a triumph. Readers of Lawrence who are curious, as we should be, about how these poems came into being – their provenance and history, how each one is related to Lawrence's circumstances at the moment of his writing and where it stands in the complex development of his thought – have every reason to be grateful, both to Christopher Pollnitz, the editor, and to the press. This is an immense achievement. The information it provides is easy to deal with but also, if the reader wishes, to ignore. The first volume – chronology, introduction, poems – is a beautiful thing to have in one's hands. The second, equally beautiful, is a useful and reliable one to have close by on a shelf.

Each lover of Lawrence's poems will have his own story of first contact with a new and unique consciousness. Lawrence was the first entirely modern poet I was presented with and, except for what I had picked up from films – the accidental influence, in Hollywood movies of the late thirties and early forties, of German Expressionist theatre and décor and, on the soundtrack, German contemporary music – the first modernist sensibility. I was twelve, going on thirteen, in my first months at Brisbane Grammar. As the bright Latin form, we were skilled at the sort of analysis and parsing that in those days was regular drill in Queensland primary schools, so we did nothing in our English class but read. The Lawrence poem in our class anthology was 'Snake', and it was like no other poem I had ever heard – I say 'heard' because poetry always began for me in those days as a reading aloud. I did with it immediately what I had been encouraged to do with any poem that in some way stuck me, or which puzzled or cluded me. I got its music into my head (*prima la musica*), and its logic or lack of logic, by learning it off by heart. Like many poems learned by heart at that time, it is still with me.

What mesmerised me was the poem's rhythms, and the perfect ease with which the lines, long or short, contained each thought and added it to the 'story'. And the openness of that story as confession. Lawrence's readiness, with no hint of self-consciousness or posing, to give himself away. I had never struck anything like that either. I took it as a kind of lesson in how I might deal with my own feelings, even the ones I was ashamed of.

In learning the poem by heart, what it had to tell – the experience it embodied but also the rhythms of its discoveries, each one as it arrived – became mine; I had made it mine, along with the voice that expressed it. This might have robbed the thing, through easy familiarity, of its challenges. Instead, odd lines, in my head as they now were, stood out suddenly and confronted me so that I had to confront them.

'The voices of my education said to me / He must be killed' – but Lawrence did not want to kill the creature; could the voices of our education be wrong? I had never been presented with *that* idea. And clearly, in this case, they *were* wrong. In attacking the snake Lawrence had sinned – but wasn't the serpent the very embodiment of sin? *This* serpent, in opposition to what the Bible asserted, was holy, because it was another creature like us, part of a *Creation* that was also holy – was that it? So the Bible was mistaken on that score also. Everything in the poem seemed to question and reverse what I had till now been told. There was a new sort of pleasure in this, each line as it turned was full of surprise and discovery.

There is a good deal in that schoolboy response that I would stand by still, and re-reading the poems in *Birds, Beasts and Flowers* (1923), I experienced again, in their simple-seeming but complex statements, line after line, the same discomfort and release of that twelve-year-old. But what strikes me now is how carefully prepared I had been to meet this challenge by all those long afternoons with our State School Readers; through the three weeks we had spent on the *Rime of the Ancient Mariner* in the *Queensland School Reader* in Grade Seven, and our explorations, in Grade Six, in the story of Pluto and Persephone (along with

Lord Leighton's vivid illustration), of the pagan underworld Lawrence was evoking and inviting me, if I was daring enough, to recognise as my world also and share:

> *And I thought of the albatross*
> *And I wished he would come back, my snake.*
> *For he had seemed to me again like a king,*
> *Like a king in exile, uncrowned in the underworld,*
> *Now due to be crowned again.*
> *And so I had missed my chance with one of the lords of Life.*

Lawrence's move – between September 1920, when he writes the first full poems in *Birds, Beasts and Flowers*, and the completion of the manuscript in February 1923 – out of a strictly human and personal world into the world of the creatures, is an extraordinary liberation. These winged, beaked, taloned creatures, these slow-moving earth-creatures with carapace shells, and fish, bats, snakes, mosquitos – nature's fantastic work of invention and play; these infinite variations on a life force that responds, with elegance and surprise and every condition of large and small, of quick and slow, in designs of so much surprise and utility and grace, call up in Lawrence a similar spirit of playful and inventive *making*. In his own spirit of fantasy, and with the liveliest humour and wit, he becomes a psalmist and celebrant of the animist creed – lyric, parodic, lightly critical; a master of reflective observation; an imitator of nature's own utilitarian caprice.

No more brooding on whether or not he is loved. No more stewing over the smallness of human needs and views, or the way 'mind' perverts and desecrates the purities of sensation. The creatures are above or beyond all that. Their world is all instinct and immediacy, but clean, and since they know nothing of the moralities, guiltless. The joy Lawrence takes in their otherness is childlike, as Blake's was; of a kind where innocence is a state beyond experience, but where one needs to come *through* experience to reach it. He never puts a foot wrong. Rhythm and cadence both follow and preclude sense, and contain and fix it. Entering *into* becomes a form of reflection, but also of self-reflection, each encounter producing its own tone and truth:

When did you start your tricks,
Monsieur?
. . . Are you one too many for me
Winged Victory?
Am I not mosquito enough to out-mosquito you?
'Mosquito'

Your life a sluice of sensation along your sides
. . . joie de vivre, and fear, and food,
All without love.
To have the element under you like a lover
I didn't know his God.
I didn't know his God.
Which is perhaps the last admission that life has to wring out of us.
'Fish'

A twitch, a twitter, an elastic shudder in flight.
In China the bat is symbol of happiness.
Not for me!
'Bat'

Challenger,
Little Ulysses, fore-runner,
No bigger than my thumb-nail,
Buon viaggio.
All animate creation on your shoulder,
Set forth, little Titan, under your battle-shield.
'Baby Tortoise'

Alas, the spear is through the side of his isolation.
His adolescence saw him crucified into sex,
Damned, in the long crucifixion of desire, to seek
His consummation beyond himself . . .
Doomed to make an intolerable fool of himself
In his effort toward completion again.
And so behold him following the tail
Of that mud-hovel of his slowly rambling spouse.
'Elle et Lui'

Still, gallant, irascible, crooked-legged reptile,
Little gentleman,
Sorry plight,
We ought to look the other way.
'Tortoise Gallantry'

Lawrence's work on *Birds, Beasts and Flowers*, from the first free-verse notes of July 1920, through the Tortoise poems of September and 'Snake' in 1921, to the 'new, "complete" MS' of February 1923, coincided with his various attempts to produce the essay on Walt Whitman that was to form the final chapter of his *Studies in Classic American Literature* (1923). It was because Whitman was so important to him that the essay gave him so much trouble, and it is in Lawrence's attempts to get at the 'quick' of Whitman's practice – what he sees as the origin and process, physical and psycho-sexual, of it – that we see what Lawrence was aiming at in his own: the process, but also, in moral and aesthetic terms (which increasingly for Lawrence became one), its justification.

The first version from 1918 has not survived, and so far as we know, no one ever saw it. It was too controversial, perhaps, in its openness about the sensual life. The 1919 version immediately adopts a contradictory stance:

> Whitman is the last and greatest of the Americans. He is the fulfilment of the great old truth. But any truth, the moment it is fulfilled, accomplished, becomes *ipso facto* a lie, a deadly limitation of truth . . . In Whitman lies the greatest of all modern truths. And yet some really thoughtful men, in Europe at least, insist even today that he is the greatest of modern humbugs, the arch humbug. A great truth – or a great lie – which? A great prophet, or a great swindle.
>
> Both!

Lawrence has no doubts about the quality and significance of Whitman's verse. 'The primal soul,' he tells us,

> utters itself in strange pulsations, gushes and strokes of sound. At his best Whitman gives these throbs naked and vibrating as they emerge from the quick. They follow, pulse after pulse,

line after line, each one new and unforeseeable. They are lam-
bent. They are life itself. But in the whole, the whole soul
speaks at once, sensual impulse instant with spiritual impulse,
and the mind serving, giving pure attention.

This is also, we may assume, how Lawrence hopes that his own
verse, at its best, may work. It is a matter of the relationship
between the lower or sensual body and the mind, with the mind
serving, and in it here that he sees Whitman, in that he chooses
finally the way of 'sensual negation', failing to take 'the next
step'. The language in which he describes Whitman's failure to
complete the process is drawn from *Fantasia of the Unconscious*,
a book already completed but not to be published until October
1922.

> Whitman, singing of the mystery of touch, tells us of the pro-
> cess. He tells of the mystery of the touch of the hands and fin-
> gers, those living tendrils of the upper spiritual centres, upon
> the lower body. But the touch of the hands is only the begin-
> ning of a great involved process. Not only the fingers reap the
> deep forces, but the mouth and tongue in kissing and so
> on . . . All this Whitman minutely and continually describes.
> It is the transferring to the upper centres, the thorasic and cer-
> vical ganglia, of the control of the deep lumbar and sacral gan-
> glia, it is the transferring to the upper sympathetic centres,
> breast, hands, mouth, face, of the dark vital secrets of the
> lower self. The lower sacral centres are explored and *known* by
> the upper self.

It is this transferring of everything into the upper self and the
'mental consciousness' that makes Whitman, for Lawrence, 'a
shattering half-truth, a devastating half-lie'.

Whitman also falls short in another respect. 'Every soul,' Lawrence insists, 'before it can be free, and whole in itself, sponta-
neously blossom[ing] from itself, must know this accession into
Allness, into infinitude. Thus far Whitman is a great prophet.
And he shows us the process of oneing; he is a true prophet.' The
falseness creeps in when we accept this 'oneing' as a goal, and
not as a process, a means to a different end, which in Lawrence's

terms, as he has been working towards it in *Look! We Have Come Through!* (1917) – in 'New Heaven and Earth' and 'Manifest' and 'Wedlock' – is 'the human soul's integral singleness':

> *And yet all the while you are you, you are not me.*
> *And I am I, I am never you.*
> *How awfully distinct and far off from each other's being we are.*
> *Yet I am glad.*
> *I am glad there is always you beyond my scope.*

What Lawrence rejects in Whitman is the insistence on 'merging', on 'fusion'. Lawrence himself aims at something different. He calls it a 'delicately adjusted polarity'.

> There is a final polarisation, a final current of vital being impossible(e) between man and woman. Whitman found this empirically. Empirically he found that the last current of vital polarisation goes between man and man. Whitman is the first in modern life, truly, from sheer empirical necessity, to reassert this truth . . . It is his most wistful theme – the love of comrades – manly love . . . The vast mysterious power of sexual love and of marriage is not for Whitman . . . He believes in fusion. Not fusion, but delicately adjusted polarity is life. Fusion is death.

Still, there is, beyond all this, Whitman's verse. There, at its best, 'the whole soul follows its own free, spontaneous, inexplicable course, the contractions and pulsations dictated from nowhere save from the quick itself . . . There is nothing measured or mechanical. This is the greatest poetry.'

But even this statement of the case is not satisfactory and in 1921–22 Lawrence sets out to resolve his own contradictory views in yet another version. 'Whitman,' he begins, 'is the last and greatest of the Americans. One of the greatest poets in the world, in him an element of falsity troubles us still. Something is wrong; we cannot be quite at ease with his greatness. Let us get over our quarrel with him first.' He then goes on to make a distinction between:

all the transcendentalists, including Whitman, and men like
Balzac and Dickens, Tolstoy and Hardy, who still act direct
from passional motives and non inversely, from mental provocations. But the aesthetes and symbolists, from Baudelaire and
Maeterlick, and Oscar Wilde onwards, and nearly all the later
Russian and French and English novelists, set up their reactions in the mind and reflect them by a secondary process
down on the body. It is the madness of the world today. Europe
and America are all alike, all the nations self-consciously pro-
voking their passional reactions from the mind, and *nothing*
spontaneous.

The last part of this version then moves into the murky area of
mystical fascism. Whitman, Lawrence tells us,

> shows us the last step of the old great way. But he does not
> show us the first step of the new. His great Democracy is to be
> established upon the love of comrades. Well and good. But in
> what direction shall this love flow? More *en masse*? As a matter
> of fact the love of comrades is always a love between a leader
> and a follower filled with 'the joy of liege adherence'.

What Lawrence ends up saluting, in a move away from 'en masse
democracy' to 'the grand culmination of soul-chosen leaders', is
'the final leader . . . the sacred *tyrannus*. This is the true democracy.' 'Onward,' he urges, 'always following the leader, who when
he looks back has a flame of love in his face, but a still brighter
flame of purpose. This is the true democracy.'

Whitman in this is largely forgotten. The best Lawrence can
do is to repeat his earlier endorsement:

> Whitman. The last of the very great poets. And the ultimate.
> How lovely a poet he is. His verse at its best spontaneous like
> a bird. For a bird doesn't rhyme or scan – the miracle of spon-
> taneity. The whole soul speaks at once, in a naked spontaneity
> so unutterably lovely, so far beyond rhyme and scansion.

Then, in November 1922, a new version in an entirely different
style: demotic, staccato, 'Modernist'; all capitals, expletives and

ironic or dismissive side-swipes; a parody of Whitman's own 'stridency' and splenetic exuberance:

> *Post mortem effects?*
> *But what of Walt Whitman?*
> *The 'good grey poet'*
> *Was he a ghost, with all his physicality?*
> *The good grey poet*
> *Post mortem effects. Ghosts.*
> *A certain ghoulishness. A certain horrible potage of human parts.*
> *A certain stridency and portentousness. A luridness about his beatitudes . . .*
> *I AM HE THAT ACHES WITH AMOROUS LOVE*
> *CHUFF! CHUFF! CHUFF!*
> *CHU-CHU-CHU-CHU-CHUFFF*
> *Reminds me of a steam engine. A locomotive . . .*
> *Your Self*
> *Oh Walter, Walter, what have you done with it? What have you done with yourself? With your individual self? For it sounds as if it had all leaked out of you when you made water, leaked into the universe when you peed. Oh Walt, you're a leaky vessel . . .*

And so on, via a piece of scurrilous gossip about Whitman in old age dancing naked in his yard and showing himself off in an excited state to schoolgirls, to

> *Only we know this much. Death is not the goal. And Love, and merging are now only part of the death process. Comradeship – part of the death process. The new Democracy – the brink of death. One identity – death itself.*
> *We have died, and we are still disintegrating.*
> *But IT is finished.*
> *Consumatum est.*

– before the whole essay degenerates into incoherent rambling about Jesus and the Holy Ghost. Barely a word in this version about Whitman the poet. Only Whitman, the leaky vessel, as thinker and man.

The 1923 version, the one that at last makes it all the way to publication as the final chapter of *Studies in Classic American Literature*, takes up the 1922 version and uses it – expurgated of its scurrilous slander and a few turns of phrase that would at the time have been seen as 'indecent' – as far as 'But IT is finished. *Consumatum est.*' It then drops its aggressive, expletive tone and embarks on something more sober and considered, more warmly personal:

> Whitman, the great poet, has meant much to me. Whitman the one man breaking a way ahead. Whitman the one pioneer. And only Whitman. No English pioneers, no French. In Europe the would-be pioneers are mere improvisers.

He recognises Whitman as 'the first to smash the old moral conception that the soul of man is something "superior" and "above" the flesh'.

> 'There,' he said to the soul, 'stay there! Stay there. Stay in the flesh. Stay in the limbs and legs and in the belly. Stay in the breast and womb and phallus. Stay there, o soul, where you belong.'

There is praise too for Whitman's enunciation of 'a morality of actual living, not of salvation':

> The soul is not to put up defences round herself. She is not to withdraw inwardly, in mystical ecstasies, she is not to cry to some God beyond, for salvation. She is to go down the open road, as the road opens into the unknown, keeping company with those whose soul draws them near to her, accomplishing nothing save the journey . . .
> The Open Road. The great home of the soul is the open road. Not heaven, not paradise. Not 'above', not even 'within'. The soul is neither 'above' nor 'within'. It is a wayfarer down the open road . . . The soul is herself when she is going on foot down the open road.

He even forgives Whitman at this point his great error, of mistaking 'sympathy' for Jesus' Love or St Paul's Charity. But he has come now to a more doctrinaire vision of what art itself is, what poetry is, that will determine from this point his own life as a poet:

> The function of art is moral. Not aesthetic, not decorative, not pastime and recreation. But moral . . . But a passionate, implicit morality, not didactic. Changes the blood rather than the mind, changes the blood first. The mind follows later, in the wake.

This looks ahead to the various prefaces Lawrence would write, between Christmas 1928 and April 1929, to *Pansies* (1929) – Pensées – the second of which tells us:

> Each little piece is a thought: not an idea, or an opinion, or a didactic statement, but a true thought, which comes as much from the heart and genitals as from the head . . . Live and let live, and each pansy will tip you its separate wink.

Between 1923 and 17 November 1928, when *Pansies* was begun, Lawrence was continually on the move, in Mexico, England, France, Italy; at work preparing ('what a sweat'), and in the case of the earlier poems rewriting, his *Collected Poems* (1928). 'I do bits of things,' he writes on 14 November 1927, '– darn my under-clothes, try to type up poems.'

The *Pansies*, written at Bandol on the French Riviera between 17 November 1928 and 10 March 1929, and the 'stinging pansies' or *Nettles* (1930), which he began in February 1929 and took up again between 17 April and 18 June in Mallorca, start out as insights into the quick of things – sensory moments, the lives of elephants in a circus – but end up in disgruntlement and general contempt for 'the dirty drab world': its hypocrisy, cowardice, snobbery, money-grubbing; its blindness and vanity – 'the whole damn swindle'. Then, on 10 October 1929, just five months before his death, he writes the first poem in the *Last Poems* (1932) notebook, 'The Greeks are coming', and we might recall what he had written of Whitman: 'Whitman would not have been the great poet he is if he had not taken the last step and looked over into Death.'

There are hints, towards the end of the *Nettles* notebook of Lawrence's last great poems; in 'Butterfly'(I) and (II), in 'The State of Grace', 'Glory of Darkness' (I), which is in fact an early version of 'Bavarian Gentians', and 'Ship of Death':

> *Blue and dark*
> *the Bavarian Gentians, tall ones*
> *make a magnificent dark-blue gloom*
> *in the sunny room . . .*
> *How deep I have gone*
> *dark gentians*
> *in your marvellous dark-blue godhead*
> *How deep, how deep, how happy*
> *How happy to sink my soul*
> *in the blue dark gloom*
> *of gentian here in the sunny room!*
> 'Glory of Darkness' (I)

But it is Glory of Darkness (III) that takes the last step and finds its way back to the Greeks, to the old dark underworld of 'Snake':

> *Blue and dark*
> *Oh Bavarian gentians, tall ones . . .*
> *They have added blueness to blueness, until*
> *it is dark beauty, it is dark*
> *and the door is open*
> *to the depths*
> *It is so blue, it is so dark*
> *in the dark doorway*
> *and the door is open*
> *to Hades.*
> *Oh I know –*
> *Persephone has just gone back*
> *down the thickening thickening gloom*
> *of dark blue gentians*
> *to Pluto*
> *to her bridegroom*
> *in the dark . . .*
> 'Glory of Darkness' (III)

And with the simplicity, the spontaneity of this, what he called, in Whitman's case, its 'throbs and pulses', Lawrence finds his way to the last poems on which his own greatness rests.

> *God is older than the sun and moon*
> *and the eye cannot behold him*
> *nor voice describe him.*
> *But a naked man, a stranger, leaned on the gate*
> *with his cloak over his arm waiting to be asked in.*
> *So I called him: Come in, if you will –*
> *He came in slowly, and sat down by the hearth.*
> *I said to him: And what is your name? –*
> *He looked at me without answer, but such a loveliness*
> *entered me, I smiled to myself, saying: he is God!*
> *So he said: Hermes!*
> *God is older than the sun and moon*
> *and the eye cannot behold him*
> *nor the voice describe him:*
> *and still, this is the god Hermes, sitting by my hearth.*
> 'Maximus'

Lawrence is a difficult poet to come to terms with; it is easy to quarrel with him as he quarrelled with Whitman. He is various, contradictory, irascible, over-insistent; he too easily takes offence and insists again. It is easy, as well, to be put off by his preachiness. He begins in the tone of a non-conformist Bible-banger, develops his own religion and bangs away at that. He is most easy with his soul when he embraces the dark gods and goes quietly underground, and best of all when he stops protesting and lets the world in, in the form of a snake, a baby tortoise, the smoking dark blue of gentians, or in the form of the psychopomp Hermes, and breathes easy again. Lets the breath and the energy of its natural rhythms create the poem.

As he puts it in the Note to *Collected Poems* of 12 May 1928, excusing his rewriting of the early poems, 'A young man is afraid of his demon, and puts his hand over his demon's mouth and speaks for him. And the things the young man says are rarely poetry. So I have tried to let the demon say his say.'

DAVID MALOUF

Lawrence makes it difficult for the reader, as well as for himself, by speaking up too soon; by insisting, performing, working out his questions, his quarrels, in public. We too, in seeking out the best in him, have to choose between the 'demon' and the man. We should be grateful to these two volumes from the Cambridge Press, and to its editor, for making this easier than it might otherwise be in the muddle of so much material; the byproduct of so much passionate energy and engagement, and of a life that was seldom orderly or still.

At his best, Lawrence is one of the finest poets in the world. There is no poet, at his best, who gets closer to what he calls the 'quick' of things, or brings us closer with him; and when he is at ease with his own spirit, his own extraordinary energy, his rare demon, there is no poet we find it so easy to love. It is all here in these two hefty volumes: the muddle, but also the magic of the man's greatness; the pathos, the wonderful coincidence of language and feeling; a sensibility almost too actively aware of the tension between singularity and oneness that is at the heart of being.

Sydney Review of Books

Poems of a Lifetime

Clive James

When I was young, cartoons by James Thurber were so widely known that people would refer to them in conversation just by quoting the captions. I remember not quite understanding the reference in one caption: 'I said the hounds of spring are on winter's traces – but let it pass, let it pass'. I thought the line very funny at the time but I didn't know that Thurber was quoting Swinburne's 'Atalanta in Calydon'. You don't need to get the reference to get the joke; but the joke eventually got me to Swinburne, who would gradually turn out to be the most accomplished poet that I couldn't stand. Spenser, in *The Faerie Queene*, would occasionally throw in an alliterative line for effect ('Sober he seemde, and very sagely sad') but Swinburne wanted the whole poem to be that way: a meal of popcorn. Sometimes, in his blizzard of alliteration, he failed to notice that he had written an identity rhyme instead of a rhyme:

> *And time remembered is grief forgotten,*
> *And frosts are slain and flowers begotten . . .*

Perhaps he noticed but thought we wouldn't, intoxicated as we were bound to be by his sonic hurtle. But for a poet to be all sound is nearly as bad as for a painter to be all paint. After several attempts over the years to detect any signs of an underlying strength, I still find that a Swinburne poem affects me like a painting by John Bratby: there is so much impasto that the only tension lies in your wondering whether it will slide off the picture and fall on the floor. I have to give up on Swinburne; there is no time to go on quarrelling; and anyway there are problematic poets with whom one can quarrel to more purpose.

Look into Chapman's Homer and you can see what alliteration once did, long before Swinburne arrived to overdo it. Agamemnon kits himself out before going into battle:

> *Then took he up his weighty shield, that round about him cast*
> *Defensive shadows; ten bright zones of gold-affecting brass*
> *Were driven about it, and of tin, as full of gloss as glass,*
> *Swelled twenty bosses out of it . . .*

While the 'defensive shadows' are good, 'as full of gloss as glass' is beyond good: it's brilliant. Just don't let Swinburne hear about it. But you can't stop poets finding inspiration in the heritage, and no doubt to be as learned as possible is not just a duty, but a good thing; and yet you can't help wishing that some of the learned poets since Shakespeare had been blessed with the knack of forgetting what they had read.

For much of his life, Milton needed his memory because he couldn't see. When he considered how his light was spent, he didn't complain about being too often driven back into his remembered books. Perhaps he didn't see the problem. But my quarrel with *Paradise Lost* – man against mountain! – begins with how Milton's beaver-dams of learning turn streams of invention into stagnant ponds. One of the several Miltonians among my friends kindly goes on telling me that the displays of learning were part of the invention. Milton obviously believed that to be true. But here I am, once more submitting myself to *Paradise Lost* in the hope of being caught up; and once more realising that the famous clash between T.S. Eliot and F.R. Leavis on the subject of Milton (Leavis did most of the clashing) was not a quarrel about nothing. It was really about a monumental example of poetic genius defeating itself; because the question of the possible insufficiency of his single most important work would never have arisen if it did not seem to pride itself on undoing things that Milton well knew how to do. A consummate lyricist faced with his biggest opportunity, he strained every muscle to be bad. Let one illustration serve, from Book IX. Eve has just spoken, and now she is described:

> *Thus saying, from her Husbands hand her hand*
> *Soft she withdrew, and, like a Wood-Nymph light,*
> *Oread or Dryad, or of Delia's Traine,*
> *Betook her to the groves, but Delia's self*
> *In gait surpassed and Goddess-like deport,*
> *Though not as shee with Bow and Quiver armed,*
> *But with such Gardning Tools as Art, yet rude,*
> *Guiltless of fire had formed, or Angels brought.*
> *To Pales, or Pomona, thus adorned,*
> *Likest she seemed – Pomona when she fled*
> *Vertumnus – or to Ceres in her prime,*
> *Yet virgin of Proserpina from Jove . . .*

Such passages, and there are scores of them, are impoverished by their riches: erudition distorts the picture, whose effect divides into the poetic and the encyclopedic. This element of Miltonics can be called uniquely his only because he did the most of it: in fact, it's a hardy perennial. In the previous century, Spenser had been often at it, as when he loaded a library on top of his two swans in 'Prothalamion':

> *Two fairer birds I yet did never see:*
> *The snow which doth the top of Pindus strew,*
> *Did never whiter shew,*
> *Nor Jove himself when he a Swan would be*
> *For love of Leda . . .*

Even those among his readers who knew nothing about Greece might possibly have known that Pindus was its principal mountain range, and everybody knew about shape-changing Jove and his attentions to Leda. Similarly, readers of Marvell's 'Bermudas' probably knew that Ormus – still in business at the time, although soon to decline and vanish – was a kingdom notable for wealth:

He hangs in shades the Orange bright
Like golden Lamps in a green Night.
And does in the Pomegranates close,
Jewels more bright than Ormus shows.

But here we see where the trouble with this aspect of Miltonics really starts: when an encyclopedic reference is outclassed by its poetic surroundings, like a fake jewel in a fine setting. The line about the lamps in the green night is one of Marvell's best things, and poor old Ormus pales beside it. (Milton, too, dragged Ormus in, and to even less effect.) One hesitates to rhapsodise about the pure spring of inspiration, but there is such a thing as clogging the pipes.

The awful thing about the apparent success of Milton's unyielding stretches of leaden erudition was that the plumbing of English poetry was affected far into the future. Without Milton's example, would Matthew Arnold have taken such pains to burden his 'Philomela' with this lumbering invocation of a naiad and her habitat?

Lone Daulis, and the high Cephissian vale?
Listen, Eugenia . . .

But surely Eugenia has stopped listening, and is checking the menu for room service. At least we can say, however, that Arnold, by perpetrating such a blunder, helped to define what makes 'Dover Beach' so wonderful: apart from Sophocles, nobody from classical times makes an appearance, and even his bit is part of the argument, not just a classical adjunct parked on top of the edifice like a misplaced metope. Milton, of course, schooled himself well in the trick of pulling a learned reference into the narrative texture, but all too often, no matter how smoothly the job is done, the most you can say of it is that it sounds good.

But sounding good can't even be called a requirement. It's a description. A poet who can't make the language sing doesn't start. Hence the shortage of real poems among the global planktonic field of duds. In the countries of the Anglosphere, the poet's first relationship is with the English language even when the poet is indigenous. There is therefore no mystery, although there is some sadness, about the shortage of Australian Aboriginal poets. Until the corrective opinion of such inspired Aboriginal leaders as Noel Pearson prevails, it will go on being true that too few people of Aboriginal origin are masters of the country's principal language. Published in 2009, the Macquarie PEN anthology attempted to compensate for this imbalance artificially by including anything in English from an Aboriginal writer that might conceivably be construed as a poem, even if it was a political manifesto. It wasn't the first attempt in Australian literary history to give Aboriginal culture a boost into the mainstream. From the 1930s to the 1950s, the Jindyworobak movement did the same, with whitefella poets rendering themselves unreadable by using as many of the blackfella's totemic terms as possible. New Zealand might have been in the same position with regard to the Maoris, had it not been for the advent of Hone Tuwhare (1922–2008), in whose poem 'To a Maori Figure Cast in Bronze Outside the Chief Post Office, Auckland' the bronze figure speaks thus:

> *I hate being stuck up here, glaciated, hard all over*
> *and with my guts removed: my old lady is not going*
> *to like it . . .*

After twenty-five lines of brilliantly articulated bitching, the statue signs off: 'Somebody give me a drink; I can't stand it.' Tuwhare was himself a Maori, so the argument was over. Finally it is the vitality of language that decides everything, and this hard fact becomes adamantine as one's own vitality ebbs.

That's not all: as time runs out, the mind is weighed down with a guilty mountain of the critical duties that won't be attended to. There is barely time to read Elizabeth Bishop's poems again and pay them a less stinted praise. When I first wrote about her, thirty years ago, I tried to be clever. It was a failure of judgement: she was the clever one. Will I get myself off the hook just by saying that I ended up with almost as many lines by Bishop in my head as by Robert Lowell? What one feels bound to acknowledge fully is her artistic stature. Of her moral stature there can be no question. The big book of her letters, *One Art* (1994), is a mind-expanding picture of a difficult yet dedicated life, and a smaller book of letters, *Words in Air* (2008), by collecting her correspondence with Lowell, defines the ethics of a historic moment: a moment when poetry, queen of the humanities, took a step towards the opportunistic privileges of totalitarianism. Lowell wanted her endorsement for his bizarre temerity in stealing his wife Elizabeth Hardwick's letters to use unchanged in his poetry. Bishop refused to approve; and surely she was right. Students in the future who are set the task of writing an essay about the limits of art could start right there, at the moment when one great poet told another to quit fooling himself.

The business of poetry is now much more equally distributed between the sexes than it was even in the period after the Second World War, when women seemed to be taking up poetry as if it were a new kind of swing shift, the equivalent of putting the wiring into silver bombers. There had always been women poets, from Sappho onwards, and a few, such as Juana Inés de la Cruz, defined their place and time; but in English poetry, a small eighteenth-century triumph like Anne, Countess of Winchelsea's poem 'The Soldier's Death' did little to remind the literary men of the immediate future that there could be such a thing as a poet in skirts. They might remember the poem, but they didn't remember her. True equality really began in the nineteenth century: Christina Rossetti, for example, wrote poems of an accomplishment that no sensitive male critic could ignore, no matter how prejudiced he was. (There were insensitive male critics who ignored it, and patronised her as a cot-case: but the tin-eared reviewer is an eternal type.) Elizabeth Barrett Browning was spoken of in the same breath as her husband. He might have been the greater, but nobody except devout misogynists doubted that she was in the same game.

In the twentieth century, Marianne Moore achieved the same sort of unarguable status: she was acknowledged to be weighty even by those who thought she was fey. Back in the late 1950s, I would listen to an all-poetry LP that included Moore reciting 'Distrust of Merits' and come away convinced that she had the strength to make seriousness sound the way it should. When she said, 'The world's an orphans' home,' I thought hers was the woman's voice that took the measure of the war in which the men had just been fighting to the death. Leaving aside Emily Dickinson, Marianne Moore would have been enough on her own to make women's poetry seem like an American thing. She was a Special Forces operative in a black tricorne hat. But there was also Edna St Vincent Millay, whose sonnets, despite their wilfully traditionalist structure and diction, looked more and more original to me as time went on, to the point where, in my mind, I was casting the movie about her affair with Edmund Wilson. Edna and Edmund could easily have become as famous as Ted Hughes and Sylvia Plath, if not for one vital factor: Plath was the formative woman poet for whole generations throughout the English-speaking world, whereas Millay has never really caught on. But then, hardly anyone has ever caught on like Plath. In the whole of literature's long history, Plath must be the supreme example of a poet breaking through to masses of people who know nothing about poetry at all. Fans of Byron had read verse before.

But if we look only for a big impact, we are treating women's poetry as a commodity. The important thing is that women's poetry has joined men's poetry in the harsh realm of art, where nothing except quality can survive the perpetual bushfire of time. Donne, in one of his regrettably few statements about how 'Metricall compositions' are made, referred to the putting together of a poem as 'the shutting up'. An unfortunate term, and we could use a better one; because there can't be much doubt that the shaping of a poem is also a pressure, in which the binding energy of the poem brings everything inside its perimeter to incandescence. If that were not the prize, then the great women poets of our time would not have worked so hard to join the men.

I still make plans to live forever: there are too many critical questions still to be raised. Most of them can never be settled, which is the best reason for raising them. Who needs a smooth technique after hearing Hopkins's praise, 'All things counter, original, spare, strange'? Well, everyone does, because what Hopkins does with the language depends on the mastery of mastery, and first you must have the mastery. And how can we write as innocently now as Shakespeare did when he gave Mercutio the speech about Queen Mab, or as Herrick did when he wrote 'Oberon's Feast', or even as Pope did, for all his show of craft, when he summoned the denizens of the air to attend Belinda in

Canto II of *The Rape of the Lock*? Well, we certainly can't do it through ignorance, so there goes the idea of starting from nowhere. Better to think back on all the poems you have ever loved, and to realise what they have in common: the life you soon must lose.

Times Literary Supplement

Reading Geoff Cochrane

Carrie Tiffany

Equinoctial
by Geoff Cochrane
> *A hand's turn or two*
> *A hand's turn or two*
> *And my work is done for the day.*

> *~*

> *Behold my suit of meats*
> *and fat tarantulas. Check out my cloak of knives*
> *and pinkest heliums.*

> *~*

> *Our lilies are broken by the wind.*
> *Broken by the wind, and then they rust.*
> *Broken by the wind, and then they rot.*

> *~~*

> *A habit I seem to have formed (and can't afford):*
> *Each morning at eleven, a latte at the same place,*
> *At the same table, my own inviolable spot*
> *Downwind of the non-smokers.*

> *~~*

> *Coffee. What a racket. I must be nuts.*
> *But I'm making an attempt to live, you see;*
> *I'm conducting an experiment in living.*

When I was a child I had two dolls in a box. Each night I placed the dolls on the floor of the box and covered them with a sheet of black paper. Sometimes the dolls required reassurance. I told them that the day was finished in their country, that it was no longer time for speaking and that all of the world was asleep.

I meet these two New Zealanders. They are brainy and handsome; they live in an old workers' cottage on the edge of Melbourne. There is a pāua shell ashtray. There are postcards of Colin McCahon. *Kia ora*, they murmur, when they pick up the telephone. I'm there one day when a relative arrives off the plane from Wellington. An old cardboard suitcase is snapped open; cake from a teashop on Lambton Quay, jars of bubbled honey, custard powder in an orange packet. The soft comforts of home . . . I score a slim volume of Geoff Cochrane. It's 2001 and this is how it begins.

It doesn't happen instantly. The Irish hold the ground. You duke it out, those first few years, with the American poet Donald Hall. But *Hypnic Jerks* (2005) seals it for me. I think of you each time I'm hooked back from sleep. I think of you in your crummy pad – the few forks and knives shivering in their drawer when the bus stops outside. I think of the view from your flat; pines, drainage ditches, rugby posts like gallows, wooded hills, a soft drink plant, red leaves that bounce like crisps, rain that inks the road.

I read your lines and I make you up. I foist you on to the few Australian poets and readers of poetry that I know. I take you out to dinner. I take you to London. I do a number on you in an interview for the women's hour on the BBC. The doughy host looks over her glasses at me. She pronounces *New Zealand* so archly the face powder on her soft English cheeks lifts and talcs the air. I take you to Calgary, Mildura, Ubud, Leeds, Port Hedland. I take you to Auckland where I mention you to a bookish crowd in a hotel bar. One of the drinkers is your publisher. I leave.

I read your lines and I follow them like tracks. There you are walking down the long hill towards Antarctica, watching the shunted clouds, taking in the smell of gorse fires, the sky is the colour of wet salt. I learn not to clarify. The waxy eye of the Kōwhai? She is not a bird; she is a tree with a yellow flower hanging limply penile. The poem is dead to me; the bird of my imagination forever tangled in its rhythms.

Your life is hectic, lonely, full of innocence and sin. Your books sit aslant on the table next to my bed. The white covers are not weathering well. The dentist's chair tilts and sinks, I think of you. The extractions, the full clearance, the needle's spiteful sting. There is your knowledge of household paint, cigarette lighters, pencils, addiction.

You write and you walk. You walk to resist the abyss. You walk to the supermarket at the foot of Tinakori Hill. You walk Wellington's ribboned pavements; you walk its harboured curve. You were walking before Sebald reached the Pacific and we sat in cafés discussing the *flâneur*. I sense you in my ankles at St Kilda as I hesitate on the kerb.

News comes. You have been seen in a shop. You are thin. I hear there are stacks of your manuscripts waiting for attention on your publisher's floor. The thought of all those poems spooling out in front of you – hovering voluptuously on the brink of being read. In *Vanilla Wine* (2003) you say you have a readership of perhaps twenty-three people. I make them up too.

The world is full of people we will never know, sitting at home, coughing quietly in their countries. It can be hard to bear the thought of these people who will always be remote, never in relation. When the day is finished in my country and I pull the black sheet over my face you are already in deep night. If I can't sleep I'll reach for you. Your poems have travelled across the sea from your island to mine in a kind of double movement – a silent athletics of writing and reading. I don't believe the poems you make are a symptom of estrangement, but of over-feeling. Although, who am I to say? I made you up. But you started it, Geoff Cochrane; you started it all those years ago when you sat down in your country and began to write.

Griffith Review

Vale Doris Lessing

Robyn Davidson

So the Big D has gone. Hardly unexpected. She was ninety-four and ill; we had talked about her impending death the last time I visited her in London. Yet when I heard the news, the kickback of knowing there would be no more of that consciousness in the world was enormous.

She would no doubt say something crisp like, 'Robbie, you must stop *emot*ing.'

As always, the most banal wish: that I had said simply, 'I love you, I admire you. I am profoundly grateful to you, difficult and prickly though you sometimes were.'

So what comes to mind immediately? The chaotic and prodigious English garden with bits of Africa scattered through it (pumpkin vines among the David Austin roses). Kittens following her up the stairs to her eyrie – a small bedroom cum writing room. The piles of washing-up, letters, postcards and books (always books) in the kitchen. The piles of magazines and books in the loo. Feeding the birds on the back porch. The way she noticed everything from that back porch, as people raised in the country do. However urban you become, that way of noticing the natural world remains.

The food. From the chaos of her small kitchen came food for fifty. Delicious, wicked food, with lots of fat and cream. Sunday lunches there would see an unlikely assortment of people – literary, famous, oddballs, old friends, lost souls she had taken under her wing, penniless immigrants (quietly, she would make sure they had money and shelter), her agent, her publisher, her son Peter sitting in his armchair, saying cryptic things . . . all of us expected to get along with one another, all felled by the calorific food and red wine, the new ones looking bewildered on the cat-haired sofa or sitting on the floor amid the piles of books. Not for her the English socialising in which status, placement and food portion are carefully considered.

The older she got, the less she gave a damn what accolades or criticism came her way. There wasn't time for such trivia. 'Oh Christ,' she said on hearing she had won the Nobel prize for literature. And those of us who knew her laughed and said how typically Doris that was. All the fuss over something so unimportant; it would eat into her time. 'Oh Christ,' as she hauled the bags of shopping up steps that were becoming more difficult to negotiate because of the pain in her collapsing back. No point in complaining – about pain, or difficulty, or death. (What do we think life *is*, after all?)

She took me in not long after I'd crossed the Australian desert, in 1978. In the arrogance of youth, I had written to her. I had said how 'useful' her books were. She wrote back, saying, 'If you can write a good letter, you can write a good book.' We corresponded for a while. I decided to write *Tracks*, the story of that journey through the desert. I went to London. I met her. I adored her. Six months later, she invited me to live in the little flat at the bottom of her house. I was editing *Tracks* for publication by then. We seldom talked about writing, though we did talk about books. I remember complaining to her one day, 'Doris, everything I write sounds the same.' She burst out laughing and said, 'My dear, that's called having a style.'

And later, when *Tracks* came out, and it was apparent it was going to be a bestseller, she advised, 'Don't bother reading what people say about you or the book. Reviews will tell you nothing useful about your work, only about the current fashion.' I took her advice and have found it to be sound.

Another time, she came down to sit by the fire with me. She was having trouble with a book. 'Some come out so easily, and others just won't budge . . . Why? Why?' I was astonished that this woman who seemed to push out a novel every five minutes could suffer from something like writer's block.

She was both friend and mentor, someone I felt deeply in tune with (that colonial background, perhaps, the dislike of limit and of being categorised, the mistrust of 'ism' and ideology, anything that trapped you or hemmed you in or limited your range of thinking and imagining) and at the same time shy of. In awe of. She was mother substitute and literary mother. Not because her books were 'feminist' but because they took on so much and indicated how far outside the usual boundaries a female intelligence could go.

She gave so many of us younger women a cardinal point to help us navigate. She gave us something to admire. To emulate. She showed us that we did not have to be nice so much as we had to be courageous.

I ignored her books until I was in my mid twenties; I ignored them because they were by a woman. My reasoning was that I already knew how a woman thought and that I needed to understand how men thought, how power worked. Then someone gave me *The Golden Notebook*. I found it, as I so gormlessly said, 'useful'. And how.

There are great human beings in the world who are not publicly visible. And there are great writers and public figures who are not great human beings. It is exceedingly rare, in my experience, that a great writer is also a great human being. Not perfect, not easy, not infallible, but great. Containing multitudes.

The Monthly

Cry When We're Gone

Neil Murray

In January 1980 I arrived in Papunya, 260 kilometres west of Alice Springs, because a whitefella was needed to drive the store truck. An Aboriginal bloke couldn't drive the truck. Kinship obligations would require him to give away the food to family members. The store would lose money. Driving that truck proved a difficult enough job for me. I delivered food and supplies to surrounding outstations where people lived in semi-traditional camps, out bush, away from the government-established settlement of Papunya and its many problems: overcrowding, chronic illnesses, grog, violence, the sedentary lifestyle its people led. It seems clear to me now that my real reason for coming to Papunya was a quest for meaning, for a greater sense of belonging, and intuitively I felt Aboriginal people were the key to all that. I wanted to be with them, work with them, learn from them. Within a week I had a visitor.

He wanted to see my electric guitar: a gold Les Paul copy I'd saved up for and bought new at Allans Music shop in Melbourne. He cradled it admiringly, then for several minutes he made a sweet sound come out. Soon we were jamming. He was thoughtful, didn't say much, a handsome cat who could peel off stunning solos and find chords and rhythm without ever second-guessing. Sammy Butcher was his name.

Sammy brought in his brothers and other interested young men. They chucked in sit-down money and scrounged up drum kits, other instruments, amps, a rough PA. One or two nights a week we held concerts in the corrugated iron shed that was Papunya Town Hall. We'd play what we could: Chuck Berry, Beatles, Stones, Little Richard and AC/DC covers, R&B and country stuff. We swapped line-ups with each genre. For the rock & roll stuff I'd be at the microphone singing and cranking out rhythm guitar while the others played with their backs to the audience, because of *kurnta*, or shame.

A few kilometres east of Papunya was a low hill known as Warumpi. It was a honey-ant dreaming site. Had you sat up on those rocks, any one of those late afternoons in 1980, you'd have heard a jangle, jive and echo wafting up from the huddle of dusty buildings, piercing the quiet of the ancient, sleeping land. People called us the Warumpi Band. We pooled a few battered Holdens for our first away gigs, playing Hermannsburg on a Friday then travelling to Jay Creek next morning. On the road out we gave chase to a perentie – with a brilliant throw of a stone our bass player, Dennis, knocked it over. It was my first taste of road kill, and of how in the years ahead we'd never miss an opportunity for a feed.

Before entering Jay Creek community we stopped at a creek bed where a group of men sat drinking. One had an acoustic guitar. I've since encountered many blackfella songwriters, and invariably you meet them outdoors: in creek beds, on riverbanks, in laneways or backstreets, behind fences, under verandahs and bridges, round campfires. The man with the guitar was middle-aged. He was jolly, cherubic-looking, the brow of his Akubra turned down at the front. His name was Isaac Yama and he was singing, in Pitjantjatjara, his own country-style songs. The flagon was passed my way. I took a modest sip. Isaac asked me to play a song. His guitar had scratches and dings on it. Below the sound hole the paint was worn away down to the wood. I strummed and sang about missing the country where I was from, the Grampians region of western Victoria. Isaac nodded. Later that evening, outside the hall, before our show, I felt him touch the skin on my arm.

'See that,' said Isaac, 'that's nothing, that's only skin colour. You got the same heart like us.'

*

By August I had hardly touched the didge I got in the top end. Blackfellas, or Anangu, in central Australia don't traditionally use didge, or *yidaki*. Instead, with boomerang percussion, they concentrate on chanting song cycles, wielding a transformative power of enormous antiquity. One sleepy Sunday I gave my *yidaki* a drink of water and blew it a while, thinking I'd be bothering no one, on the verandah of my square one-roomed flat, the only serviceable space left in a block of four. The other three flats were trashed. Walking my way along the dusty street came a skinny fella in jeans and a denim jacket. He looked darker than the local desert blokes. His head was a shock of fluffed, frizzy hair. As I blew, attempting some rudimentary calls and rhythms I'd learnt from old David Blanasi at Barunga, the skinny man quickened his stride, angling across and into my front yard and landing, with a couple of steps, on the verandah, simultaneously clapping his hands and singing gustily in lingo.

I stopped. Had I done something, transgressed – flipped open a forbidden door?

'Don't stop. You got it. That's Bungaling-Bungaling.'

'I don't know much,' I stammered, 'that's all I know.'

'Give it here. I'll show you.'

He took the didge. Out came a rich, deep, guttural throb that was precise, intricate – the proper score of what I'd been trying to play.

I was gushing. 'That's great.'

He wasn't listening. He'd noticed something lying on the swag in my room.

'Ah, you got a guitar!'

'Yes.'

'I'm a singer man.'

'Are you now?'

'What time you havin' band?'

'Later in the hall.'

'I'll see you there.'

That afternoon, at Papunya Town Hall, I learnt his name was George Rrurrambu and he hailed from Elcho Island. He'd come south to marry Suzina, the sister of Sammy. With George as Sammy's new brother-in-law there was no way he wasn't going to be in the band. We had our frontman. He even faced the audience.

For the next twenty or so years I watched him develop until all he had to do was slip into his super Koori outfit – black jeans, sneakers, Aboriginal-flag waistcoat – flash an irresistible grin, leer into the microphone, strike a cocky pose, legs apart, stamp a foot, and the crowd would be his.

'You wanna listen to Warumpi Band? You wanna listen or what? Don't be shy cause I'm black. You want rock & roll? You'll cry for us when we go. All right, all right, don't panic we'll play all night.'

We made three albums, played countless gigs, in Australia and overseas. All that time George was out front, exhorting the audience to join him, or else falling into a front row of girls and me and our manager David Cook having to yank him back on stage by the legs. Odd, quiet moments – him and me in a hotel room, listening to distant thunder, and George suddenly telling me a special word that could make a storm go away; both of us running a lap of a paddock through chilly twilight air to make ourselves really alive and alert before hitting the stage in Canberra.

But by mid-June 2006 I didn't want to see George anymore. We'd had our blues and I had said this before. This time I was adamant. That month, six years after the Warumpi Band's official retirement, we played a rare gig at the Dreaming Festival in Queensland. George's stamina and voice weren't there. Neither was he – he didn't want to be with us, preferring to hang with the other rock stars, get stoned with them, follow them round. I was disgusted at his subservience to others and disregard for us. I wanted to get the gig done and get out. But when it came time to leave we couldn't find George. Then when we did he was in a foul mood for us having interrupted his socialising. I wanted to leave him there. We all had planes to catch. He was angry and so was I. We almost came to blows. His were the usual complaints: he was being treated badly, I was to blame, I'd taken money or royalties, it should be his money.

'Just get your bag and get in the car,' I seethed.

'This my festival. Go find your own festival. Don't come round my festival, fuckin' prick.'

We overnighted in a motel near Brisbane airport. Next day he was still angry. When he threatened the tour manager I had to confront him. Here we were, nudging our fifties – I didn't want to fight him. Thankfully it did not come to that. He merely refused to acknowledge me. We reached the airport, caught our respective flights, and I set my mind to forgetting all about him. Six months later Sammy rang.

'You heard from George?'

'No.'

'He's not well, he collapsed in Melbourne they say. He's in Darwin now. He's having tests. Something's wrong. You should call.'

'I don't really feel like it. Not after what happened.'

'*Yuwa* – look, don't think about the bad times. Just think about the good times. You should call him. They saying he might have cancer.'

I remembered his diminished energy, his negative attitude; it all squared up. But it was not without apprehension that I phoned him.

'I hear you are crook.'

George's voice came back croaky. '*Yo*, can't hardly walk,' he said, indignant.

'That's no good. What's the doctor say?'

'Don't know yet.'

He made no mention of our disagreement. Neither did I. I sensed he was short of breath.

'Have you got anyone looking after you?'

'*Yo.*'

'What you need is a feed of stingray.'

'*Yo*, I'm trying for that one now.'

'Get those Birdwave boys to help you.'

Birdwave were three young Adelaide guys on bass, drums and Hammond organ, George's backing band. Less than a month later Sammy rang again: George was diagnosed with lung cancer and back on Elcho Island with his family.

'They saying he might only have three weeks,' said Sammy.

My whole history with George telescoped into the moment. I recalled an argument on a bus after a jail gig at Canning Vale, in Perth, when George was being particularly congratulatory about *his* performance and *his* show. This was 1999. I'd been increasingly alarmed about this trait in George. Maybe it is a peculiar syndrome of all lead singers to become like this. I reminded him then and there that we were – I thought – still a team, a band.

'You weren't alone on that stage. We were there with you, backing you up, making the show work too.'

'No, I did it myself. I made them all get up.'

He was getting on the nose. Quietly I proffered: 'Okay, who writes the songs?'

George glared. Rising angrily in his seat, he roared – 'Yes, you write the songs, but they get the message from me. I sing them! Me Rrurrambu! They get it from me!' He thumped his own chest for emphasis.

For George, the singer was more important than the song. For me, the song is paramount. Made for tension and drive in the band, perhaps. He had a point. So did I. I could appreciate his view. What did it matter now? George will always be the singer, the showman, the rocker, the livewire out front, the tip of the spear. Now he was dying.

As Sammy said, think of the good times. And there were plenty.

We were fat with good times. When George was on song, kicking up a storm, we'd win any crowd, hold ourselves against any band in the country. The energy that took over when we played was greater than the sum of our parts. That's what defines a good band. We'd made our mark. We'd made Aboriginal people proud. We'd sung the truth of blackfella experience and put it on the mainstream map. We couldn't have done it without George. He was the one to deliver that message. Would I never see his laugh, that cocky smile – George in all his dynamic glory – again?

Four years before, when my father died, I rang George to tell him. He broke into sobs, muttering, 'Daddy's gone to his home.' His instant empathy and display of grief startled me. Now I had to make that call, give something back.

'Hello, George?'

'*Yo.*'

'You in Galiwinku?'

'*Yo*, at my island home.'

'*Manymak*, are you comfortable? Have you got painkillers?'

'Nothing, only Panadol. Hey, brother, can you send me CD,

Warumpi Band CDs? My kids wanna listen.'

As soon as you send them, Warumpi Band CDs disappear. They spirit out of houses, rooms, cars, bags. Vanish into scrub. No one person retains them very long.

'*Yo*, I'll post them.'

A silence. I think, is this the last time we'll speak? A freight of emotion arrived.

'I love you and I'll miss you,' he sobbed.

'I love you too.' I was choking up. 'I'll see you down the track one day.'

'Is it heaven?'

He was asking me the question. He really wanted to know: would he go to heaven? I sensed fears, and a guilt he was struggling with.

'*Yo*. I'll see you there, brother.'

Three weeks came and went. George was alive. Two months later I found myself in Nhulunbuy for a show with Shane Howard. George was alive. I chartered a plane to Elcho Island. His emaciated body, his face shrunken into its skull, strange hospital dressings attached to his chest – even in this weakened state he managed a lazy smile. Gently I embraced him. 'I'm trying,' he murmured, 'very hard.'

George wanted to live. He loved this life. He had more to give, more to create. He had songs and recordings to do with the Bird-wave boys, who along with George's family were providing 24/7 care.

They said he'd been up all night. One of his aunties implored him, in language, to lie down and rest. George said he'd sleep when he's dead.

We went out the backyard. Someone produced an acoustic guitar. Helped onto an old bed, George lay back. I sat on a plastic chair. Nearby was his mother's grave. Softly I strummed and began singing 'Fitzroy Crossing'. *If you see me on the track way out west of Rabbit Flat . . .* George joined in the chorus, a croaky whisper. Some of his family were tearing up. I tried a couple of other song fragments. Too much for him; he didn't have the strength. We would never sing these songs again. But George remained stoic. He was, after all, surrounded by family – and he had everyone's attention. When he was momentarily distracted I took the chance to expunge a few tears. Mostly we sat and said nothing. I watched his grandchildren play. Hours passed. A heavy feeling I'd had since arriving began to lift. Finally George was helped to a chair further down the yard. I went with him. When it was just the two of us I spoke.

'You know, we did good work in the Warumpi Band. We made the country take notice. And we had the best fun.'

George struggled to get up, the emotion rising in him. 'You, me and Sammy. Warumpi Band was the first—'

That's all he could say. He stayed half-standing, leaning forward, staring at the ground, his hands clutching the chair's arms, his mouth agape as if puzzled why his body would not respond.

Out front a Toyota was waiting to take me to the airstrip, where a return flight was booked. I clasped hands with regal old Matjuwi Burarrwanga, George's father, slim, tall, long grey-white hair, a straggly beard. Nearly blind and confined mostly to a wheelchair, his intellect, authority and spiritual strength were intact. I had lost my father; now Matjuwi was losing a son. As I bid Matjuwi goodbye I hoped to convey my gratitude and respect for him as my kinship father, and for having known his son.

Everybody came out to see me off – but seeing George there surprised me. He could not stand unaided but he was showing me his spirit was buoyant. Same as it ever was. Climbing into the Toyota, I turned to him.

'Goodbye,' I said.

'Goodnight,' he said – a parting quip.

From out the Cessna's window I stared blankly while we accelerated along the asphalt before lurching into the air, a slab of turquoise sea opening up beneath the plane's wings, and as we swung left over the community I tried, in vain, to pinpoint George or his family's house before they were swallowed by the scrub, then the shore.

*

In a studio in east Balmain, where I was recording my second solo album in 1991, I had a visitor one evening – not unusual, musos were always dropping in, generally to see one of the producers, either Mark Moffatt or Jim Moginie. This muso was different. He was Yolngu. And he was blind.

Gurrumul entered and stood quietly, an interested smile on his attentive face as he listened to the studio sounds. I remembered seeing him play with Yothu Yindi. I knew he was gifted. We touched hands briefly, softly, and I sensed respect and admiration, also connection – via my long-time association with one of his countrymen, George. I hoped to reciprocate the same feelings to him. We didn't engage in conversation. He was pleased just to say hello and soak up the studio ambience. I had the distinct feeling this was where he wanted to be: in a recording studio, so he could paint the colours of the sounds in his head. The next time we shook hands he would be a multi-platinum artist.

*

The last song of Paul Kelly's set at a 1993 gig I played with him in Dee Why was a moving ballad called 'Took the Children Away' – written, he announced, by Archie Roach. Afterwards PK asked if I'd heard of him. Archie was originally from Framlingham in south-west Victoria, less than an hour's drive from where I was born and raised, but of course I couldn't possibly have known him: Archie was taken away, aged three. In my local district Aboriginal people were absent, or at least not conspicuous. Somehow I formed the idea they were all up north and set a course for the Northern Territory. Paradoxically, it was only by going to Papunya that I came to realise what had been lost in my home country – and what could be gained.

When Archie and I finally met at the Annandale Hotel that same year he said straight off: 'We like the Warumpi Band – that George, he's really something.' I told him I was from the Lake Bolac district. 'It's funny,' said Archie, 'how a lot of us from western Victoria got into music.' Amy Saunders, Shane, Damian and Marcia Howard, Rose Bygrave, Richard Frankland, Dave Steel, Brett Clarke, Lee Morgan . . . Discovering that Archie and others came from where I came from became a cumulative influence on my decision to return.

At first I was desperate to get close to Archie. But he was reclusive, and not forthcoming about confiding in anyone beyond his partner Ruby and immediate family. I began to realise he was struggling with his own stuff. I have since learnt a lot more when we have shared a stage, where he readily opens himself up to a live audience. He has humbled me with some generous remarks, saying my songs and writing taught him an important truth: you don't have to be Aboriginal to have a connection and spirituality with the land. When I first mentioned Archie to Sammy and George I told them, proudly, that he was my countryman.

*

Kev Carmody is from a Queensland droving family and it was Joh Bjelke-Petersen's Queensland, it seems to me, that put the fire in his belly. Kev's mission is to expose, in song, hypocrisy and truth. For someone who writes such weighty, powerful material he is jovial company. We did some music workshops in jails, and at one particular maximum-security centre in Lithgow – where indigenous inmates were grossly over-represented, just like in all the other jails – the female warden was leading us through security barrier after barrier. As we paused in a confined space before a heavily fortified door, the one that would finally get us inside, I had in my head the doors-opening-and-closing title sequence from *Get Smart*.

'You know,' said the warden, 'we've got the worst of the worst in here.'

'Oh, really, what are the inmates like?'

Kev was quick.

*

I only heard Brian Murphy after he was gone. A Tennant Creek producer and engineer, Jeff McLaughlin, kept pushing into my hands, twice in two years, a CD of Brian's songs. 'You gotta hear this,' he'd say.

People are always giving me CDs. They wave them in my face. I gotta take them. They want me to take them. I don't know why. They must think I can make something happen for them. I'm flat out making something happen for myself. Even if the stuff is good, I say, what am I gonna do? I'm not a record company. I'm not a publisher.

Back in Tennant Creek the next time Jeff was still talking about Brian – telling me of the occasion at Winanjjikari Studio when Brian turned up unannounced in a taxi with a bunch of elderly grandmothers and said, 'We're recording now.' Jeff barely had time to get the leads plugged in. Brian launched into an acoustic-driven lament, in Warlpiri, while the grandmothers fired up a traditional chant around him. It was a one-take only.

On the drive back to Alice I put on that track – 'Jipirunpa' – the final song on Brian's 2009 album *Freedom Road*, released by Winanjjikari Music through Barkly Arts. It sounds chaotic, random even, Brian alone on an acoustic guitar, and after a while he starts singing low, a melancholic refrain, and suddenly a bunch of old women erupt with a traditional chant except this chant of theirs has a totally different structure. The piece turns and repeats on itself, compelling you to take in the cyclical melody, it's enchanting, Brian's world-weary vocal rising and falling with the tough grit of the grandmothers until – finally I'm forced to concede to Jeff – it makes powerful emotional sense. 'I have heard nothing like it,' I say. 'I love it.'

Maybe I'd met Brian years ago, briefly, somewhere? Maybe at a Warumpi Band gig? We played in Tennant many times. Maybe he watched us from the shadows? Maybe I shook his hand? I would never know. Why is Brian dead?

Brian Murphy was born in Tennant Creek and raised in Ali Curung. He was of Warlpiri and Warumungu parentage. He had – as far as can be known – a normal indigenous-community childhood. His father Albert played guitar. One day Brian wagged school and stayed home to play that guitar. His father admonished him for that. In general, Brian was too smart for school and was mucking up.

Were the school or Brian's parents or Brian looking for opportunities outside Ali Curung? For when Brian was fourteen or fifteen a fateful decision was made. Somehow it was arranged for Brian to go – indeed, he went willingly – to Darwin, to a white man. In 1987 the man took Brian to Papua New Guinea. Brian's family thought Brian was in boarding school. For four years Brian was the victim of sexual abuse and exploitation. He poured himself into music, learning all he could. At nineteen, and presumably too old for the man (who had 'adopted' another, younger boy), Brian was sent back to Tennant Creek.

When Brian returned he brought with him dozens of cassettes. Songs were burning in his chest. He formed Band Nomadic, one of the Barkly region's top bands of the late '80s and early '90s. Brian's voice was deep, fearless, heartfelt. It was the authentic voice of painful lived experience yet capable of great tenderness. His songs – stunning lyrically and melodically – expressed the anguish, pain, loss and love in his own life and his people's lives. He had a grasp of Western song structure far ahead of his peers. One song, 'The Rock', about the 1985 handback of Uluru to its traditional owners, was recorded by popular Top End band Blekbala Mujik. Brian received no acknowledgement or royalties.

He found it difficult to resettle and cope with family pressures in Tennant Creek. Alcohol and drug abuse went hand in hand with petty crimes that escalated to him spending time in and out of prison. Jasmin Afianos, editor of the *Tennant & District Times*, was one who knew him well. 'Brian emerged from his childhood experiences so very torn,' she says. 'Torn between two cultures, heterosexuality and homosexuality, success and failure, love and hate, and good and evil. He often tumbled from the tightrope into a dark, raging, angry void, surfacing only to the sounds of music.'

When in jail Brian continued to write and record; Jeff has dozens of recordings made in prison. When out of jail he often took off interstate. He made a living busking around Flinders Street Station and jammed with musicians such as Joe Camilleri. Jeff, trying doggedly to complete the recording of many of Brian's songs, tracked him down in Melbourne. They recorded a vocal take live onto a laptop beside the Yarra River. Afterwards, Jeff recalls, Brian passed out in a bar.

With warrants out for his arrest, Brian kept ahead of the police. He went to Adelaide. He had family there. He busked around Hindley Street and Rundle Street mall but was always falling in with unsavoury types. And alcohol, drugs and hard living were taking their toll. He succumbed to serious illness, ending up in an Adelaide hospital, where he died in June 2010. His body was flown home and buried in Tennant Creek. That August, Brian was posthumously inducted into the Northern Territory Music Hall of Fame.

All we have are the songs he left us, which ring resonant, clear and irresistible to all those who seek them. If royalties ever eventuate his family want to erect a headstone for him.

It happened in the Gulf Country. I was booked to do a gig at a mine where a lot of local indigenous people were employed. They knew me from decades ago with the Warumpi Band, and they also knew that with the passing of the lead singer that band was no more. When I got the phone call to come and play I was incredulous.

'You sure you want me? I'm not in the pop charts. I'm not even in the mainstream.'

'We're not in the mainstream either, bro. We want you.'

I didn't need a publicist. Blackfellas don't forget you. Later we were having a few post-gig beers in the warm night air, insects chucking themselves at the yellow lights blazing above the accommodation dongas, and me being introduced to some indigenous men I'd never met but who seemed keen to meet me. Some were near my age, most were younger. Gig organisers Patrick Wheeler and Alec Doomadgee were doing the introductions. One young man, waiting patiently in the shadows, came forward when it was his turn and clasped my hand in his.

'If not for your music, I wouldn't be alive now.'

The other blokes nodded. They must have known the lad's history. Suddenly the decades of struggle, sacrifice and hardship in the music game mattered naught.

'Brother,' I said, 'that is the best thing I've ever heard. Thanks for telling me.' I glanced around. 'And what about this mine? Is it a good thing?'

'If we had our way,' said Alec, 'we'd say fill in the hole, put it back the way it was. But what can you do? We got no right of veto, only to negotiate. If we don't negotiate they gonna dig it up anyway. So we try to make the best of a bad situation.'

The Best Music Writing Under the Australian Sun

The War of the Worlds

Noel Pearson

The inspiration for *The War of the Worlds* came one day when Wells and his brother Frank were strolling through the peaceful countryside in Surrey, south of London. They were discussing the invasion of the Australian island of Tasmania in the early 1800s by European settlers, who hunted down and killed most of the primitive people who lived there. To emphasise the reaction of these people, Frank said, 'Suppose some beings from another planet were to drop out of the sky suddenly and begin taking over Surrey and then all of England!'

— MALVINA G. VOGEL, 'Foreword' (2005)
to H.G. Wells, *The War of the Worlds*

A personal quadrant of the Australian landscape

I came upon this foreword some years ago when sharing an enthusiasm of my youth for H.G. Wells's *The War of the Worlds* with my young son. Even as he makes his way through his own all-consuming passions of boyhood – Thomas, the Crocodile Hunter, *Pirates of the Caribbean*, *Lord of the Rings*, Minecraft and now Harry Potter – I indulge my own nostalgia by sharing those things that possessed me when I was a boy. We've done *Richard III*, to which we will doubtless return. We've read Charles Portis's masterpiece *True Grit*, and watched the original John Wayne film and the Coen brothers' remake a hundred times. We've acted out the shoot-out scenes; he's always Rooster. We are yet to get to Sir Arthur Conan

Doyle and *The Hound of the Baskervilles*. His younger sister and I have started *Great Expectations*.

First turned on by Jeff Wayne's musical version of *The War of the Worlds* in early high school, aware of Orson Welles's radio hoax and having read the Wells book, I was stunned to have been unaware of the inspiration for the idea of a Martian invasion of England – its origin in what was called the 'extirpation' of the original Tasmanians. I was disquieted that the source of this extraordinary production in world culture was unknown to me. I knew it was likely unknown to everyone around me, and to almost all of my fellow Australians. How come?

H.G. Wells knew of the original Tasmanians, but that did not mean he felt empathy for the fate of this 'inferior race' at the hands of the British. Instead he subscribed to the scientific racism of his era, believing them 'Palaeolithic', and writing, 'The Tasmanians, in spite of their human likeness, were entirely swept out of existence in a war of extermination waged by European immigrants.'

In *The Last Man: A British Genocide in Tasmania* (2014), the English historian Tom Lawson shows how the destruction of the Tasmanians played out in British culture. We will return to Lawson's contribution to the debate on genocide in Tasmania soon, after we lift the scales from our eyes concerning some of the most revered figures of that culture in the nineteenth century.

The novelist Anthony Trollope, in his emigration guide *Australia and New Zealand*, demanded his British readers squarely face the fact that colonisation involved the theft of land and the destruction of its original owners – which fact was not morally wrong but an advancement of civilisation. Lawson writes that Trollope cannot be taken as other than calling for genocide when he wrote: 'of the Australian black man we may say certainly that he has to go. That he should perish without unnecessary suffering should be the aim of all who are concerned in this matter.'

Charles Darwin, the century's greatest scientist (whom Lawson calls 'a self-conscious liberal humanitarian'), while opposing polygenist theories that various races were distinct species, nevertheless proposed culture as the basis of inferiority and superiority (Lawson: 'indigenous Tasmanians in Darwin's formulation had been swept aside by a more culturally developed, more civilised people'). Lawson writes: '*The Descent of Man* was Darwin's answer to that new political context, in which he asserted that while biologically the human race *was* singular there were in effect cultural differences that allowed for some form of racial hierarchy. The Tasmanians appeared at the bottom of this hierarchy.'

Darwin wrote:

> when civilised nations come into contact with barbarians the struggle is short . . . Of the causes which lead to the victory of civilised nations, some are plain and simple, others complex and obscure. We can see that the cultivation of the land be fatal in many ways to savages, for they cannot, or will not, change their habits.

Of course, the deformation of Darwin's theory of natural selection into social Darwinism and the scientific racism of the latter half of the nineteenth century and the first half of the twentieth was the source of much misery for indigenes throughout the colonial world. Darwin was not entirely innocent of this conflation of biology and culture, which gave scientific authority to an ideology of inevitability about the demise of the Tasmanians and others of their ilk in the face of European superiority.

I expected Charles Darwin. But I didn't expect Charles Dickens.

Of the century's greatest English novelist, the author of *Great Expectations* and an immortal canon, Lawson writes, 'Dickens famously attacked . . . the humanitarian idealisation of the "noble savage" in June 1853, in a furious denunciation that amounts, to use modern-day language, to a call for genocide.'

Dickens wrote:

> I call him a savage, and I call a savage something highly desirable to be civilised off the face of the earth . . . my position is that if we have anything to learn from the Noble Savage, it is what to avoid. His virtues are a fable; his happiness is a delusion; his nobility nonsense. We have no greater justification for being cruel to the miserable object, than for being cruel to a William Shakespeare or an Isaac Newton; but he passes away before an immeasurably better and higher power than ever ran wild in

any earthly woods, and the world will be all the better when his place knows him no more.

I am yet to work out whether, how and when to tell my girl that the creator of Pip, Pumblechook and that convict wretch Magwitch may have wished her namesake great-great-grandmother off the face of the earth.

Ironically, when one's identification with the magnificent literary treasures of England turns out so, there is a Dickensian pathos to the crestfallen scene. One is acutely conscious of what Robert Hughes called 'anachronistic moralising', but the bridge between our contemporary values and those of Dickens's time should surely be a universal and timeless humanity – but alas not.

I don't know whether it is hard for all Aborigines, but it certainly is for me, to read this history with a historian's dispassionate objectivity and without the emotional convulsions of identification and memory. As a child, I loved my mother's mother most in the world; her humour, generosity and ill-temper I often detect in myself and in the various countenances of my children. An irascible, pipe-smoking, bush-born lady, she bustled with her portmanteau on perambulations to her numerous grandchildren growing up in the Daintree and Bloomfield missions, and the Hope Vale Mission of my childhood. She could have been Truganini, but less travelled and from a smaller rainforest world than the nineteenth-century Tasmanian whose passing in 1876 was a world-historical event, marking the assumed extinction of a race. It was a reverberation I would feel when I learnt her name in primary school and the awful meaning of her distinction.

How many Australians born in the 138 years since Truganini's death learnt her legend and scarcely thought deeper about the enormity of the loss she represented, and the history that led to it? Her spirit casts a long shadow over Australian history, but we have nearly all of us found a way to avert our eyes from its meaning.

That small item in the primary-school curriculum of my childhood would have been learnt by all my generation. Maybe it wasn't a formal part of any syllabus, but it was one of those salient facts of Australian society that every child absorbed, like Don Bradman's batting average and Phar Lap's outsized heart. It would have been learnt by John Howard and Paul Keating. By Gough Whitlam and Robert Menzies. I don't know if they teach kids about Truganini today.

As a student of history but not a historian, I am as well read as many, but I too have skirted this history. Learning later in life of the descendants of the original Tasmanians, and the offence of the assumption of extinction, seemed to lessen the imperative to face the question of Truganini's moral legacy. Maybe the scale of the horror diminished as the country accepted the fact of the continued survival of Tasmania's Aboriginal community. But surely the fact of the descendants' survival does not in any way alter or diminish the profundity of what happened to their ancestors.

In his 1968 Boyer Lecture, W.E.H. Stanner spoke of the 'Great Australian Silence':

> inattention on such a scale cannot possibly be explained by absent-mindedness. It is a structural matter, a view from a window which has been carefully placed to exclude a whole quadrant of the landscape. What may have begun as a simple forgetting of other possible views turned under habit and over time into something like a cult of forgetfulness practised on a national scale. We have been able for so long to disremember the Aborigines that we are now hard put to keep them in mind even when we most want to do so.

This excluded quadrant of the landscape was not just a national phenomenon: it was personal. Forgetfulness was not just a cult: it was resorted to by individual Australians, descendants of both the invading Europeans and the Aborigines. Australians who, like me, struggle to work out how we might deal with the past.

The cult of forgetfulness
I had hoped to avoid the past – for sheerly political reasons. In this essay I seek to make a case for constitutional reform recognising indigenous Australians. This must by definition be a unifying cause. If we don't have an argument that can persuade 90 per cent of the nation, then the cause of constitutional reform is lost. Any successful case must transcend the natural political and cultural polarities of Australian society, and seek and seize political

bipartisanship. This can only happen if Australians faced with a constitutional proposition are led by the better angels of our nature.

The risk with history is that it may provoke partisanship and division, both among the cultural and political tribes of the nation at large, and between indigenous and non-indigenous Australians.

We witnessed this in the History Wars of the 1990s and 2000s, when the 'black armband' historians and political leaders were pitted against the 'white blindfold' historians and political leaders. Led by Keith Windschuttle on the one hand and Robert Manne and Henry Reynolds on the other, the wars were a bitter and not always illuminating affair.

But the wars were unavoidable.

Following the Great Australian Silence at the end of the 1960s, from the '70s through to the '90s there was a burgeoning of Aboriginal history, led by scholars such as Reynolds. In hindsight, given the intense relationship between indigenous policy and politics and the representation and interpretation of the nation's history, the rise of a counter-narrative in the form of Windschuttle's *The Fabrication of Aboriginal History* (Volume 1, 2002), was inevitable. No discourse can lean one way for long. No wind can blow from one direction without restraint.

The public contributions of the doyen of conservative historians, Geoffrey Blainey, were the first indications of the discomfort of those who held the settler Australian narrative. Blainey would have been better qualified to steady the ship of the nation's narrative had he done so as a historian. Instead he did so as a polemicist. His caricaturing of the new frontier history as the 'black armband' view made for a tribal fight in the public square, rather than a debate within the discipline of history. Blainey's commendable record on Aboriginal history was obscured in the ensuing debate: he was not contemptuous of the Aborigines; he wanted to defend settler traditions. It was most unfortunate that Blainey made his case in this manner. A serious point in an unserious way.

Over the past three decades, I have read Henry Reynolds's numerous books, and I well understand the grounds upon which conservative and nationalist readers of his histories baulk at his interpretations. It seems to me that Reynolds's lifelong contribution has been a liberal pursuit of a shared history for the nation.

He has been about finding grace for the nation by breaking the silence on Aboriginal history and all the time being faithful to Australia.

But there are two problems with Reynolds's project. First, he comes to the case from a patently political background. His wife, Margaret, was a Labor senator for Queensland during the Hawke years, and the couple came at politics and indigenous issues from a certain Labor left perspective. There is a strongly Fabian tone to his arguments, and trenchant advocacy frames his books. In the acknowledgements of *An Indelible Stain? The Question of Genocide in Australian History* (2001), Reynolds tellingly reveals: 'My family – Margaret, John, Anna and Rebecca – have been, as ever, supportive and have frequently reinforced my commitment to progress along the often difficult road of human rights advocacy.' Which, for his critics, raises the question whether he was primarily engaged in academic history or human rights advocacy, and perhaps suggests that more dispassion and less politics might have better enabled Reynolds to secure a shared history for his fellow Australians.

I will say at this point that I am at one with Henry and Margaret Reynolds on the human rights side of the equation, but at odds with them on the responsibilities side. They have been and are mute on the social crisis of Aboriginal Australia; indeed, I have observed that the policies needed to tackle indigenous misery – economic integration, social order and welfare reform – have been championed by the right, and in 2006 noted that 'Windschuttle and [Gary] Johns are more attuned to many of the necessary policies than the progressives'.

The same thing struck me about rock star and former Labor politician Peter Garrett as the former senator Reynolds. No greater friends when it came to indigenous rights and paying the rent and decrying the burning beds of history, but completely silent about the unravelling social crisis of the present – and, to the extent they thought about what needed to be done, mostly wrongheaded. It is strange that people who would insist strongly on Aboriginal agency in the past would turn a blind eye to such passivity in the present.

Second, I find persuasive Bain Attwood's critique of Reynolds's oeuvre as consisting overmuch of 'juridical history': the telling of history as if presenting evidence in a legal case before a court. I share Attwood's view that Reynolds's core trilogy – *The Other Side of the Frontier* (1981), *Frontier* (1987) and *With the White People* (1990) – is unimpeachable. But much of the rest has the features of juridical history, and too many contentions seem to be submissions to a court case rather than based on a proper grappling with the political economy of the time and circumstances of which he writes. Therefore some appear thin.

In a 2007 essay for *Griffith Review*, I analysed the dynamic of the political discourse between progressives and conservatives. I observed that the conservative camp comprised a broad spectrum, ranging from true denialists such as Windschuttle to those who, in their cups, would admit the truths of Aboriginal history, but who were defensive of their own heritage and of the accomplishments of their forebears. John Howard was not a denialist; he was defensive about his settler heritage. Of course, an inability to deal with the psychological meaning of this historical legacy often means the default position becomes a version of denialism – or is strongly coloured by denial. After all, the long, 150-year reign of the Great Australian Silence was about denial.

On the other hand, I observed that progressives were prone to use racial discrimination and historical denial as political bludgeons against their conservative opponents, and their advocacy for an honest confrontation with the colonial past degenerated into moral vanity. The result was that progressives reinforced victimhood of the indigenes while their opponents denied their victimisation.

Having said this, I now turn to the volatile question of the extirpation of the original Tasmanians.

I hoped to avoid the past, but it is not possible. I hoped to disremember the past, but it is not possible.

The question of genocide in Australia

The use of the term 'genocide' and the rhetoric of the Jewish Holocaust is incendiary. The destruction of the Tasmanians was an event of world history long before the Nazi genocide of the Jews. It was well established in the discourse of British and Australian history long before the 1948 Genocide Convention. It was referred to around the world during the course of the nineteenth century and throughout the twentieth.

Whether you use the word most common in colonial times – 'extirpation' – or other words also used – 'extermination' or 'extinction' – or the word 'genocide', they speak to the same meaning. And that meaning is the loss to the world by the passing of a people from history by killing and mass death. The fact that a descendant community survived this history does not negate or reduce the profundity of the loss. When as a primary schooler I was told the significance of Truganini was that she was the last 'full blood' of Tasmania, I understood clearly what was meant. The language of racial composition was commonplace in that time, and still is, among black and white Australians, despite its contemporary disreputability. It is not to deny the fact of the survival of the descendant community, and neither is it to impugn their identity, to remember the enormity of the fact that Truganini's death marked the passing from the world of one of the last Tasmanians without mixed lineage. A lineage that had occupied that land for more than 35,000 years.

Those last sentences were hard to write. I was not sure I could get it right, and still don't know whether I have. I mean not to offend contemporary Aborigines of Tasmania. I mean not to return to the mind-frame of racialist eugenics that has so tangled the history that I wish untangled. I just do not want to deny or diminish the tragedy of Truganini and the old people of Tasmania.

Of course, as a reader of history and not a historian, I can hardly untangle this history. I can only say how I respond to and deal with it, as an Aboriginal and an Australian.

History is never resolved, and we should not make a shared future contingent on a shared past. For this reason I cannot abandon the examination of genocide as readily as some eminent historians in the wake of the History Wars prescribe.

I will not deal with the debate on whether the removal of children, identified by Michael Dodson and Sir Ronald Wilson in the *Bringing Them Home* report of 1997, constituted genocide. I will also not deal with the debate on whether the colonial history of mainland Australia – particularly my home state of Queensland – involved genocidal episodes. Instead I will confine my discussion to what happened in Tasmania in the first half of the nineteenth century.

Among historians who have been at the forefront of Aboriginal history, there is some respectable consensus against the use of the term 'genocide' in this context.

Henry Reynolds's *An Indelible Stain?* centres on official correspondence from secretary of state for the colonies Sir George Murray to Tasmania's lieutenant governor, Sir George Arthur, on 5 November 1830. Murray referred to the 'great decrease which has of late years taken place in the amount of the aboriginal population' and his apprehension 'that the whole race of these people may, at no distant period, become extinct'. He wrote:

> But with whatever feelings such an event may be looked forward to by those of the settlers who have been sufferers by the collisions which have taken place, it is impossible not to contemplate such a result of our occupation of the island as one very difficult to be reconciled with feelings of humanity, or even with principles of justice and sound policy; and the adoption of any line of conduct, having for its avowed, or for its secret object, the extinction of the native race, could not fail to leave an indelible stain upon the character of the British government.

Reynolds's discussion focuses on the coining of the term 'genocide' by the Polish Jewish jurist and American émigré Raphael Lemkin, in the 1940s, and its adoption in the Genocide Convention of 1948, following the Holocaust. Lemkin was clear that while the term and its establishment as a crime in international law was new, its occurrence in history was not. Lemkin specifically assumed that the events in Tasmania which I am discussing here constituted such an occurrence.

Applying the definition of the crime of genocide to events before the enactment of the Convention involves retrospectivity, and indeed its application to the Holocaust was necessarily retrospective. It was applied by Lemkin and is generally not considered anachronistic when applied to the history of the Armenians at the hands of Turkey in 1915. How far back does retrospectivity turn into anachronism?

But anachronism is not the only objection to taking terminology invented in the 1940s and applying it to events in colonial

Tasmania. In his discussion in *An Indelible Stain?* and *Forgotten War* (2013), Reynolds comes down against the application of genocide to Australia because the 1948 Convention requires *intention* on the part of the offending state. The absence of an explicit intention on the part of the colonial authorities, who frequently expressed concern at the treatment of indigenous peoples at the frontier, ultimately underpins Reynolds's conclusion. It is a lawyer's conclusion. The lawyer in me protests that the circumstances and the evidence clearly speak of a constructive intention on the part of the colonial authorities, but this debate is not merely a legal argument. John Docker's point is apposite:

> We must also remember that in Lemkin's 1944 definition . . . the cultural and political were both strongly present as part of the manifold ways the essential foundations of life of a group were being destroyed. Lemkin's 1944 definition and the Lemkin-influenced definition enshrined in the 1948 convention have acted in subsequent thinking about genocide like a double helix – neither reducible one to the other nor wholly separable. The definition of genocide, that is, always has a double character: both discursive and legal. In my view, we should not base the historical study of genocide on a legal definition alone; indeed, we should not base the historical study of any phenomena on a legal definition alone.

Inga Clendinnen, an authority on the Jewish Holocaust and respected Australian historian, also baulked at the application of the genocide definition to the Australian context:

> I am reasonably sophisticated in these modes of intellectual discussion, but when I see the word 'genocide' I still see Gypsies and Jews being herded into trains, into pits, into ravines, and behind them the shadowy figures of Armenian women and children being marched into the desert by armed men. I see deliberate mass murder.

Bain Attwood's *Telling the Truth about Aboriginal History* (2005) was a fine circuit-breaker to the History Wars. He showed clearly that Keith Windschuttle's role in these debates was not as a historian.

Windschuttle is a reader of history and public intellectual, not a historian, and *Fabrication* is a work of historiography, not history. I consider Attwood's book a good starting place for Australian readers of history to think about how we might come to terms with our past. I therefore take his view seriously:

> In my opinion, genocide is neither a necessary nor a useful concept for the task of understanding the nature of the white colonisation of this country.

But I remain unpersuaded that these views should be the final word. Let me enumerate my reasons.

First, the fact of Truganini.

Second, Michael Mansell's point that 'the British had more impact on Aborigines than the Holocaust had on the Jews' is particularly apt in respect of the history of his people. The old people of Tasmania are no more. Only their descendants remain. (Lawson: '. . . if the destruction of their ancestors was not total, it was comprehensive. All original communities had been destroyed since the British invasion, and the population reduction was greater than 99 per cent.')

Third, I bridle at assessments that derogate from the gravity of what happened to the Tasmanians. In this respect I am resistant to Attwood's approach:

> in becoming the universal trope of trauma [the Holocaust] can also simultaneously enhance and hinder other historical and memorial practices and struggles. In the Australian context, it had undoubtedly done both. My concern here, though, is the way in which invoking the Holocaust has become, in some hands, a means by which other crimes are cast as minor by comparison to its absolute evil. As Peter Novick has argued, making the Nazi genocide the benchmark of atrocity and oppression can 'trivialise' crimes of lesser magnitude. This is not merely a distasteful mode of speaking, but a truly disgusting one, he points out. Yet, as he suggests, it is one that readily occurs when something like the Holocaust becomes the touchstone in moral and political discourse.

Without in any way diminishing the Holocaust (as if it could be diminished), I cannot accept any moral comparison that diminishes the fate suffered by the Tasmanians.

Fourth, the accounts – both from the oral histories of Aborigines and from the documented sources of colonial times – referring to the death of Aborigines on the frontier speak to me of the profoundest moral problem of this history: the heavy discounting of the humanity of the Aborigines. It is not the horrific scenes of mass murder that are most appalling here; it is the mundanity and casual parsimony of it all. No people on earth were considered lower. No people rated lower on the ruling scales of human worth, and their deaths elicited the least level of moral reproval. My point is that while the reproof of the time reflected the morality of the age, the racism that underpinned that calculus cannot hold sway today. The Tasmanians were human beings. They were gone within half a century. And only their descendants remained.

Fifth, there is Tom Lawson's thesis in *The Last Man*, to which I now turn.

The Scylla and Charybdis of colonialism

Tom Lawson is professor of history at Northumbria University in the United Kingdom. His book *The Last Man*, published this year, is subtitled *A British Genocide in Tasmania*. If his thesis has any power, it is to make plain that the consensus view outlined above is a long way from having resolved these questions. He puts forward a compelling counter-interpretation.

I will avoid a summation of Lawson's book, for it is better read in its own right. It is worth reading in its own right. Even if you come to these questions with scepticism or indeed indignation, you have a duty to hear out his scholarship.

If you read Lawson after Reynolds's *An Indelible Stain?*, you will be struck by a subtle but critical point made by the Briton about who would wear the indelible stain. For Reynolds:

the question that Murray's words still confront us with is whether our history has left an indelible stain upon the character and reputation of *Australian* governments – colonial, State and federal – and upon the colonists themselves and their Australian-born descendants. [emphasis added by Lawson]

But in response, Lawson notes that:

> George Murray had not himself been that interested in the
> moral implications of genocide for the colony, but for the metro-
> pole. The 'indelible stain' that Murray feared was, it is worth
> repeating, upon the reputation of the *British* government.

It is a crucial reorientation of Reynolds's framing. The discussion
of what happened to the Tasmanians in the first half of the nineteenth century is about a British colony run by the British government. The principal players in this history, Governor George
Arthur, his predecessors and successors, his superiors back in
Downing Street and their agents, such as George Augustus
Robinson, on the colonial frontiers were members and agents of
the British government, acting under the ultimate authority of the
Colonial Office. They administered British policy, and this would
remain the case until responsible government was vested in
Tasmania in 1856.

It probably required a Briton to face this matter squarely. We
might want to discuss the legacy bequeathed to subsequent pre-
and post-Federation Australian governments and the colonists
who were protagonists in and inheritors of this history, but Lawson's first point is that the destruction of the Tasmanians occurred
in a British colony governed by the British Crown:

> This was a British genocide, carried out on the other side of the
> world by British men, articulating British ideas, discussed in
> British newspapers and ultimately embedded in British history
> and remembered in British museums.

This is Lawson's account of how an island population of several
thousand was reduced to an official figure of seventeen inhabitants in fifty years:

> Some indigenous people in Tasmania died at the hands of set-
> tlers who wished to exterminate them. Some died in the process
> of being removed from land that settlers wished to develop.
> Some died in the process of being removed from the land and
> 'civilised' into Europeans. Some died from warfare between the

island's nations that was promoted by their declining resource bases, a result of British presence. Some died of imported diseases. And, of course, some survived, but with little or no access to a culture that the British considered worthless and had attempted to destroy. This happened over the course of a colonisation played out during more than 50 years.

It is not Lawson's contention that there was a state project aimed at genocide – 'clearly there was no state project of extermination in either Tasmania or continental Australia' – but rather that the colonial project itself had a fatal logic – 'genocide was the inevitable outcome of a set of British policies, however apparently benign they appeared to their authors' – because 'even those aimed at protection . . . ultimately envisaged no future whatsoever for the original peoples of the island'.

And this is the point that Lawson makes which is so compelling to me, and which is so important to grasp: indigenous Tasmanians were nearly extinguished between the Scylla of extermination and the Charybdis of protection.

These two pincers served the same ends: the preservation and continued prosecution of the colonial enterprise without relent, with sparing pity, but with no pause to the destruction it was so obviously causing the native peoples of the land being colonised, and of which the colonial authorities were acutely conscious long before the bitter end was reached.

This is how Lawson puts it:

the British government knew explicitly that it had unleashed a destructive process that would eradicate those societies. Its representatives disavowed, and indeed even regretted, the exterminatory impacts of their presence, yet they never faltered, never sought to roll back colonial development. Indeed, they even developed an understanding of the world that saw as inevitable the dying out of 'inferior' indigenous races.

Coming to terms with the past

Lawson's is a perspective-shifting analysis for me: that frontier destruction and protection served the same colonial logic. A logic that envisaged *no future* for the native peoples, whose homelands were to be usurped and societies swept aside by the expanding colonies. Which, in the case of the Tasmanians, led to utter destruction.

Of course, I have always understood that protection worked in concert with frontier dispossession, and facilitated it. It is just that protection seemed to be, if not pulling in an opposite direction, then at least divergent – ameliorating the harshness of frontier colonisation. Instead, protection pulled in the same direction as the frontier – which is what Lawson shows so powerfully in the case of its conception and inception in Tasmania.

I am a third-generation legatee of mission protection. The Lutheran mission at Cape Bedford started in 1886 was the initiative of Johann Flierl, a Bavarian missionary en route to German New Guinea. Waylaid in Cooktown, he started the mission after seeing the devastation of the Guugu Yimidhirr peoples in the wake of the Cooktown gold rush of 1873. The following year his successor, George Schwarz, took up Flierl's mission. The mission was an initiative of its society back at Neuendettelsau, not of the colonial government of Queensland, but following the *Aboriginals Protection Act 1897* (later replaced by the *Aboriginals Preservation and Protection Act 1939*) the mission and the Queensland state became entwined. Pursuant to these laws, in 1910 my grandfather was removed from the bush as a boy. Dispossession on the frontier and the state's protection apparatus – native police 'dispersing' the frontier tribes, protectors removing children to the missions, and Aboriginal reserves – led to what would be called the stolen generations. Protection provided new souls for the mission. What began in the 1880s as a safe haven for young women and an enticement for young men wanting partners, from 1900 turned into a receiving station for masses of huddled young, separated from their families.

Protection and preservation were not there for nothing. For the other side of Queensland's frontier had been and still was a charnel house: consisting of moments when the pitiless logic of colonialism ended in genocidal doom for some groups. As Queensland lacks the defining sea boundaries of the Vandemonian island, the annihilation of tribes on the frontier is more obscure. But there is a wide consensus in Aboriginal histories that the fiction of *terra nullius* was turned into the remorseless fact of *homo nullius* in some parts of Queensland.

As inheritors of the mission's religion and traditions, people like me necessarily hold complex perspectives on this history. The missionaries' kindnesses and humanity were mixed with the racialism of the time, and their objection to and support for various aspects of the colonial enterprise does not tell a simple story.

This dialectic has been part of my life and identity. The dingoes and sheep of my own exploration of our mission history as a student at Sydney University spoke to this historical and spiritual turmoil.

I will not get into the permutations of the protection regimes that emerged across the Australian mainland following George Augustus Robinson. The Tasmanian model was ameliorated with the setting aside of Aboriginal reserves in other states and the Northern Territory. The attitudes of the churches towards indigenous cultures, languages and heritage – and the conviction and vigour with which they sought to deracinate their charges – varied widely, according to the proclivities of particular denominations, individual missions within denominations, the personalities of key missionary figures, and the period of history. Therefore, while many missions and government settlements destroyed indigenous cultures and languages, others actively preserved them, and unofficially (and later sometimes officially) allowed Christianity to coexist with native religious beliefs. The language of the Guugu Yimidhirr survived because of Missionary Schwarz's conviction that their mother tongue best conveyed the Gospels to their hearts. Robinson's prototype house of confinement at Wybalena, Flinders Island, might have been the most extreme example, but its original logic remained at the core of all subsequent protection regimes.

So how is this to be dealt with? I cannot let Lawson's thesis on the Tasmanian genocide be set aside, and I also know that without the Lutherans my people would have perished on the Cooktown frontier. It is for me no longer an ambivalence; it is a clear understanding of the good and bad in the past. Yes, it is often said that history has many shades of grey, but this appreciation of complexity and nuance should not provide refuge from the truth that our nation's history includes times of unequivocal evil and times of redeeming goodness.

Whatever the ideological and symbolic villainy he represents to Aboriginal people, there is no mistaking Captain James Cook's extraordinary courage and stature as a seafaring explorer. Indeed, it is ridiculous to dispute it. For me, it is the same with Schwarz. I still cleave to my testimonial to the old man, published in the *Australian* on the eve of the parliamentary apology to the stolen generations:

> The nineteen-year-old Bavarian missionary who came to the year-old Lutheran mission at Cape Bedford in Cape York Peninsula in 1887, and who would spend more than fifty years of his life underwriting the future of the Guugu Yimidhirr people, cannot but be a hero to me and to my people. We owe an unrepayable debt to Georg Heinrich Schwarz and to the white people who supported my grandparents and countless others to rebuild their lives after they arrived at the mission as young children in 1910. My grandfather Ngulunhdhul came in from the local bush to the Aboriginal reserve that was created to facilitate the mission. My great-grandfather Arrimi would remain in the bush in the Cooktown district, constantly evading police attempts to incarcerate him at Palm Island and remaining in contact with his son Ngulunhdhul, and later his grandson, my father. My grandmother was torn away from her family near Chillagoe, to the west of Cairns, and she would lose her own language and culture in favour of the local Guugu Yimidhirr language and culture of her new home. Indeed, it was the creation of reserves and the establishment of missions that enabled Aboriginal cultures and languages to survive throughout Cape York Peninsula. Today, those two young children who met at the mission have scores of descendants who owe their existence to their determination to survive in the teeth of hardship and loss. Schwarz embodied all of the strengths, weaknesses and contradictions that one would expect of a man who placed himself in the crucible of history. Would that we were judged by history in the way we might be tempted to judge Schwarz – we are not a bootlace on the courage and achievement of such people.

My childhood home was on the first street on the northernmost side of the village, named after Flierl. Next is the main street named Muni, a rendering of Schwarz's Guugu Yimidhirr name. These parallel streets name the key figures of our mission history in succession. The third is named after Wilhelm Poland, who, supporting Schwarz, raised a young family in the earliest years of the mission. A prolific writer and translator, he gave an account of the capture by troopers in July 1888 of Didegal, one of the Guugu Yimidhirr still living in the bush, who was suspected of killing a white man three months before. Didegal was treated as an outlaw, like my great-grandfather. Arrimi eluded police all his life, but Didegal did not:

> But, this time, Didegal's fate was sealed; he was the victim of his own treachery. On the following morning, his pursuers had little difficulty in tracing the clear imprint of his footsteps through soot and ash, and had completed their mission before midday. The man who was still planning mischief 24 hours previously now stood before us in irons, but with that characteristic look of sneering disdain still dominating his dark features. I must admit, I felt a certain compassion towards him. Was he not, after all, a poor, misguided heathen?
>
> After a short break, the troopers saddled their horses, shouldered their guns, indicated to the captive that he was to follow them, and made their way back into the privacy and secrecy of the bush.
>
> No one ever saw Didegal again. Some distance from the beaten track the party was ordered to a halt, a shot was fired, and Didegal was dispatched for good. He was, after all, only a black fellow.

This is what I mean by the casual parsimony of killing on the frontier. Anonymous, extrajudicial, unreported, mundane. Like eradicating vermin. Or inferior beings of human likeness.

A Rightful Place

Burning Men: An American Triptych

Guy Rundle

Pete Seeger

There are people who die at a great age, and it seems impossible they were still alive. When the writer Edward Upward, a quint-essentially 1930s writer, Berlin and cabbage soup and railways, died in 2009, amid Facebook and convenience stores, it seemed like a sort of trick of the century. That is not the case with Pete Seeger, the musician and activist, whose passing at the age of ninety-four marks the end of a long continuity.

Last year he was playing at gatherings at the tail-end of the Occupy movement; he did the first of these in the late '30s, a tall young man of ferocious energy, wielding a five-string banjo, the then somewhat obscure instrument he'd heard played at a square dance in North Carolina. Before the guitar went electric, the banjo was electrifying, its sharp strings and hard shell giving it an urgent intensity. Seeger sang and played it for strike parties, union benefits, hunger marches, peace rallies; later, for civil rights rallies, antiwar rallies, counterculture gatherings, anti-nuclear concerts, the global anti-capitalist movement, Iraq War rallies, and Occupy. He played protest songs and old folk ballads, songs of war and love, and thousands of children's songs. He revived and sharpened 'We Shall Overcome', wrote 'Where Have All the Flowers Gone', 'Turn! Turn! Turn!' and dozens more, made famous 'The Lion Sleeps Tonight' and dozens more.

He was the straight and continent man to Woody Guthrie's

tempestuous, tormented – and tormenting – short existence, and the carrier of much of his memory to new generations. He was part of a vast undertaking, a movement as wide as the century, and his name stands for thousands less well known, or not at all. But he was also a leader, a regrouper, someone who pulled people together and sent things in a certain direction.

In the '40s, he organised the Almanac Singers, and then the Weavers, groups that took folk into the mainstream. Much of that music, smoothed out for commercial use, seems anodyne today – the Seekers, as the name maybe suggests, were pretty much a mildly rocked-up copy of the Weavers – but it introduced folk into the bloodstream of American culture. The Weavers' reunion concert at Carnegie Hall in 1955 – after they had been blacklisted from TV and radio for several years – and the album that came from it marks the start of the folk boom that would explode in, and in part shape, the '60s.

But Seeger was as much an activist pure and simple as a musician who did benefit gigs. His politics were initially hard-Left. Coming from a prosperous liberal family – he was at that North Carolina square dance because his father was taping the music there, in the manner of many at a time when genuine folk cultures were falling victim to highways, cities and radio – he went into the Communist Party in the late '30s, at a time when Communism seemed to many to be the only movement capable of resisting Fascism. That he stayed it in through its peregrinations in the '40s – playing anti-war songs in the period of the Nazi–Soviet pact, and then Leftist patriotic ones after the USSR was invaded – was something he would later be rueful about. His seven years or so with the party will doubtless form the nub of much right-wing commentary. But retrospect is kind. Just as everyone who does past-life regression discovers themselves to be Cleopatra or Caesar, everyone who judges decades past imagines they would have been Orwell. Since there was only one of him, and not many more others like him, it is a rather self-serving delusion.

Feted in the anti-Fascist '40s, Seeger rapidly became a target of the blacklist. The process was altogether more brutal than it is often represented to be, since the intent was not merely to bar people from media access, but also to deny them employment and destroy them psychologically. Families were targeted, and even extended families. The numerous resulting suicides were really homicides.

Yet many at the time bore this and other dangers – beatings, and worse, at civil rights rallies – and stayed upright, and Seeger was one of them. After being jailed for refusing to name names before the House Un-American Activities Committee, he was banned from TV and many venues until the late 1960s. He began playing at colleges, effectively sparking off the college entertainment circuit, and writing and publishing musical how-to books. In the '50s, he and his wife, Toshi, who died last year after seventy years of marriage, built a cabin up the Hudson River and began campaigning for the clean-up of what had become an outfall pipe. Their campaign of sailing the river and raising awareness was an early model of a localised, site-specific campaign with a global message. He also created children's music organisations for ghettoised urban kids to get to sing and play, funded by the royalties that came in from recordings that were adaptations of traditional songs.

In that respect, as much as being a radical, he was a conserving, conservative figure – a reminder that a section of the Left, over this century, did the work that many conservatives contributed little to, allied as they were with a nihilistic modernising liberalism. We conserved the cities, the buildings, the habitats, the folk culture and the commitment to serious art that the Right were happy to see swept away by market forces. Seeger was an essential part of that, because he and others saw the way in which the disappearance of a folk culture – dying from the late nineteenth century onwards, crowded out by an industrially produced culture – was theft, an alienation of our lives, of the immediate simplicity that such a culture offers. The effort to reintroduce it was part of a great cultural renewal in the 1960s, when we began to push back against the creation of monolithic suburbs, the destruction of living cities, the imposition of a drab and conformist lifestyle.

Too successful, perhaps; the folk revolution changed, above all, the way we do early schooling, the songs we learnt, the stories we heard, the forms of organised play. It fused itself with a philosophical search for authenticity in a commodified world and became, through a transformed popular music, the voice of that search.

It was inevitable that that would come to be the thing we would flee from, whether through Bob Dylan's turn to electric music or the punk rendering in which the authentic was necessarily the pessimistic – or now, through our simple distancing from it, via a movie like *Inside Llewyn Davis*, which treats the era that Seeger helped create as one as distant as the Pharaohs. But by now, the historical work of its content has been done. We regained a dimension of life we had lost, even if endless primary school singalongs or *Sesame Street* rejigs make it impossible to now hear the rawness and exuberance that 'If I Had a Hammer' or 'Guantanamera' had on first hearing, among the lush and overproduced lounge music of the '50s.

Seeger was dubbed 'Mr Saint' by those around him. Unquestionably, it was not a simple compliment, but neither was it purely sarcastic. He left the Weavers when they decided to do a cigarette commercial; he donated his fees on 'The Lion Sleeps Tonight' back to the composer, Solomon Linda, when he found out it was not a traditional song (the song's US publishers stole the fees back again). Like many who live long and are famous in this game, he was quite possibly impossible and imperious at times, and may well have got credit due to someone else.

The dust-bowl aesthetic he took on – never as stagily as Guthrie – was no doubt as irritating to his contemporaries as Bruce Springsteen's born-again fauxletarianism was in the '70s. Time has elided the fact that he was the private school–educated son of a New England, New Deal family. Black-and-white film has done its work, rendering the past authentic in a way that we feel we have lost. But of course that is a little true: Seeger and Guthrie and others were not trying on a new image, they were committing to a movement and a world; that world took them on and changed them, and Seeger at least lived long enough to be part of the years when everything turned, turned. That may be an occasion for nostalgia, but it can also be one for self-renewal.

In an era when the gains are small and the scope for change has become modest, it is easy to take refuge in a pessimism, a paranoia, an idea of permanent dissidence that aims for no more than to make known its refusal of consent. Pete Seeger's long life reminds us to think otherwise. When he began, at the tail-end of the Depression and the beginning of a total war, black people were being hanged from trees on a harsh word, on mistaken identity, on a whim; the world was carved up into a number of European and American empires; a casual and near universal anti-Semitism girded and protected its violent and vicious expression in Germany and Eastern Europe; a woman could be sacked from her half-pay job for getting married, for kicking back against a sexual shake-down; a child could die because no one could afford the price of a doctor. In whole areas of the world now, these things do not happen, not as a matter of course, and when they do it is an exception, not a rule, and the word goes out worldwide. When a gay man is killed in Idaho or a woman pack-raped in India, a synagogue attacked or a footballer abused, there is outcry.

Some of it, maybe much of it, is self-serving and hypocritical, or silly, or feeds a sense of self-satisfaction. Some of it is used to obscure other acts that it is inconvenient to note: the burning and bombing of mosques, for example. Some things go backwards at a rapid clip. But the world where such things could get no more than a shrug of the shoulders is fading fast to sepia. If it feels some-times that a radical spirit has departed the place, that is because we live after a great surge towards that new time, the period from World War II to the end of the '60s, to be seen properly as a single unified period, a great social revolution.

If it often seems like we missed the best of it, well, we missed the worst of it, too, both the delusional pursuits of utopia – as such things are often portrayed – and the grim choice between armed camps, as they more often were. And if it looks like the one thing we did not achieve was a greater economic equality, some sort of democratic control over the means of how we live, then it's worth remembering how poor poverty was for many, and how thread-bare of opportunity was even prosperity; if it feels like we have exchanged those limits for a plenty that is immersing us in a cul-ture of glut, surplus, waste, atomisation and spiritual damage, well, that is the next battle to be won, the next thing to make vis-ible. If the struggle to stop lunatics from torching the planet feels like playing on defence, it isn't – this battle was always going to come, not simply to restrain a bunch of criminals and psycho-paths, but to reassert the global ownership of the shared resources of a finite existence.

All this is encompassed by Pete Seeger's long life – all that, and the thousands, less well known or not at all, who worked with him, influenced him, taught him. There are times when the image of someone like Pete Seeger – standing ramrod-tall, singing defiance, before a crowd over six decades, all over YouTube – seems impossible to live up to. But the example is there, not to allow us to reproach ourselves for the time when the strength or the vision fails; it is there to encourage us to stand back up again when we have fallen or been knocked down, with as much spine as we can muster. No one can ask more of us or themselves than that; we cannot give more than that because that is all that is in our power to give.

That is what I take from Pete Seeger's life, and we shall overcome, someday.

True Detective

'Someone once said to me, "Time is a flat circle."' Leaning back in the plastic chair in the untidy interview room, the interrogatee, scrawny, mustachioed, wild-haired, is waxing philosophical to two bemused cops questioning him. 'So Death invented time to grow the things it wanted to kill.' 'You boys ever heard of the M-brane universe?'

What else could this be but *True Detective*, the latest greatest-ever television series from HBO, eight one-hour episodes ostensibly centred around a single crime, focused on a detective duo, Marty and Rust (Woody Harrelson and Matthew McConaughey), one a family man, apparently uncomplicated, the other single, driven, dark. Based in the hinterland of Louisiana, a mid-range American no-space, swampy land, boxy towns, car parks, low-slung houses, trailers, broken-down gas stations, *TD* starts with the discovery of a murdered girl's body, ritually arranged, antlers attached to her body, in some form of ritual killing.

Twenty years ago, it's the sort of murder no one would put in a TV show; now, thanks to fourteen seasons of *Law and Order: SVU*, it's a commonplace, almost a little below par. What, only a ritual satanic murder in the Bayou? Will this really sustain eight hours? But *TD* quickly moves into a more complex mode, split across past and present – and then more than that. The story itself is coming out of the recent past, recounted by both Marty and Rust separately, in long police interviews. Maybe a decade, maybe fifteen years separates the two times.

Marty wears a better suit, has grown chunky, having clearly ridden up the chain of command; Rust is the wildman, with the frontier hair and the powerful thirst. Something, in the interim, happened, and not just to him. What, we don't know. We don't know why they are being questioned, whether it relates to the case that unfolds through their recounting, or something that happened between those two events, how past/present/future connect. Soon we have more dimensions to deal with. Rust, it transpires, has joined the Louisiana PD after years undercover in Texas, an extended 'mission' as a drifting minor drug dealer, elements of which come roaring back into the 'present' of the core story. Yet at episode five, after the pair triumphantly bust a neo-Nazi meth outfit with a sideline in child rape, the story lurches forwards, six years, to the early 2000s.

The partnership, having had years of coexistence, has started to collapse inwardly. Marty is content to work cases as they come, and maintain a fragile relationship with the wife he had humiliated by serial infidelity six years earlier; Rust has continued to pursue a line of inquiry that takes in lost children, fundamentalist preachers, swamp people, the police department and much else. But it all comes apart when Marty's wife fucks Rust, out for revenge after Marty's lapse into infidelity – with a woman he had tried to rescue when she was a child prostitute. They half kill each other, Rust departs, is gone for a decade, and the questioning occurs after he has returned. The story closes up, and the present becomes an excavation of the past.

To thus summarise, and oversimplify, and omit crucial facts for the sake of those yet to see it, is, it all but goes without saying, entirely to miss the incantatory feel of the series. *True Detective* grows out of the Louisiana swamp like sweetgrass, a place that is in the South, but not of it, an outpost of France's Caribbean empire, full of pirates and vodou, old, old families and long, long decline. New Orleans – the Big Easy, margaritas and cast-iron balconies – never makes an appearance. But nor do we see ever see a Starbucks or a McDonald's. Corporate America – the wholly branded environment – never makes an appearance.

In part that is simple verisimilitude – the rural South is so poor that whole stretches of it are devoid of the big brands that we have come to think of as the ubiquitous texture of American life (helped by product-placement funding of TV and films, which appears to be absent here). But it is also a way of creating an America that is not so much mythical – this is no story of a lost 'real' place – but interstitial. *TD* America hangs somewhere between the '70s, '80s, '90s, 2000s and now. The bars are deliciously scummy, the houses are cookie-cutter exurbia, the popular culture is the sort of stuff – Juice Newton's hit 'Angel of the Morning' – that hangs around for ever on FM radio, that all but seems to have no beginning at all.

That it is a wrecked America goes without saying. America has been wrecked for so long that the portrayal of a hopelessly fallen world, a place of fragments, is now simply the default setting. *The Wire* (and *The Shield*) spent a hundred or so hours describing an America which was a rotting shell of a once vibrant body politic – their worlds only made sense as dysfunctional successors of a once whole-world, places where cities were not ruins, and work and neighbourhood were the centre of life, crime the margins of it. *SVU* became a vast catalogue of big-city life as a charnel house of paedophilia, incest and rape, domesticating those crimes in the same way as crime fiction of the '20s domesticated conscienceless murder as something routine rather than a shocking measure of degeneration in a world after the death of God. Each of these series found a way to mark that decline in its storytelling – such as the moving closing scenes of the fifth season of *The Wire*, a long, wordless montage of a dying city waking up, its depleted docks starting work, its once-great newspaper shredded, and *Breaking Bad* in which the decline is the story.

In *True Detective*, this wreckage is simply assumed. We never – until right at the end – see any of old Louisiana (of which there is plenty); no French Quarters, seaside towns, restored wooden mansions. The place is simply what it has been for decades: one of the poorest worst states of the US; bad housing, cracking freeways and poisoned waterways. This is how it has always been, how it will always be, the flat circle of southern decline. *True Detective* joins its particular field of decline – the slow winnowing of the US, through four decades following the end of the post-war boom – with the longer decline, that of a defeated slave-civilisation, dying these hundred and more years.

TD, though by its name it appeals to the pulp tradition, is in the mainline of southern gothic, something of an understatement.

With Rust, its death-driven wall-eyed obsessive sprouting Nietzsche, its erotomaniac women, its swamp people, its black mamas wit' de vodou secrets – if it were any more Faulkner, it would have its own station on the Upfield Line. Its creator and sole author, Nick Pizzolatto, has a prize-winning volume of short stories to his name – impressive but arty, somewhere in the post-MFA hinterland between McCullers and McCarthy – and a neo-pulp novel *Galveston*, a mark of transition from high to genre fiction, i.e. from one genre to another. That makes him the first real high-culture writer to create a full TV series, and it shows.

David Simon of *Homicide* and *The Wire*, Paul Attanasio of *House*, Vince Gilligan of *Breaking Bad* – they are all first-class writers and producers, but they're coming from pop-culture or journalistic traditions. *True Detective* is a repository of high-culture technique, especially in the rendering of Rust, a character who will not settle into a space on the standard grid of mass-culture character differentiation. He's a man who has done a lot of thinking, too much, of a type that sets him apart from the people he sees around him ('You people – you let your young be eaten as long as you got something to salute,' he says, as he leaves the force, in 2002), but none of which has brought him a wisdom that might bring a sort of peace. His meditations fuse police procedural with a serial monologue of batty speculation about the circular nature of time, the irreducible solipsism of existence (the 'locked room', police slang for an interview, becomes a metaphor for the impossibility of escaping your own consciousness to a 'real') and how this relates to new theories of the cyclic universe, of endless Big Bangs creating and collapsing the same world over and over. Rust's musings come with an explicit death wish – his marriage gone after their infant daughter died – and he regards a potential bullet in the head from infiltrating a bikie gang as a 'zero risk' option. His musings on death, suffering and life are hardly unique to mass cultural style – *SVU* is a psychodynamics casebook, weekly – but what makes them distinctive is their particular mix: cosmic speculations drawing in the mind-boggling world of physics with older early-twentieth-century vitalist speculations about life and death forces, eternity and time.

This sort of thinking works without falling into self-parody because it is not unmoored from the genre it seeks to evoke. It is a glance back at a lot of the *True Detective*–style pulp of the mid-twentieth century, when such musings on the nature of life, death and eternity were bubbling into the culture. This is particularly so with the ideas of Nietzsche – the centrality of Will and a life force, and living according to it – which took America by storm in the first decades of the century. As Jennifer Ratner-Rosenhagen noted in *American Nietzsche*, everyone imbibed this idea of a force in existence independent of morality, 'from anarchists to baptist ministers', because it gave an oomph to an American individualism become jaded in the cogs and wheels of a mass society. In *True Detective*, Rust ain't the only one harking back to Germanic ideas of a terrifying universe that we must try to tame: the neo-Nazi speedfreak apprehended, and then murdered, talks of a 'circular universe' moments before Marty murders him, enraged at his lethal rape of children. 'That Nietzsche shit,' Rust mutters. Later, he will play it back to the detectives interviewing him in the 'present', and uncoil his whole cosmology, the notion that Being is Death – static and unchanging at its root, originator of Time, for it could not be Death without Life.

This is the sort of stuff – out of Schopenhauer, and before him, the ancient Hindu Upanishad texts – that makes Nietzsche sound like a bubbly life coach. Rust scorns self-serving versions of it – that Nietzsche shit – because its notion of making meaning through an exercise of Will is as much a denial of the truth of the universe as the Judeo-Christian notion of redemption it seeks to displace. Rust is not going to war against evil, against suffering – he is going to war against Will itself, against the wayward notion that desire acted on is any sort of action at all. Marty counterpoints him, blowing up his own life through infidelities lacking even the swagger of passionate love, losing his family absolutely, winding up in an efficiency flat, eating TV dinners.

(Yes, *TD* is very male. *Existenz* is something men struggle with, and women – most of whom bear a striking resemblance to the silhouette Playboy logo – love and hate the men as they struggle with das Being. One could say that the women are portrayed as the sane ones, but that hardly compensates. One simply has to take it as part of the genre – or read against it, as a portrayal of the manner in which masculinity is a machine for turning desire into philosophy, for its own purposes.)

The philosophising would verge on pseudo-intellectual flim-flam were such content not mirrored in the form. For *TD* uses long-form TV's most distinctive resource – tense shifts and multiple time streams – to give that sense of circular action. Time flows in *TD*, but more like the intersecting runnels of a bayou than as a river, criss-crossing, expansive and formless. Multi-stream TV series have hitherto used different stocks (or video imitations thereof) and filters to separate past and present. There is none of that here, and the absence of external markers of different eras means that the story happens both in time and all at once – made more complex by the fact that the series repays multiple viewings of each episode. The muted particularities blur the line between subjective and objective is this happening, in this order, in the world, or in the mind? If so, whose? Crucial events happen because characters have lied in earlier time streams – so we do not know that the story is the story. Have we been lied to? Is there a series of lies behind those revealed? Is the actual, final revelation a decoy? The possibility, and a few well-placed remarks in episode eight, leave open a continuation in further seasons – although it is difficult to imagine Rust, a hard-eyed adamantine performance by McConaughey, having anything like the impact or gravitas in a second season.

Difficult to know, too, how something like *TD* will hold up, in five years, ten, fifty. Gunplay and speculation on the eternal is pretty much the essence of a certain type of hard-boiled crime fiction, but the nature of the speculation tends to change. Ultimately, philosophical preoccupations tend to be framed by the era in which they take place, and the world of *True Detective* is one in which imposing will hasn't gone too well for quite a while. Whatever chance the place had to break out of its ancient torpor has been sealed over by more recent torpor, with the same families and forces receding ever further behind the scenes.

True Detective is an example of the much-celebrated 'new golden age' of US television, but what is of most significance is that the television comes together as the US comes apart. The long-form series has become the empyrean in which one can get the measure of an empire which can no longer comprehend itself. History, when it runs out of Time, invents Culture to grow the things it wants to kill, and that is where we are now, waiting for season two.

Elliot Rodger

Last Sunday afternoon, I made a cup of coffee, fired up the laptop, went online, noticed that the 'manifesto' of Elliot Rodger, the Isla Vista killer, had been posted, clicked on to it – and didn't get up for two hours. I didn't move, save to scroll down, and at one point to feel my jaw drop.

If you haven't read Rodger's 140-page document, you may well not want to. It was described in the news as a 'rambling manifesto'. If only. It is neither. A narrative of his life up to the point where he started on the series of killings, 'My Twisted World' is no manifesto, nor is it rambling. Repetitive, yes, as Rodger recounts his perceived humiliations and injustices, and above all his rejection by women. But what it is is relentless, driving, as beat by beat Rodger draws us towards the event that happened soon after it was sent to friends and associates – the stabbing murder of three people in his apartment, and the drive-by shooting of three more, two of them young women outside a sorority house – just as he had said it would. It is a terrifying read because you know what's coming, and because it has the structure of a thriller and may well have been shaped by the genre.

Having detailed a happy early childhood up to the age of six, Rodger starts to paint a picture of things going wrong and a struggle to join the world of love and connection. Then, around a hundred pages in, the 'Day of Retribution' appears. The 'Day of Retribution' is – well, exactly what happened. Rodger begins suggesting it after he has started to fume with obsessive misogyny, snobbery and casual racist elitism: women are animals who cannot recognise a great man like himself when they see him, black people and poor whites are sub-human. He does not want to start the Day of Retribution, he says; he will try to rejoin humanity (on his own terms). Eventually, he concludes that there is no alternative. He must take revenge on both women and men – women as a whole because they have rejected him, men because they have been accomplices to such rejection. The narrative finishes with him musing that he will have to kill his housemates in order to complete his plan. This is exactly what he appears to have done.

'My Twisted World' is an appalling document, because of the events that occasioned its publicity, but it is also a revealing one. It is the meticulous record of a man suffering a total collapse of mind, subjectivity and selfhood, from a very specific and pure form of narcissistic disordering. Various pundits have tried to attach more complex, and tendentious, diagnoses to Rodger's behaviour – most of them relying on spurious neuro-psychiatry – but what is plain, as a first-order description, is that Rodger was poisoned by dysfunctional narcissism. By 'narcissism' we mean a basic inability to get the relationship between self and world right. The correct idea of that relationship is that we are limited selves in a world with other people, who have their own projects and motives. The narcissistic reversal is that the world is seen only and always as a function of the self, which is always morally blameless. We are all sufficiently narcissistic to function as subjects, organising the world around us. But we recognise our reality in it – that we fall short in our actions, that we are limited in our powers, that reality is a resistant other that we negotiate.

Occasionally, our narcissism gets off the leash – when we overestimate our worth, underplay our culpability in our failures, forget the otherness of others and the legitimacy of their worlds. For some very small number of people, that narcissistic disordering becomes jammed on, totalising, and consumes whatever real assessment of the world they can make. Such people are everywhere, everybody knows one – those in the entertainment industry know many. They usually blaze bright young – and, if they make a sufficient success of it, can accrue sufficient social power to make people put up with their shit. Those who don't, when they fall, fall far, become malign. They're the office sociopath, the paranoid in the MP's waiting room, the adult child who blows up the family at Christmas, and on, and on. Rodger's record of his decline and fall is a portrait of someone at the very extreme of that disordering – not simply because he ended it with mass murder, but because the record of his life is so relentlessly miserable and wounded.

Like many such afflicted people, Rodger's world-perception seemed to go wrong pretty early: he records that from the age of eight he was having great problems connecting with other children, attaching, simply being lost in activity. Whether that was actually the case when he was eight is less important than that he had come to believe it was. His record of friendships from that age is coloured by this lack of attachment – and then by the beginnings of narcissism, the overvaluation of self, to compensate for the perceived disdain. Rodger's narrative is a meticulous record of the way in which such a narcissistic shell forms: he becomes increasingly approving of his own appearance (he was blessed/cursed with being conventionally attractive), and then by stages masculinist, racist and snobbish. What developed early, it seems, was a haughtiness – a belief that people should come to him to be friends. When adolescence hit, that was extended to girls. By the time he had passed through five years of the daunting US high-school system, he had lost all capacity to connect or to make a way in the world. By the time he was eighteen, these failures had left him delusional about his own status. He was not recognised as great and a superior mate, so all women must be fools, animals; all men who were not Eurasian as he was were crude and ugly (he seemed to take pride in the received notion that Eurasian men have 'elegant' features); two roommates, geeky types assigned to him by his college, show him friendship, but are 'obviously' too low-class to connect with. And so on.

As a record it is loathsome, it is pathetic, but above all it is deeply, deeply sad, for it is a record of someone locked in a prison of self, of the eternal defence of a bounded self. In the culture we have now, it is an easy trap to fall into.

Sadder still, however, was the reaction to the killings, and to Rodger. Though he had said he would kill women for their slights against him, he killed more men than women. He was a classic 'universalist' killer, not greatly different from the McDonald's mass killers of the 1980s and '90s, the school and cinema killers of the 2000s. Yet because of his writings, his act was quickly recuperated as a misogynist killing – a simplistic and self-serving interpretation. The act, evil, futile and despairing, was given a meaning it did not possess, in service to a set of social causes. Cause and effect were reversed. Being narcissistic-disordered, Rodger had gradually acquired various hatreds, which explained to him why he felt so rejected. But anyone reading 'My Twisted World' ought to see that the original thought was not programmatic. There was just pain and then hate as a way of transmuting it.

You would not have known this to read the reaction to the event and to the writings. One of the things that was most shocking was the annihilating disdain directed at Rodger – or at his meme, the man himself was dead – as a way of dealing with his atrocious act.

Because he had thematised his general killing spree as particular – said that he was killing women, when he in fact killed more men – he was dismissed as a 'loser', 'garbage' and much more, on Twitter, Facebook and elsewhere. People tried to outdo each other in heaping abuse on his memory. There was also a counter-reaction – men on bodybuilding and 'pick-up artist' sites lauding his dark existential act. Everyone seemed eager to construct a general killing as specific, for their own cultural-political ends.

This served several purposes. First off, it was atavistic, like the mediaeval practice of putting dead people on trial for their misdeeds and rehanging them. No five-minute hate session directed at this very disturbed human being was going to bring back the people he killed, so what of it? It was designed to deal with our anguish – especially the anguish of Americans at a process they cannot control, because violent, disturbed people can get handguns. There are any number of Elliot Rodgers walking around London, Sydney, etc., today, seething and bubbling with hate – but they do not live in a culture that is both violent and which offers easy access to the means of delivering violence.

But there was another purpose to it, far from consciously perceived, and that was the advancement of an ideology – that of a cultural-political elite focused on highly branded oppression. Rodger's sin was against the six people he killed, but the chaotic randomness of his acts makes less of a story than that it was a specific killing, for misogyny. The lesson drawn is that insistence on the 'wiping out' of misogyny, and on a sort of heightened self-vigilance about one's negative thoughts, would serve to lessen the violence.

As Jeff Sparrow suggests in a perceptive *Counterpunch* piece, that is to mistake the specific for the general. One could add that it would also be counter-productive. The idea that dark, murderous and irrational impulses can be legislated out of existence, and that this is the lesson we should take from the event, is not only ludicrously misplaced, it also has a narrow class agenda. The people imposing such a specific cultural order, such a regime of good thoughts, are the essentially the people who run the higher levels of a post-industrial society, the controllers of discourse. Their particular ideology – which they regard as an eternal truth – is that all racist, sexist, etc. thought should be wiped out at the level of thought rather than at the level of public discourse and action.

The obvious effect of trying to achieve this is that such thought comes to be regarded as more authentic the more it is suppressed, giving it a gloss of liberation. The past thirty years or so have been shaped by this extended culture/class war, whereby fractions of the diminishing working and lower-middle classes have reacted to their loss of power through a sort of deliberately crude cultural resistance. You can see how this bubbled up in popular culture, especially in stand-up comedy, which acts as a social release valve. The more people insist on a no-tolerance policy towards 'rape culture', the more stand-ups, male and female, gleefully fill their set with rape jokes. So it goes. In this class war, which often has a faux proletarianism about it, Elliot Rodger is treated as a scapegoat, to be loaded up with the sins of society and sent into the wilderness. The overall purpose is to deny that social processes produce such tormented, and very, very occasionally violent, individuals.

But the plain fact is that if you have a hyper-individualist society, you will produce people such as Elliot Rodger. His account of his life is illuminating because it is such a record of cultural emptiness. Rodger lived in a world of placeless suburbs, decommunalised schools and screens, screens, screens. It is our world, the one we have made, and one whose overwhelming characteristic is atomisation. The passage from childhood to tweendom to adolescence today is one in which, to a historically unprecedented degree, people must be 'entrepreneurial subjects' – they must assemble their own social context, rather than being able to rely on given networks of family and neighbourhood/culture, something that people could rely on (and be stifled by) until the 1960s. Thus, for every three or four people who succeed at this, there will be one who fails – and as society becomes more disconnected, the ratio will become more brutal.

Jeff Sparrow gives a Marxist account of this, suggesting that the market form creates the alienation that feeds – in very rare cases – the murderousness of an Elliot Rodger. That is only half the story. At the root is a deeper cultural problem: the atomisation of a high-tech (a)social life, the disintegration of the self that cannot project. Trying to talk about this is difficult, because one effect of this atomisation has been a diminished capacity for people to think about individual selfhood as a social product. As common sense, everyone knows this to be true – any classroom of kids will produce a bell curve of nerds, geeks, drones, normals, outlaws and freaks, and they will essentially define each other into the roles – but for a couple of decades now we have been blasted with the liberal ideology that we are somehow self-choosing sovereign minds.

It is an utterly incoherent idea – who would choose to be as fucked-up as Elliot Rodger? – but it is powerful because it dovetails with notions of consumer choice. Thus the resulting problems of social subjectivity – increasing numbers of children who become dysfunctional and unhappy in adolescence – can be seen as at first a failure of will, and then a brain malfunction, and treated with drugs. In a final move, this connects with narrow thought-policing notions of anti-sexism, and anti-racism, and so on, by which a deeply disturbed person can be dismissed as human 'garbage' on the same grounds – that he could not maintain a mental sovereignty which would allow him to exercise restraint over his most violent urges. It is another example of the way in which an ostensible progressivism serves as an ideological cover for a neoliberal triumphalism. Sheer self-interest suggests that such simplistic notions be knocked on the head.

Toxic narcissism is to our current social order what rickets was to nineteenth-century capitalism – pervasive, so common as to be half-hidden, a byproduct of the system itself. Your child is not going to gun people down – such symbolic, grotesque acts are vanishingly rare (and fifteen women in the US have been murdered in boring, unremarkable fashion by their partners since the Isla Vista massacre happened) – but he may be the one who falters, at the age of eight, eleven, thirteen. It is more likely that this will happen to him than it would have been thirty, fifty, 100 years ago. It is more important than ever that we think about subjectivity and selfhood as a complex social process rather than simply ape the winners-and-losers model pushed on us relentlessly by the culture we are being shaped by. And that we still extend, to even the most destructive among us, the notion of a shared humanity, and the possibility that things could have been otherwise.

Crikey/Daily Review

May Day: How the Left Was Lost

Christos Tsiolkas

It is May 2013, a week after Orthodox Easter, and for my final night in Athens my cousins have taken me out to dinner at a taverna in the working-class neighbourhood of Kipoupoli. It is a warm night in the Greek capital, the alcohol is flowing, and after finishing our meals we all take out our cigarettes and puff away under the English-language no-smoking sign.

I have spent a fortnight in Greece, and every day has been a reminder of the social death brought on by the financial crisis and austerity measures: banks of homeless people sleeping on the streets near the university, the sullen and resentful faces of the refugee prostitutes soliciting clients behind the markets in Omonia, police in riot gear congregating on street corners in the Plaka, teenage heroin-users sharing needles in the parks, a pensioner blowing his brains out at Syntagma Square because he could no longer keep up with his bills. But tonight I am drinking, and I am reminded of the hospitality and anarchic spirit of the Greeks. Tonight, just for a few hours, in food, drink and song, we can forget the cuts to wages and the pensions, the International Monetary Fund, the European Commission and the European Central Bank – that bloody Troika and its austerity. Tonight, I can feel proud of my Greek heritage.

I find myself in an intense and exhilarating conversation with a nineteen-year-old law student. Dimitri is intelligent and erudite. He offers a devastating critique of both neoliberalism and social democracy, arguing that the global financial crisis has extinguished the post–World War II consensus between capital and labour. For Dimitri, the ideologies of the past century have little relevance and they no longer offer any social or economic value. His contempt not only for Greece's parties of the centre-left and centre-right, PASOK and New Democracy respectively, but also for Syriza, the radical left coalition that he dismisses as social democracy cloaked in Marxist rhetoric, is matched by his distrust and abhorrence of the European Union. As I listen to him, I tell myself that even though youth unemployment is scraping sixty per cent, even though his generation is one that free-marketeers, social democrats and economists have collectively forsaken as 'lost', this cohort will defy the bankers, bureaucrats and politicians. I interrupt his impassioned flow to ask a question.

'What does the European Union mean to you? Do you feel European?'

He is taken aback. I have asked this question of cosmopolitan Germans, Brits, Dutch and Danes. Publishers, academics, human rights activists and artists, they have answered me with conviction, that yes, they are European and for them the EU is the future. But not for Dimitri.

'Do you want to know what the EU means to me?' He points his cigarette towards the no-smoking sign over my shoulder. 'The EU means anti-smoking laws and copyright laws. That's what the EU cares about. It doesn't give a fuck about the people hungry in my country. It doesn't care that my generation won't know what it means to work.'

I ask him another question. 'So who did you vote for last year?'

There is no hesitation this time. 'Me? I voted for the Golden Dawn.'

He voted for the Fascists.

*

Greece is radically and violently transformed into the land field of 'wasted lives' in the giant trashcan of global capitalism. Witnessing as I do this novel form of social necrophilia that eats alive every inch of human life, workspace and public space, I cringe at the sound of the words 'sacrifice', 'rescue' and making Greece, according to the claims of Greek PM Antonis

Samaras, a 'success story'. Whose sacrifice and whose rescue?
Who succeeds and who loses?
— Panayota Gounari, 'Neoliberalism as Social Necrophilia:
The case of Greece', 2014

*

My mother and my father, Greek immigrants to Australia, were Paul
Keating's 'true believers'. Their commitment to the Australian Labor
Party was unshakeable. For years I used to boast that I went to my
first demonstration when I was ten years old. It was outside Melbourne
Town Hall, where the governor-general, John Kerr, was to attend a
function not long after the dismissal of the Whitlam government.
My father took me along with a bag of tomatoes to throw at the
miserable royalist dog – his words. It was only recently that my
mother informed me that this wasn't my 'first' demonstration, that
when I was still a toddler she had taken me to one of the anti–
Vietnam War marches. Thinking those protests the preserve of stu-
dents and the radical Left, I expressed my surprise at her involvement.
   'Don't be an idiot,' she responded curtly. 'I had two young sons.
Of course I marched against that stupid imperialist war.'
   Unlike my generation, my parents had first-hand experience of
war. First there was Germany's occupation of Greece during World
War II, and then the wicked testing ground of the emerging Cold
War that was the Greek Civil War in the late 1940s. Those two
calamities destroyed the rural peasant class of Greece, the class to
which my parents belonged. Their families were on opposite sides
of the tragedy, my mother's Communist and my father's anti-
Communist. But though the tragedy of the civil war arguably poisoned Greek politics for three generations, my parents both
believed that in the 'new world', whatever the cost of exile, those
differences could be put aside and replaced by an affirmation of
a political party, the ALP, that took seriously their status as immigrants and as workers. Both my parents were denied education –
that was the privilege of the bourgeoisie in mid-twentieth-century
Europe – so they did not speak in the language of social democracy. But their faith in the ALP centred on that party's commitment to public education, to public health, to industrial rights for
workers and to its opposition to imperialist power.
   The neoliberal economic reforms ushered in by the Hawke and

Keating Labor governments were never explained to my parents and their peers. They extended a faith in both Bob Hawke and Keating, a faith in the ALP, that these reforms were necessary and would not undermine their conditions as workers. But these men and women, who supplied labour for the so-called 'unskilled' textile, car parts and manufacturing industries of the post-war boom, distrusted the language of competition and globalisation that accompanied the reforms. In the late '90s, I interviewed my father and a few of his colleagues, long after they had retired, and all of them expressed a preference for collective bargaining, for a system of arbitration that negotiated between capital and labour as equal partners. It wasn't that they assumed *all* bosses would be mercenary and unjust but they knew that plenty *were*. My father could never understand the logic where the shareholder took priority over the worker; he saw the share market as analogous to the gambling table upon which he and his mates used to play poker or manila. People who moaned over losses on the stock market made him laugh. 'It's gambling,' he would say. 'You win some, you lose some.'

I emerged a relative winner in the era of globalisation. I had to confront the enervating reality of recession in the early 1990s, but by the end of that decade I was part of a cosmopolitan, educated professional class that assumed mobility and flexibility in work, education, living standards, technology and travel. I didn't say it to their faces, but I thought the old people's anxieties and concerns were merely nostalgic, and that they were too uneducated to understand how Keating had saved us from descending into a 'banana republic'.

What I didn't understand then was how crucial that extension of faith from working-class constituencies had been in opening up our markets and ushering in the globalised era. This 'faith' was extended to social-democratic parliamentary parties across the Western world. Towards the end of his life, my father lamented how the public education and health systems had been undermined, and he mistrusted the consensus among democratic parliamentary parties to privilege productivity over equity and the market over civic and community life. He believed that the faith he had placed in the ALP had been betrayed.

I too experienced a betrayal, years later, but for my peers and myself the betrayal was the result of the party's vacillations over asylum-seeker policy and its muted response to climate change, especially when contrasted to the urgency and passion of the Greens. It wasn't that I thought education, health and industrial rights were unimportant – far from it – but in some sense I took them for granted. Unlike my parents, I hadn't known a social order in which they hadn't existed. And as I took them for granted, they were no longer the focus of my political belief, my political commitment.

*

But what if we treated humiliation itself as a cost, a charge to society? What if we decided to 'quantify' the harm done when people are shamed by their fellow citizens before receiving the mere necessities of life? In other words, what if we factored into our estimates of productivity, efficiency, or well-being the difference between a humiliating handout and a benefit as of right? We might conclude that the provision of universal social services, public health insurance, or subsidised public transportation was actually a cost-effective way to achieve our common objectives. Such an exercise is inherently contentious: How do we quantify 'humiliation'? What is the measurable cost of depriving isolated citizens of access to metropolitan resources? How much are we willing to pay for a good society? Unclear. But unless we ask such questions, how can we hope to devise answers?

– Tony Judt, 'What is Living and What is Dead
in Social Democracy?', 2009

*

In 2007 I escorted my mother to the Greek consulate in Melbourne. Her sister was involved in a property dispute in Athens, and my mother needed to sign an affidavit of support, to be witnessed by a member of the consulate staff. We were eventually ushered into a small office where a young Greek man obsessively texted throughout my mother's appointment. He had a bulky gold watch strapped across one wrist; his shirt was neatly pressed and clearly expensive. He hardly said a word to my mother, and I had to stop myself leaning across the desk, grabbing the phone and throwing it against the wall. At one point, my mother, in an attempt to be friendly, asked him what part of Greece he was from. The question made him look up at her for the first time.

'Why? What does it matter?'

My mother, humiliated, mumbled a response.

'I'm Athenian,' he answered shortly, returning his gaze to the screen.

My mother started telling him of when she was a young woman in Athens in the early 1960s, of how hard it was to leave and migrate to Australia, how much she still missed the city. He interrupted her.

'Look, that was a different time,' he said. 'I really can't be bothered with all these old migrant stories. We're European now. The Greece you are referring to doesn't exist anymore.'

My mother and I were both so shocked at his rudeness that we were speechless. She was shaking as we left the consulate.

'They really don't care about us, do they?' she said to me, meekly, and meekness had never been something I had associated with my mother.

A year later, when the global financial crisis had hit, and the news of the human cost of the turmoil in Greece began to filter through to Australia, my first thought was of this young man with his expensive shirt and his gold watch. I wondered if he still had his job. I wondered if he was still proud of being European.

The political tumult of contemporary Greece cannot be separated from the economic turmoil across Europe. But unlike those of Iceland, Ireland and to some extent even Italy, Portugal and Spain, the crisis that Greece now finds itself enduring is also existential. There is a language of retribution directed towards the nation, an accusation that the Greeks had it coming. Stories of wholesale tax avoidance, overly generous pensions and a moribund and bloated public sector have been integral to the reporting of the crisis and its effects. In Australia, it doesn't matter how much I attempt to steer conversations towards questions of EU culpability in blindly bankrolling the Greek state, of how decades-long deregulation of financial markets precipitated the economic collapse, of how social cohesion in Greece is being destroyed by the Dublin Regulation of 2003 (a directive that forces asylum seekers to be returned to the country through which they first entered the EU, which has meant that the countries of southern Europe have had to deal with a disproportionate number of asylum seekers and refugees). In the end, I am always challenged to defend the culpability of the Greek people themselves.

There is a peculiar dissonance between, on one hand, this understanding of the Greek character as lazy, entitled and culpable for the economic mess they now find themselves in and, on the other hand, Australia's recognition of the hardworking Greek migrants who helped build and transform our nation. Is it the challenge and experience of migration itself that defines the Greek Australian? A recurrent cliché of multiculturalism is that migrant communities, wrenched geographically, linguistically and temporally from their homes, maintain a nostalgic and an ahistorical conception of their cultures of origin. When I first returned home to Australia after visiting Greece as a young adult, I crowed mercilessly to my parents that the stories they had told me were no longer true, that the history that had formed them had now vanished. My cousins in Athens had laughed at me when I called older people *théa* and *théo*, auntie and uncle. They saw this as residue of an old peasant and rural past that was irrelevant to their highly urbanised late-twentieth-century nation. 'You're stuck in the past, Mamá and Papá,' I insisted. 'Greece has moved on.'

But just as the Greeks in Greece have changed over the last quarter of a century, so have the Greeks in Australia. The successive waves of immigrants and refugees who came to this country over the past fifty years didn't *bring* multiculturalism with them. Multiculturalism emerged as a consensus within the body politic of the nation, as it negotiated the changing demographics once the White Australia Policy, and the legacy of colonial nationhood, had begun to be dismantled. Multiculturalism has had an impact as much on migrants and refugees as it has on indigenous Australians and Anglo-Celtic Australians. Whatever the contest over what the concept means, whatever the petty or serious racisms still expressed in our country, it's a given now that we're a multi-ethnic society home to numerous religions.

Multiculturalism was never part of the Greece I have been visiting over the past thirty years. It wasn't part of the Greek conception of nationhood before the global financial crisis, and it certainly isn't part of how Greeks have seen themselves since then. And not only in Greece: the antagonism towards multiculturalism is rife throughout the EU. The financial crisis has only exacerbated existing tensions over immigration in Europe. Here it is important to separate the politics of immigration from the politics of asylum. Immigrants in Europe, and their children, remain non-European in both political and popular language. The right-wing parties on the rise throughout the continent – in Holland and Denmark, Sweden and Hungary, the Czech Republic and France – are not only anti–asylum seeker but also anti-*immigrant*. In Australia, mired for more than fifteen years in the toxic politics of border security and asylum, we can easily disregard the importance of this distinction.

The argument propounded by the right in Europe is that immigration is one of the main reasons the social democratic consensus has shattered. Fears are largely directed towards Asian, Arab and African immigrants but there is also a resentment of Balkan and Eastern European immigrants. That resentment reveals a contradiction at the heart of the EU project that has never been successfully resolved: that the economic union that arose out of Cold War politics was about *Western* European nations rebuilding and reconstructing European identity after the calamities of the world wars. According to the right-wing propaganda, the notion of who is European was decided not in national parliaments but in Brussels.

In his 2009 memoir *Returning to Reims,* translated into English last year, the French cultural critic Didier Eribon writes of visiting his family home in north-eastern France thirty years after he deliberately turned his back on the working-class world from which he emerged. In that long period of exile from his family, Eribon took on academic postings in Paris, wrote a biography of Michel Foucault, and became a prominent critic of and from within the Left. Over those three decades, he effaced his working-class heritage, and understood this denial to be necessary in order to refashion himself as a leftist cultural critic in Europe.

A call from his mother prompts the return home. His father – a factory labourer, a drinker and, from what Eribon writes, a hard and sometimes abusive man – is dying. It is his father's sexism and homophobia that has engendered the long silence between them. During Eribon's youth, his family and their community were Communists. On his return to Reims, he is shocked to discover that his parents and his brothers have abandoned socialism and now vote for the far-right Front National.

Eribon never reconciles with his father. He does not attend the old man's funeral. He can't abandon the rage of his adolescence, and he seethes at the xenophobia, casual sexism and homophobia of his brothers. He finds it hard to understand how they have remained untouched by the liberating social movements that have defined his life after Reims. But what remains unanswered in the book is the question of how his family were to make sense of such cultural transformations if Eribon himself saw it as a precondition of his liberation that he break his link to family and to his class. Eribon's portrait of his family is not distant; it is familiar and recognisable. As is the paradox of his avowal of socialist and social democratic principles while at the same time deploring and rejecting the working class itself. I am not sure what the French term for 'bogan' might be, or even if there exists an equivalent in the language, but the distaste, shame and fear that Eribon expresses when he writes about his family are contained in that word, in how it is used here in Australia.

Australia has escaped the worst manifestations of the global financial crisis. There is great wealth here, and unemployment levels are comparatively low. On returning to Melbourne from Athens, I found myself fulminating, in ways not too dissimilar to Eribon, at the complacency and entitlement of my nation. But my rage was tempered when I left the inner city to visit family and friends in outer suburbia.

If many of them were now indeed 'cashed-up bogans', just as many were unemployed. Many were on welfare, many on drugs both illegal and prescribed. Even among the 'cashed-up bogans', there was a real fear about how long this period of extended prosperity was going to last. And unlike my friends in the inner city, they worked in trades and jobs that still required hard physical labour, or they worked in retail, or as domestics, or in health services, where repetitive constant movement – from scanning a barcode to stripping and making up a bed to mopping a floor – could also lead to long-term physical damage. They were fearful of a rise in interest rates and in rents and of the loss of permanent jobs to casualisation. If I complained to them about so many of us entering the private health system or sending our children to private schools, they pointed out that the nearby public schools and the public hospitals were strained and over-committed.

Did they care about same-sex marriage? Some did, some didn't. Did they agree with the bipartisan insistence on offshore processing for asylum seekers? Most did, some didn't. Did they think that the media's treatment of Julia Gillard had been misogynistic? Some did, some didn't. Were they worried about climate change? Some were not, most keenly were. But none of these issues were central to their concerns. The cost of living, the uncertainty of employment, the erosion of public health and public education – that's what mattered.

*

I think more of the little kids from a school in a little village in Niger who get teaching two hours a day, sharing one chair for three of them, and who are very keen to get an education. I have them in my mind all the time. Because I think they need even more help than the people in Athens.

– CHRISTINE LAGARDE, managing director,
International Monetary Fund, 2012

*

It was on the drive from Athens airport to my aunt's house on the western outskirts of the city that the immense transformation wrought by the global financial crisis hit home. Along the motorway, the billboards were all bare; there was only mile after mile of skeletal scaffolding. The Greek economy had come to such a standstill that no one was bothering to advertise anymore. This was a first-world nation, part of the EU, and yet capital had drained from it. The empty billboards seemed to presage an apocalyptic future.

The architects of austerity promise that the advertising will eventually return, that the ruthless measures introduced are necessary and will result in a more productive and economically sustainable Greece. But as anyone who has lived through unemployment understands, the social cost of this economic experiment will be paid by the present generation and the generation to come.

It was a central component of the social democratic consensus across the Western world that parliamentary democracy, hand in hand with the welfare state, would guarantee productive and sustaining labour for working-class people. For all of our outrage and mockery when Gina Rinehart extols the cheapness of African labour compared to Australian labour, at its essence the sentiment is not so different to Christine Lagarde's privileging of a sub-Saharan child's poverty over that of an Athenian child. Of course, it is a matter of degree, and only a fool would deny it: the poverty in the developing world is incalculably more pernicious and inhumane. But the faith my parents placed in Hawke and Keating's neoliberal reforms was predicated on the promise not that they would democratise poverty but that they would democratise opportunity. That too was the promise of social democratic parties of Europe. That has been the promise that has been betrayed.

I came to claim a very different left-wing politics to the faith of my parents. My mother's politics were forged from a personal experience of superpowers meddling in the political affairs of Greece. Her anti-imperialism grew stronger here, both from Australia's involvement in Vietnam and watching from afar as the United States supported the military junta in Greece in the late '60s and early '70s. Subsequently, it was my parents' experience of a migrant working-class life that determined their alliance with the party that represented labour. My politics, on the other hand, emerged from an intellectual and university-trained engagement with the identity movements of feminism, queer, anti-racism and anti-colonialism. These were forms of politics that, to put it most simply, replaced the idea of empowerment based on labour rights with principles of empowerment founded on human rights. It is neither my want nor my belief that a choice needs to be made between these two forms of political alliance, but it is clear that social democratic and labour parties have for a quarter of a century increasingly privileged the latter over the former.

There is a reasonable logic to that privileging: there has been the collapse of Communism and with it the collapse of faith in state control over economies, the inexorable pace of globalisation, the obduracy of sections of the union movement (best exemplified by the suicidal lunacies of the UK unions in the 1960s and '70s, which laid the ground for Thatcherism to emerge and smash them). And yes, the success of social democracies in educating and professionalising the children of workers *has* led to substantially increased mobility in terms of aspiration and identity. But a politics of rights, classically liberal and universalist, has never been adequate in addressing the conflicts between labour and capital. I might have a right to work, but what is the nature of the work available to me? Have I a right to a minimum wage? Then how and by whom is that minimum to be decided? The EU has a Charter of Fundamental Rights, including industrial rights, given force by the Treaty of Lisbon in December 2007. One can read through this document and applaud the language of dignity that suffuses it. But as my friends and family in Greece have discovered, including those who are still working though their wages are only intermittently paid, the document, for all its splendid rhetoric, is chicken shit.

In *Returning to Reims*, Eribon can't answer the question he poses at the beginning of his book: Why has his traditional working-class family turned from the left, instead supporting Marine Le Pen? In part, he can't answer it because he refuses to hold himself accountable for the thirty years he spent rejecting his roots. Still wedded to his allegiance to the sexual politics of identity, he wants his family to 'return' to him, to reconstruct themselves as feminist, queer-friendly, Green and anti-racist. But surely there was a possibility beyond estrangement?

Maybe a clue to the paralysis of contemporary social democracy lies in our very use of the word 'traditional' to describe people whose life choices and experiences are defined by labour and by familial and communal kinship rather than by professionalism, tertiary education and cosmopolitanism. Tradition assumes conservatism, and that is the preserve of the Right, whereas we progressives claim a politics of consistent change. That this change has seen a possibility for greater mobility and opportunity is undeniable, but so is the fact – made clear by the financial crisis – that this mobility and these opportunities are not evenly shared.

The austerity measures in Greece may well result in greater future economic productivity, but the fear that animates many of my friends and family there is the suspicion that it will also destroy aspects of their 'Greekness' that may not be quantifiable but are just as important to them: family obligation taking precedence over work, a notion of time that isn't held hostage to the twenty-four-hour clock of globalisation, and a pride in the historic and cultural specificity of their national identity.

For too long, like Didier Eribon, I didn't listen to the questions and fears my parents and their generation of the working class were expressing. I pounced on any yearning for traditional values as being inherently right-wing, as counter to progress. But I now consider the silencing of such voices to be a disastrous mistake. It has meant that as far as working-class people are concerned, the mainstream parties – whether of the left, right or centre – are all advocates for markets *first*. Real fears for job security and unemployment are dismissed or papered over by talk of 'green jobs' or 'service jobs' as if such euphemisms need no further explanation. But what skills will be required in these new jobs? What opportunities exist? For whom do they exist? Are these jobs permanent or casual?

Working-class people are repeatedly being told that the welfare state can no longer function as it has, that the age of entitlement is over, but what is ignored is that this questioning of its efficacy has been occurring in working-class communities for decades now. If we had been listening, we'd have realised that the talk isn't of cutting the dole or pensions but of how to reverse the penalties built into welfare for those who depend on casual or intermittent work or for single mothers who enter relationships.

As Noel Pearson has most eloquently expressed about the indigenous community, the conversation about welfare dependency, its dangers and tragedies has been occurring for years. The answer is not abolishing welfare but tackling the cycle of dependency. And if we had been listening, we'd have heard that people do want better schools but they know that it takes more than increased funding or increased teacher salaries to halt the deterioration of public schools, that we also must take seriously people's concerns over discipline, curriculum and streaming. The knee-jerk reaction to such questions – as conservative or right-wing or traditionalist – is an indictment of the Left. Why has the traditional working class here and in Europe turned against social democratic parties? Maybe because we haven't been listening.

Listening cuts both ways, and in contrast to Eribon's experiences, I found a way to speak about my politics to my parents, to have them listen to me. They initially had little sympathy for the identity politics that are part of my leftist heritage. But in time they came to understand my commitments to anti-racism, to feminism and sexual identity. They might not have agreed with all of my positions, but nor did I agree with all of theirs. I describe my politics as socialist but equally as libertarian, and the latter doesn't always find favour with many of my own peers.

I believe the challenges facing the parties of the Left and social democracy are serious, potentially terminal, and that smugness, obstinacy and purity when it comes to political beliefs are harmful. I think that multiculturalism has been one of the continuing strengths of Australian society. I also know I have to defend this position, including to the people who challenge me on it. Especially to the people who challenge me on it.

It was a truly frightening moment when the bright young student in Athens told me that he had voted for the party of fascism. At that moment I also came up against the futility of a politics of 'listening to' that I have tentatively sketched above. There are principles and issues that are lines in the sand and that divide us. The party he voted for wants the forced repatriation of immigrants, and its leader denies the Holocaust. Golden Dawn members have attacked refugees and murdered left-wing activists. Sometimes there can be no common ground.

My voice trembling, I explained that I was a son of immigrants, that whatever my complaints about my nation, and I had plenty, I was proud of its multiculturalism. I told him that I abhorred, absolutely detested, the party he had voted for.

Dimitri went quiet, and when he spoke again he sounded chastened. He explained how he feared that he would be unemployed his whole adult life, how his mother worked three shifts a day as a cleaner, rising at dawn and returning late at night, how his father's pension had been cut by thirty-five per cent, and how his parents were supporting Dimitri and his unemployed sister. He wondered if he could ever afford to marry, to raise a family. He told me how he wished his grandparents had moved to Australia as my parents had done. He spoke of friends who were applying for visas to Canada, the US, Australia, but these rich countries were no longer taking in Greek immigrants. He spoke of a friend who had found work in construction in the Emirates, that maybe he could go there, maybe he could find work as a builder in Dubai or Abu Dhabi. 'I just want a job,' he kept repeating. 'I just want to work.'

We shared cigarettes under the English no-smoking sign. We smoked in silence because neither of us had any answers.

The Monthly

The Dream Boat

Luke Mogelson

It's about a two-and-a-half-hour drive, normally, from Indonesia's capital city, Jakarta, to the southern coast of Java. In one of the many trucks that make the trip each month, loaded with asylum seekers from the Middle East and Central Asia, it takes a little longer. From the bed of the truck, the view is limited to a night sky punctuated by fleeting glimpses of high-rise buildings, over-passes, traffic signs and tollbooths. It is difficult to make out, among the human cargo, much more than the vague shapes of bodies, the floating tips of cigarettes. When you pass beneath a street lamp, though, or an illuminated billboard, the faces thrown into relief are all alive with expectation. Eventually, the urban pulse subsides; the commotion of the freeway fades. The drooping wires give way to darkly looming palms. You begin to notice birds, and you can smell the sea.

In September, in one of these trucks, I sat across from a recently married couple in their twenties, from Tehran. The wife, who was seven months pregnant, wore a red blouse stretched over her stomach; the husband a tank top, thick-rimmed glasses and a faux hawk that revealed a jagged scar (courtesy, he said, of the Iranian police). Two months had passed since they flew to Jakarta; this was their fourth attempt to leave. Twice, en route to the boat that would bring them to Australia, they were inter-cepted, detained and paid bribes for their release. Another time, the boat foundered shortly after starting out. All the same, they were confident this trip would be different. Like everyone else's in the truck, theirs was a desperate kind of faith. 'Tonight we will succeed,' the husband assured me. They were determined that the child be born 'there'.

Our drive coincided with a violent tropical downpour that seemed to surge, under pressure, more than fall. Each asylum seeker had brought a small bag with spare clothes and provisions. Those who packed slickers dug them out. The storm was amusing at first, then just cold and miserable. The children, who earlier delighted in our clandestine exit from the city, now clung to their parents. An old man, sitting cross-legged beside me with a plastic garbage bag on his head, shivered uncontrollably, muttering prayers.

Around three in the morning, the truck braked and reversed down a rutted dirt road. The rain had stopped as abruptly as it started. No one spoke. We knew we had arrived. The rear hatch swung open, and we piled out. A second truck was parked behind us; people were emerging from it as well. We were in a dense jungle whose tangled canopy obstructed the moon. Several Indonesians corralled the crowd and whispered fiercely to keep moving. 'Go! Go!' they urged in English. The road led down a steep hill and ended at a narrow footpath. As people stumbled in the dark, the Indonesians prodded them along. At the bottom of the footpath was a beach. It appeared as a pale hue through the trees, its white sand giving off a glow. The asylum seekers, fifty-seven of them, huddled at the jungle's edge.

We were in the shelter of a wide bay, its arcing headlands, dotted with lights, repulsing the windward waves. Two open-hull skiffs with outboard motors idled offshore, bobbing gently in the swells. Behind us, the clamour of the truck grew distant and was gone. Suddenly, the Indonesians began pushing people toward the sea.

'You, you. Go!'

Two at a time, the asylum seekers raised their bags above their heads and waded out. The cool water rose to waists and armpits. It was a struggle to climb aboard. Whenever someone had to be hauled up, the skiff pitched steeply, threatening to tip.

We were ferried to a wooden fishing boat: a more substantial vessel than the skiffs, though not much. About thirty feet long, with open decks, a covered bow, a one-man cockpit and a bamboo tiller, it was clearly not designed for passengers. Noting the absence of cabin, bridge, bulkheads and benches, I wondered whether anyone else shared my deluded hope: that there was another, larger ship anchored somewhere farther out, and that this sad boat was merely to convey us there.

With frantic miming, the two-man Indonesian crew directed us to crowd together on the deck and crouch beneath the bulwarks. They stretched a tarp above our heads and nailed its edges to the gunwales. Packed close in the ripe air beneath the tarp, hugging knees to chests, we heard the engine start and felt the boat begin to dip and rise.

*

Our destination was an Australian territory, more than 200 miles across the Indian Ocean, called Christmas Island. If the weather is amenable, if the boat holds up, the trip typically lasts three days. Often, however, the weather is tempestuous, and the boat sinks. Over the past decade, it is believed that more than a thousand asylum seekers have drowned. The unseaworthy vessels are swamped through leaky hulls, capsize in heavy swells, splinter on the rocks. Survivors sometimes drift for days. Children have watched their parents drown, and parents their children. Entire families have been lost. Since June, several boats went down, claiming the lives of more than a hundred people.

I first heard about the passage from Indonesia to Australia in Afghanistan, where I live and where one litmus test for the success of the US-led war now drawing to a close is the current exodus of civilians from the country. (The first 'boat people' to seek asylum in Australia were Vietnamese, in the mid-1970s, driven to the ocean by the fallout from that American withdrawal.) Last year, nearly 37,000 Afghans applied for asylum abroad, the most since 2001. Afghans who can afford to will pay as much as $24,000 for European travel documents and up to $40,000 for Canadian. (Visas to the United States, generally, cannot be bought.) Others employ smugglers for arduous overland treks from Iran to Turkey to Greece, or from Russia to Belarus to Poland.

The Indonesia–Australia route first became popular in Afghanistan before September 11, mostly among Hazaras, a predominantly

Shiite ethnic minority that was systematically brutalised by the Taliban. After the Taliban were overthrown, many refugees, anticipating an enduring peace, returned to Afghanistan, and for a while the number of Afghans willing to risk their lives at sea declined. But by late 2009 – with Afghans, disabused of their optimism, fleeing once more – migration to Australia escalated. At the same time, Hazaras living across the border in Pakistan, many of whom moved there from Afghanistan, have also found relocation necessary. In a sectarian crusade of murder and terror being waged against them by Sunni extremists, Hazara civilians in the Pakistani city of Quetta are shot in the streets, executed en masse and indiscriminately massacred by rockets and bombs.

In 2010, a suicide attacker killed more than seventy people at a Shiite rally in Quetta. Looming directly above the carnage was a large billboard paid for by the Australian government. In Dari, next to an image of a distressed Indonesian fishing boat carrying Hazara asylum seekers, read the words: 'All illegal routes to Australia are closed to Afghans.' The billboard was part of a wide-ranging effort by Australia to discourage refugees from trying to get to Christmas Island. In Afghanistan, a recent Australian-funded TV ad featured a Hazara actor rubbing his eyes before a black background. 'Please don't go,' the man gloomily implores over melancholic music. 'Many years of my life were wasted there [in detention] until my application for asylum was rejected.' In addition to the messaging campaign (and the hard-line policies it alludes to), Australia has worked to disrupt smuggling networks by collaborating with Pakistan's notorious intelligence services, embedding undercover agents in Indonesia and offering up to $180,000 for information resulting in a smuggler's arrest. The most drastic deterrence measure was introduced this July, when the Australian prime minister at the time, Kevin Rudd, announced that henceforth no refugee who reaches Australia by boat would be settled there. Instead, refugees would be detained, and eventually resettled, in impoverished Papua New Guinea. Several weeks later, the resettlement policy was extended to a tiny island state in Micronesia called the Republic of Nauru.

Since then, there have been more boats, more drownings. In late September, a vessel came apart shortly after leaving Indonesia, and dozens of asylum seekers – from Lebanon, Iran and

Iraq – drowned. That people are willing to hazard death at sea despite Australia's vow to send them to places like Papua New Guinea and the Republic of Nauru would seem illogical – or just plain crazy. The Australian government ascribes their persistence partly to misinformation propagated by the smugglers. But every asylum seeker who believes those lies believes them because he chooses to. Their doing so, and continuing to brave the Indian Ocean, and continuing to die, only illustrates their desperation in a new, disturbing kind of light. This is the subtext to the plight of every refugee: Whatever hardship he endures, he endures because it beats the hardship he escaped. Every story of exile implies the sadder story of a homeland.

*

It's surprisingly simple, from Kabul, to enlist the services of the smugglers Australian authorities are so keen to apprehend. The problem was that every Afghan I spoke to who had been to Indonesia insisted that no Western journalist would ever be allowed onto a boat: Paranoia over agents was too high. Consequently, the photographer Joel van Houdt and I decided to pose as refugees. Because we are both white, we thought it prudent to devise a cover. We would say we were Georgian (other options in the region were rejected for fear of running into Russian speakers), had sensitive information about our government's activities during the 2008 war (hence, in the event of a search, our cameras and recorders), traveled to Kabul in search of a smuggler and learned some Dari during our stay. An Afghan colleague of mine, Hakim (whose name has been changed to protect his identity), would pretend to be a local schemer angling for a foothold in the trade. It was all overly elaborate and highly implausible.

When we were ready, Hakim phoned an elderly Afghan man, living in Jakarta, who goes by the honorific Hajji Sahib. Hajji Sahib is a well-known smuggler in Indonesia; his cellphone number, among Afghans, is relatively easy to obtain. Hakim explained that he had two Georgians – 'Levan' and 'Mikheil' – whom he wished to send Hajji Sahib's way. Hajji Sahib, never questioning our story, agreed to get Joel and me from Jakarta to Christmas Island for $4000 each. This represents a slightly discounted rate, for which Hakim, aspiring middleman, promised more business down the road.

A few days later, we visited Sarai Shahzada, Kabul's bustling currency market. Tucked behind an outdoor bazaar on the banks of a polluted river that bends through the Old City, the entrance to Sarai Shahzada is a narrow corridor mobbed with traders presiding over stacks of Pakistani rupees, Iranian rials, American dollars and Afghan afghanis. The enclosed courtyard to which the corridor leads, the exterior stairwells ascending the surrounding buildings, the balconies that run the length of every floor – no piece of real estate is spared a hard-nosed dealer hawking bundled bricks of cash. The more illustrious operators occupy cramped offices and offer a variety of services in addition to exchange. Most of them are brokers of the money-transfer system, known as *hawala*, used throughout the Muslim world. Under the *hawala* system, if someone in Kabul wishes to send money to a relative in Pakistan, say, he will pay the amount, plus a small commission, to a broker in Sarai Shahzada, and in return receive a code. The recipient uses this code to collect the funds from a broker in Peshawar, who is then owed the transferred sum by the broker in Sarai Shahzada (a debt that can be settled with future transactions flowing in reverse).

In Afghanistan, where many people have family living abroad and lack bank accounts, the *hawala* system mostly facilitates legitimate remittances. It also, however, offers an appealing space for illicit dealings. In 2011, the US Treasury Department blacklisted one of Sarai Shahzada's main businesses for laundering millions on behalf of Afghan narcotics traffickers. The Taliban, as well, are thought to get the bulk of their donations, from Persian Gulf and Pakistani patrons, via *hawala* transfers.

The refugee-smuggling business is conducted almost entirely through *hawala*. Hajji Sahib's man, Mohammad, keeps a third-story office overlooking the courtyard in Sarai Shahzada. When we got there, we found Mohammad sitting behind a desk papered with receipts pinned down against a squeaky fan by half-drunk glasses of tea. With long unkempt hair, bad posture and acne, Mohammad looked as if he could still be in his teens. Other young men lined the walls, hunched in plastic chairs, working cellphones and calculators. When Hakim introduced himself as an intermediary for Hajji Sahib, they all glanced up from their computations, stiffening a little.

Mohammad immediately gave a spirited endorsement of Hajji Sahib's integrity, as well as of his own. He was eager to assure us that we were in capable hands. 'We represent lots of smugglers,' Mohammad boasted. 'For Australia and also for Europe. Every month, dozens of people give us their money.' He picked up a black ledger and waved it in the air. 'Look at this notebook! I write every customer's details in here.'

We gave him our fake names and origins. ('Gorjestan?' we were asked for the first but by no means the last time.) Then, a bit reluctantly, I counted out $8000 in cash. In return, Mohammad handed me a scrap of paper with our *hawala* codes scribbled in pen. Levan: 105. Mikheil: 106. Mohammad would withhold the money from his counterpart in Jakarta until we reached Christmas Island. This, theoretically, would preclude Hajji Sahib from retrieving it prematurely. It would also ensure he would not get paid if our boat sank or if we drowned.

*

Most asylum seekers bound for Australia arrive in Jakarta by air. The day after we landed in the sprawling capital, I called Hajji Sahib and arranged to be picked up the next morning at a 7-Eleven on a busy intersection. Joel and I were sitting outside the 7-Eleven when an Indonesian man in a Hawaiian shirt appeared at the appointed time. He eyed us doubtfully, then handed me a cellphone.

'You will go in a taxi with this guy,' Hajji Sahib told me. 'He will bring you to a safe place.'

We drove in silence, for about an hour, to the northern edge of the city, where gated communities vied for waterfront with ramshackle slums on the garbage-heaped banks of Jakarta Bay. We pulled into the parking lot of a massive tower-block apartment complex and took an elevator to the twenty-third floor. Midway down a poorly lit hallway, our escort knocked on a metal security door. A young girl in a dress decorated with images of Barbie let us in. An Iranian man sat at a glass table, tapping ash from a cigarette into a water-bottle cap. A small boy lay on a bare mattress, watching cartoons. 'Okay?' asked the

Indonesian, and before anyone could answer, he was gone.

The man, Youssef, had been living in the apartment for a couple of weeks with his eight-year-old son, Anoush, and six-year-old daughter, Shahla. (All the names of the asylum seekers in this story have been changed for their protection.) Youssef had been a laborer in Tehran, refurbishing building exteriors. In order to pay Hajji Sahib, he had sold all his possessions and gave up the house he was renting. He left his wife with her parents, planning to bring her to Australia legally once he and the children were settled there. 'In Iran, there is no work, no life, no future for these children,' Youssef told me, nodding at Anoush and Shahla. 'I want them to go to school so that they can get a position.'

We were sitting at the table, in one of the apartment's three rooms. A TV and refrigerator stood against the far wall, opposite a sink and counter, with a two-burner camping stove. Whereas Youssef, plainly, was less than thrilled to have new roommates (there were only two beds, one of them a narrow twin), Anoush and Shahla were competing to one-up each other with hospitality. After Shahla complimented Joel and me on our 'beautiful beards', Anoush set about preparing us a lunch of chicken-flavored instant noodles.

Shahla said, 'People become thieves there, in Iran.'

'In Australia, I want to be a policeman,' Anoush announced. 'I want to arrest thieves, and say, "Hands up!"'

Youssef seemed to disapprove. 'They will study,' he said.

On different floors throughout the tower block, other apartments housed about thirty more asylum seekers. Some were Hajji Sahib's; some belonged to rival smugglers. A majority, I was surprised to discover, were not Afghan but Iranian. Most were from cities and the lower middle class. They were builders, drivers, shopkeepers, barbers. One man claimed to be a mullah; another, an accomplished engineer. Their reasons for leaving varied. They all complained about the government and its chokehold on their freedoms. A few said they had been targeted for political persecution. They bemoaned the economy. International sanctions – imposed on Iran for refusing to abandon its nuclear program in 2006 and later tightened – had crippled their ability to support their families. They were fathers who despaired of their children's futures, or they wanted children but refused to have them in Iran. The most common word they used to describe their lives back home was *na-aomid* – hopeless.

Shortly after we settled into the apartment, an Iranian named Rashid stopped by for a visit. Rashid had the sickly, anaemic look that I would soon come to associate with asylum seekers who languished in that place for two months or more – a combination of malnourishment and psychological fatigue. As he collapsed into a chair, elbows propped on knees, chin propped on palm, he seemed to lack even the most basic gravity-resisting vigour. After a month in Jakarta, Rashid told me, he got aboard a boat bound for Christmas Island. The engine promptly failed, leaving them adrift for days. In lieu of a bilge pump, Rashid and the other men had to use buckets to bail out the water splashing into the hull and seeping through its wooden planks. They ran out of food and water. People might have begun succumbing to dehydration if the tide hadn't carried them to a remote island. There they were arrested and obliged to pay the Indonesian police before they could be freed.

'We came back to this place,' Rashid said. 'The smuggler said, "Don't worry, we will take you again soon."'

I glanced at Joel. Over the phone, while we were in Kabul, Hajji Sahib urged us to get to Jakarta as soon as possible, saying the next boat was ready to depart.

'Our smuggler told us we were leaving tomorrow,' I said.

Rashid laughed. 'Yes, they say that.'

*

The waiting was brutal: doing nothing became the most onerous of chores. The fact that your smuggler could call at any time, day or night, meant that you were forever suspended in a state of high alert. It also meant you couldn't venture far. Most of the asylum seekers, additionally fearful of police, never left the building. Generally, they spent their days sleeping as much as possible, smoking cigarettes and rotating through one another's rooms – for a change of scenery, presumably, though they were all identical. Everyone was broke, and meals, in our apartment anyway, consisted of instant noodles, once or twice a day, on occasion served with bread. To sleep, Youssef, Anoush and Shahla shared one of the two beds, while Joel and I alternated between the other and a thin mattress on the floor. Mattress nights were coveted, because it lay at the foot of the refrigerator, which you could open for a brief but glorious breath of cool air when you woke drenched in sweat, and because, compared with the bed, it was relatively free of fleas.

Although many of the asylum seekers in the building had children, only Youssef had brought his with him. (The others expected to be reunited with their families in Australia.) It's difficult to imagine how Anoush and Shahla processed the whole experience. My sense was that the thrill of the adventure eclipsed its hardships and hassles. With nothing and no one, except each other, to play with, they kept themselves remarkably well entertained. A feather duster found beneath the sink made for a superb tickling instrument; plastic grocery bags were turned into balloons; the hot-sauce packets, included in every ration of instant noodles, could be squirted on the tabletop to create interesting designs. There was also much to explore. The tower block was a kind of self-sufficient microcity, its four lofty wings flanking a private courtyard with shops and fish fries servicing outdoor tables clustered around a concrete bandstand. Every night, wizened Indonesian men belted out karaoke covers of John Denver and Johnny Cash. There was a Muslim mosque, a Christian church, a Buddhist temple. There were giant roaches and tailless cats to chase. And most delightfully, there was a pool.

As neither of the kids had swimming trunks or a spare pair of clothes, underwear had to suffice. Applying their talents for improvisation, Shahla found a used dish rag they could both share for a towel, while Anoush, with a kitchen knife, removed a length of flexible tubing from the back of our air-conditioner (which was broken anyway), repurposing it as a snorkel. Their resourcefulness continued at the pool itself: each day, they seemed to come into possession of some new equipment – a pair of goggles, a bar of soap, an inflatable flotation ring.

While Youssef made the rounds of the rooms, Joel and I would end up watching them at the pool. We were both distressed to see that neither Anoush nor Shahla could really swim.

When I asked Anoush, who had never been on a boat before, whether he was nervous about the journey, he clucked his tongue. 'I have no fear,' he said. 'I'll be smiling.'

Their father was less carefree. Not long after we joined them, it became clear that Youssef had no money, and if Joel and I didn't buy food and water, they would simply go without. Whenever the fleas or heat would wake me in the night, I would find Youssef sitting by the window, staring out at the fires – bright islands of flame and eerily coloured smoke – where the slum dwellers were burning trash. Everyone was stressed; the strain of two kids and no cash, however, rendered Youssef especially edgy. He was given to fits of anger and with the slightest provocation could fly into rages at Anoush, as well as at the other asylum seekers, many of whom avoided him.

Then one day Youssef's family wired money. I was sitting with him in the apartment, smoking, when he got the call. The news transformed him. Beaming with joy, Youssef leapt into the air and began to sing and dance.

That night Joel and I found him in the courtyard drinking with Rashid. Anoush and Shahla ran from shop to shop, swinging bags of candy. When he saw us, Youssef insisted we sit down, then shouted loudly, at no one in particular, for more beer. A group of elderly Indonesian men, playing dominoes nearby, regarded him impatiently. Youssef didn't notice. He was slumped over the table, doodling on its surface with a permanent marker.

Rashid seemed embarrassed for his friend. 'His head is messed up,' he explained. 'Waiting here, with his kids, not knowing when we'll go. It's hard.'

Youssef nodded glumly.

'My head is messed up, too,' Rashid said. 'I'm going crazy. I have two sons in Iran. I haven't seen them or my wife in a year.'

Rashid said that before Australia, he tried to get to Europe via Greece. He made it from Turkey to Athens, where he was fleeced by a smuggler. Rather than return to Iran, he came to Indonesia. 'Every day, they tell us, "Tomorrow, tomorrow," Rashid said. 'But tomorrow never arrives.'

Anoush and Shahla appeared and asked Youssef for money. They wanted chips. Youssef pulled out a wad of bills and threw some in their direction. Several fluttered to the ground.

'Beer!' Youssef yelled at a woman passing by. Then he looked guiltily at Rashid, and added: 'Please! Thank you!'

*

Australia's decision to send all boat people to Papua New Guinea or the Republic of Nauru only compounded everyone's anxiety. Although no one allowed himself to take it seriously (if he did, he would have no option but to do the unthinkable – give up, go home), the news was never decisively explained away. 'It's a lie to scare people so that they don't come,' Youssef told me when I brought it up. Another man became agitated when I asked him what he thought. 'How can they turn you away?' he demanded. 'You put yourself in danger, you take your life in your hand? They can't.' A third asylum seeker dismissed the policy with a shrug. 'It's a political game,' he told me.

In many ways, he was right. It's hard to overstate how contentious an issue boat people are in Australian politics. From an American perspective, zealousness on the subject of immigration is nothing unfamiliar. But what makes Australia unique is the disconnect between how prominently boat people feature in the national dialogue, on the one hand, and the actual scale of the problem, on the other. Over the past four years, most European countries have absorbed more asylum seekers, per capita, than Australia – some of them, like Sweden and Liechtenstein, seven times as many. All the same, for more than a decade now, successive Australian governments have fixated on boat people, making them a centrepiece of their agendas.

In the summer of 2001, a Norwegian freighter, the MV *Tampa*, rescued 433 asylum seekers, almost all of them Afghan, from a stranded fishing boat. Rather than return them to Indonesia, the captain of the *Tampa*, Arne Rinnan, consented to their demands to be taken to Christmas Island. Australia forbade the ship to enter its territory, and the standoff that ensued led to Australia's threatening to prosecute Rinnan and Norway's complaining to the United Nations. John Howard, a conservative prime minister, who, in the midst of a re-election campaign, was trailing his opponent in most of the polls, declared, 'It remains our very strong determination not to allow this vessel or its occupants to land in Australia.' When Rinnan, concerned over the welfare of the asylum seekers on his ship, proceeded toward the island anyway, Howard dispatched Australian commandos to board the *Tampa* and stop it from continuing. The impasse was resolved only when New Zealand and Nauru agreed to accept the asylum seekers instead. Howard's action was widely popular with voters, and two months later he was re-elected.

Diverting boat people to third countries for processing – albeit with the possibility of someday being resettled in Australia – was subsequently adopted as an official strategy. Under an arrangement popularly known as the Pacific Solution, asylum seekers trying to get to Christmas Island were interdicted by the navy and taken to detention centres on Nauru and Papua New Guinea (both of which rely heavily on Australian aid). The Pacific Solution was denounced by refugee and human rights advocates, who criticised the harsh conditions of the centres and the prolonged periods of time – many years, in some cases – that asylum seekers had to spend in them while their applications were considered. Depression and other mental disorders proliferated; incidents of self-harm were common. In 2003, detainees on Nauru protested with a weeks-long hunger strike, during which some of them sewed their lips together. Last September, Arne Rinnan, the captain of the *Tampa*, told an interviewer that he had recently received a letter from Nauru, written by one of the Afghans he had rescued. According to Rinnan, the man said that 'I should have let him die in the Indian Ocean, instead of picking him up.'

After the Labor Party regained control of parliament in 2007, and the new prime minister, Kevin Rudd, abolished the Pacific Solution – his immigration minister condemning it as 'neither humane nor fair' – the UN and just about every other organisation involved with refugees lauded the move. Rudd lost his leadership of the Labor Party in 2010, and his successor, Julia Gillard, resurrected the offshore-processing strategy. When Rudd returned to power in 2013, apparently having learned his lesson, he kept Gillard's policies in place. It was in the context of another re-election bid in July that Rudd eliminated the possibility of any boat person ever settling in Australia. 'I understand that this is a very hard-line decision,' he acknowledged in a national address. He seemed anxious to make sure that voters understood it too.

Rudd's conservative opponent, Tony Abbott, would not be outdone. One of the two rallying cries that had come to define Abbott's campaign was 'Stop the boats!' (The other, referring to carbon-emissions penalties, was 'Axe the tax!') Proclaiming the influx of boat people a 'national emergency', Abbott proposed an even tougher scheme than Rudd's, dubbed 'Operation Sovereign Borders'. Among other proactive measures, this militaristic plan called for deploying warships to turn asylum seekers back at sea, before they reached Australian shores.

The elections were scheduled to be held less than a week after the night I found Youssef and Rashid drinking in the courtyard. Whichever candidate prevailed, one thing was certain: neither Youssef nor Rashid, nor Anoush nor Shahla, were going to get to the place they believed they were going. Rashid would never be reunited with his wife and sons in some quaint Australian suburb; Youssef would never see his children 'get a position' there; Anoush would never become an Australian policeman; Shahla would never benefit from a secular, Western education. What they had to look forward to instead – after the perilous voyage, and after months, maybe years, locked up in an isolated detention centre – was resettlement on the barren carcass of a defunct strip mine, more than seventy per cent of which is uninhabitable (Nauru), or resettlement on a destitute and crime-ridden island nation known for its high rates of murder and sexual violence (Papua New Guinea).

How do you tell that to someone who has severed himself utterly from his country, in order to reach another? It was impossible. They wouldn't believe it.

*

Joel and I were walking along the bay, where dozens of residents from the slums had gathered to watch backhoes on floating barges scoop refuse out of the shallows and deposit it onto the banks, when Youssef called my cellphone and shouted at us to get back to the tower – we were leaving. In the apartment, we found two young Iranian women, Farah and Rima, sitting at the table with large backpacks, while Youssef hurriedly shoved dates and lemons – thought to alleviate seasickness – into a canvas messenger bag. I noticed, too, that he was bringing the inflatable flotation ring Anoush and Shahla had found at the pool.

An Iranian man named Ayoub appeared and told us our car was waiting. By the deferential way Youssef and the women treated him – and by his assertive self-possession, in contrast to our rather panicky excitement – I gathered that Ayoub was a smuggler. He wore a military haircut and a handlebar moustache, and his sleeveless shirt displayed the words 'Life is hard' tattooed in English across an impressively sculpted left deltoid.

We all crammed into a new car with tinted windows, driven by a squat Indonesian man with long rapier-like pinkie nails that tapered into points, who belched every couple of minutes and chain-smoked flavoured cigarettes. Anoush and Shahla were elated. As we pulled onto the highway, they could not stop talking about the boat and the sea. The women adored them instantly. Farah hauled Anoush onto her lap, while Rima set to braiding Shahla's wild hair. The kids received this affection like sustenance, with a kind of delirious gratitude and appetite. It made me remember that since arriving in Jakarta, they had not only been without their mother but without any mother.

We stopped at three gas stations along the way and linked up with other drivers. By the time we made it out of the city, several hours later, we led a convoy of six identical cars, all packed with asylum seekers. It seemed a bit conspicuous, and sure enough, as we climbed a narrow, winding road up a densely forested mountain, people came out to watch whenever we passed a shop or village. It was maybe eight or nine at night when our driver got a call that caused him to accelerate abruptly and career down a side road that led into the woods. The other cars followed. Pulling to a stop, shutting off the lights and engine, our driver spun around and hissed: 'Shh! Police.'

He got out to confer with his colleagues, and when he returned, it was in a hurry. Recklessly whipping around blind turns, we retreated down the mountain in the direction from which we came. Emerging from one sharp bend, we encountered a dark SUV blocking the way. A siren whined; blue lights flashed. We slammed to a halt. A police officer in civilian clothes and a black baseball cap approached the driver's side. He peered in through the open window, registering the women and children. Then, after a moment's hesitation, he reeled back and smacked our driver hard and square in the face.

With the SUV behind us, we returned to the turnoff for the side road. The other five cars were there, surrounded by several police vehicles and a four-wheel-drive truck. A crowd had gathered. It was hard to tell what was happening. Some of the officers were taking pictures of the licence plates and asylum seekers, others appeared to be joking affably with the drivers. Everyone was making calls on cellphones. At one point, our driver stuck his head in the window and rubbed his thumb and fingers together. 'Money, money,' he said. But the next instant he disappeared again.

Eventually, with a police car ahead of us and the truck bringing up the rear, we continued along the road. It was useless to try to get an explanation from our driver, who, in a torpor of self-pity, only muttered to himself and stroked a red mark on his cheek. When Rima got hold of Ayoub, he said not to worry, Hajji Sahib was taking care of it.

We were taken to a police station, in the city of Sukabumi. There, an older, bespectacled man in army fatigues and a beret seemed to be in charge. Once more, all the drivers were pulled out of their cars, pictures were taken, phone calls were made. After about an hour, with the same escort in front and behind, our convoy was on the move again. It's hard to say for how long we drove or where we finally stopped: all I could make out were a couple of shuttered storefronts on an otherwise empty road. Curiously, when I looked out the rear window, every police vehicle save one was turning around and heading back toward Sukabumi.

The sole remaining officer, a young man in a tan uniform, leaned against a chain-link fence, smoking a cigarette, apparently uninterested in us. Soon the asylum seekers began getting out of their cars. After the officer watched with indifference as a group of Afghan teenagers briskly walked away, everyone started flagging down trucks and hopping into communal passenger vans. When a large commuter bus happened by, the officer signalled for it to stop. Those of us who hadn't yet absconded piled on.

I found myself sitting toward the front of the bus with an Iraqi family from Baghdad – a young woman in a hijab, her husband, father-in-law and three children.

'Where are we going?' the Iraqi woman said in English.

'I don't know,' I said.

Someone asked the driver.

'Bogor,' he said.

'Where's Bogor?' the Iraqi woman said.

'I don't know,' I said.

It turned out to be the end of the line. When the bus stopped, about thirty asylum seekers from Iran, Iraq and Afghanistan got out. No one quite knew what to do. It was nearly dawn, and everything in Bogor was closed. We all walked to the highway – a motley, exhausted crew, carrying backpacks and plastic bags with food and clothes – and started hailing taxis. Youssef, the children, Rima, Farah, Joel and I managed to persuade a commuter with a minivan to take us back to the tower block for $20. The sun was coming up by the time we got there. The apartment was still filthy. It still stunk. It was still hot. Youssef lit a pot of water for the noodles.

*

A few days later, Joel and I were on our way to one of the shops downstairs when a young Middle Eastern man we had never seen before approached us. 'Come with me,' he said.

We followed him to the courtyard, where we found Ayoub sitting at one of the tables, absorbed in a hearty lunch.

'Get your bags and the apartment key,' Ayoub told me, dropping a chicken bone onto his plate and loudly sucking the grease off his fingers, one at a time, from thumb to pinkie.

When we got up to the apartment and I told Youssef the news, he only nodded. The reaction was not what I expected. 'Ayoub is here,' I repeated. 'We're leaving.'

'Did he say us too?' Youssef asked. 'Or just you?'

I didn't understand. 'We're all going together, of course.'

Youssef seemed unconvinced and made no move to pack. A few minutes later, Hajji Sahib called me. I stepped into the hall.

'Are you with the Iranian family?' he said.

'Yes. We're almost ready.'

'Ayoub is already gone,' Hajji Sahib said. 'You have to take a taxi to another place. And you have to leave the Iranians there. They can't come. There is a problem with their money.'

Back in the apartment, I found Youssef at the stove. He had put Shahla in the shower. Anoush was watching cartoons.

'What's going on?' I said.

Youssef shook his head. When I told him Joel and I had to go alone, without them, there was no objection or rebuke;

however miserable, Youssef was reconciled to what was happening, and I realised he must have seen it coming. He lit a cigarette and lay down on the mattress. Shahla was still in the shower. Anoush, I could tell, hadn't missed a thing. His eyes, though, stayed fastened on the TV.

*

We took a taxi to a much nicer building on the opposite side of Jakarta. A tall, skinny Iranian in his early twenties met us in the lobby and took us to the top floor. In the apartment, we found Farah and Rima sitting with three Iranian men around a coffee table with a row of cellphones on it. The women greeted us warmly and introduced one of the men, Siya, as the 'boss'. Muscular and shirtless, with intricate tattoos of feathered wings spread across his chest, Siya was busy fashioning a sheath for a long wood-handled knife out of folded magazine pages and rubber bands.

Noticing me notice the knife, Farah said, 'For security.'

Siya told us to put our cellphones on the table and informed us that we would no longer be allowed to use them.

'Who told you to come here?' he asked.

'Hajji Sahib,' I said.

'Who introduced you to Hajji Sahib?'

'Hakim. From Kabul.'

'Hakim from Kabul?' Siya nodded knowingly. 'Okay, good.'

After a while, a middle-aged man and his son joined us. Siya embraced each of them for a minute or more. The father, Amir, was a shop owner from the Iranian side of the border with Iraq. He and Sami, a pudgy nine-year-old with glasses, were two of the friendliest people I met in Jakarta. Although he was older than Siya, Amir's meek nature relegated him definitely subordinate: a somewhat awkward dynamic that Amir, loath to make anyone uncomfortable, deflated by clicking his heels and saluting the boss (who, in turn, ordered him to execute a series of squats and lunges, counting out the sets in a mock drill-sergeant voice). Later, when Siya asked to inspect his weapon, Amir reached into his pocket and produced a flimsy steak knife.

It was around midnight when Siya got the call. He gave us back our phones, and we took the elevator to an underground parking garage, where another caravan of new cars with tinted windows was waiting. Every vehicle was already packed beyond capacity. We were all greatly relieved when, a few miles down the highway, our driver pulled into an alley, stopped behind the truck and told us to get out.

*

After the hard rain on the way to the beach, and wading out chest-deep to the skiffs, everyone was drenched. It was still dark out when the two Indonesian crew members pulled back the tarp they had nailed over our heads. The coast was a vague shadow growing vaguer. The Indonesians distributed life vests: ridiculous things, made from thin fabric and a bit of foam. The youngest children, including a girl in a pink poncho who appeared no older than four or five, were directed with their parents to a small square of open deck in the stern. The reason for this was that the farther aft you went, the less violent was the bucking as we ploughed into the swells.

As the sun broke, we got our first good look at one another. Rashid had made it, as well as several other men from the tower block. There were nine children and more than a dozen women. Aside from one Afghan man, from Kunduz Province, everyone was Iranian. Most of the elderly crowded into the covered bow or leaned against the bulwarks. The rest fit where they could on the open deck. The sea was choppy enough so that each time the boat crashed from a peak into a trough or hit a wave head-on, large amounts of water splashed against us.

The first person to become sick was Siya. It was still early morning when he started throwing up. He was a natural leader, that man, and almost everyone soon followed suit. By late afternoon, we'd lost sight of land completely, and the swells grew to a size that blocked out the horizon when they loomed above us. Some people bent over the gunwales, some vomited into plastic bags. It quickly became apparent that there were not enough bags to go around: rather than toss them overboard, full ones had to be emptied, rinsed and reused.

Siya would not be cowed. Peeling off his soaking tank top, revealing his tattooed wings – seeming to unfold them, actually, as he threw back his shoulders – he began to sing. Others joined in, breaking now and then to retch.

It was slow going. The Indonesians took turns manning the tiller and hand-pumping water from the bilge. One was older and taciturn and wore a permanent scowl; the other looked to be in his teens, smiled enough for the both of them and called everybody 'brother'. The tremendous racket of the engine belied its less-than-tremendous horsepower. Like the rest of the vessel, it was built for neither such a heavy load nor such high seas. Our typical speed was four to five knots, less than six miles per hour, and at times we seemed to make no headway whatsoever against the strong south-easterly trade winds, which whipped up white caps on the waves and kept us all alert with stinging gusts of spray. Depending on the direction of the swells, the Indonesians would signal the men to consolidate themselves on the starboard or port side of the deck and thereby mitigate our listing – which, now and then, felt alarming.

The sea was still big when the sun went down, taking with it the warmth. Those of us who had spent the day on our feet now began staking claims on places to try to sleep. The deck became a claustrophobic scrum of tangled limbs. Few could recline or stretch their legs. Each time someone tried to reposition a foot or knee, say, to restore some circulation, the movement would ripple out in a cascade of shifting and grumbling as the surrounding bodies adjusted to the new configuration.

The tarp was unfurled. There was not enough of it to cover everyone. If you found yourself on an edge or corner, someone from the opposite side would invariably pull it away the moment you relaxed your grip. In any case, it was too worn and porous to do much. The water ran down its folds and creases, streaming through the many tears along the way.

*

In the morning, everyone looked different. Sallow. Haggard. Reduced. Amir and Sami slouched limply against each other, passing between them a bulging plastic bag. The man with the faux-hawk was curled up in a foetal ball: he stayed that way the rest of the trip. His pregnant wife sat cross-legged near the bow, pale and wet and trembling. Rima was clutching Siya's arm, as if it were a lifeline. Their eyes were squeezed tightly shut, but they were too ill to sleep.

Another problem arose. There was no toilet, and absent any railing to hold on to, going over the side was too risky. The men urinated on the hull, the women in their pants.

The Indonesians had brought a box of sealed plastic cups of water, but hardly anyone could hold them down. Siya continued to sing and puke. Although a couple of the children had begun to cry, none complained. In the afternoon, two dolphins appeared and spent the better part of an hour playfully showing off. As they darted under the boat, and launched into the air, the spectacle cheered up everyone, adults and kids alike. Even Amir and Sami rallied from their stupor to watch. A few grown men became positively gleeful, vying to be the first to spot the grey shadows flitting from the deep.

That night, several of us tried to sleep atop the engine room, trading the shelter of the hull for a little extra space. It was a poor call. Every ten minutes or so, a bucket's worth of cold water took your breath away or you were pitched against a hot pair of vertical pipes spewing noxious smoke and sparks. There was nothing to do but lie there, bracing for one or the other, admiring the magnificent array of stars and the phosphorescence glowing in the wake.

*

With first light, despite the sleep deprivation, dehydration, seasickness and filth, the asylum seekers were energised by the fact that, according to the Indonesians, we would likely reach Australian territory before nightfall. Although there was still no land in sight, the arrival of birds circling overhead was unanimously interpreted as a sign that we were getting close. The sea had also calmed: no more waves crashed upon the deck. Initially, this was an enormous relief. For the first time, the sun dried us out. As it crept higher, however, it proved to be far more powerful than during the past two days, and soon, without a single cloud in the sky to blunt the blistering rays, everyone was longing for the same frigid breakers we previously cursed.

The tarp was brought back out. While blocking the sun's glare, it also trapped its heat. A couple of people, desperate for fresh air, cut up the box of water cups, which was almost empty, and made visors from the cardboard. One of the fathers in the stern, wearing a Qatar Airways sleeping mask to protect his face, found a length of string and rigged up some sheets and scarves for shade. The bow – the only covered part of the boat – reeked dizzyingly of vomit and urine. None of the dozen Iranians who rushed to fill the space when we embarked had since dared to leave it. Now they were suffering. An argument arose between them and their comrades on the open deck. The tarp was obstructing the entrance to the bow, it seemed, and smothering its already rank and humid air.

'Please,' one woman begged. 'We can't breathe in here.'

There was little desire among the deck dwellers, however, to endure direct exposure to the sun for the comfort of those who had thus far enjoyed comparatively plush accommodations.

Presently, the heat finished off anyone who might have been bearing up. The pregnant woman's condition bordered on critical. She was flushed and drenched in sweat and heaved dryly, with nothing left to give. Sami was weeping. Amir lay supine. His eyes drooped catatonically, and when I tried to make him drink some water, he weakly gripped my ankle.

'I need help,' he said. 'Call for help.'

That decision seemed to be up to Siya. There was a satellite phone on board: Siya said the plan was to contact the Australian authorities once we were well within their waters. The navy would then bring us ashore. In the past, asylum boats often made it all the way – but the landing can be treacherous (when one boat smashed on the cliffs in 2010, fifty people drowned), and now it's standard practice to request a 'rescue' before reaching Christmas Island. Although Australian rescuers, when responding to distress calls, venture much farther north than where we currently were, Siya wanted to be sure. I think it was Amir's pitiful entreaties that finally persuaded him to make the call.

An Iranian man who knew some English – the one who in Jakarta told me he was an engineer – spoke to the dispatch. The Indonesians had brought a hand-held GPS device; neither they nor the asylum seekers, however, knew how to work it. Eventually, someone offered his iPhone, and the engineer read out our coordinates.

While we waited to be rescued, the Iranians set about destroying their passports. 'So they can't deport you,' Farah told me.

Clearly, though, the task also carried some symbolic weight. Rather than simply jettisoning them, the asylum seekers painstakingly ripped out each individual page, crumpled it into a ball, and tossed it to the wind. A pair of scissors was passed around. The burgundy covers, emblazoned with the Iranian coat of arms, were cut into tiny pieces. The work was accomplished with flair and relish. Only one man seemed hesitant. Moving closer, I saw that the passport he was disposing of was his son's. When the scissors came his way, he carefully cut out the photo on the first page and slipped it in his wallet.

Soon, on the horizon, a ship appeared. A government airplane buzzed above us, swooped low and made a second pass. The asylum seekers waved shirts in the air, crying out in jubilation. The younger Indonesian performed a dance atop the engine room; he seemed amazed we had made it. Some of the men emptied their pockets, thrusting on him all the cash they had. The Indonesian beamed. 'Thank you, brothers!'

Two skiffs broke off from the battleship and motored our way. Each carried six Australians in grey fatigues, riot helmets and sidearms holstered on their thighs. The Indonesians cut the engine (and after three days of its unrelenting clamour, the silence that replaced it was startling). The skiffs manoeuvred abreast of us, one on each side.

The Australian sailors all looked like fresh recruits. One of them held a manual of some kind. He read from it in a loud voice. 'Are there any English speakers?'

The engineer stepped forward.

'Does anyone on board require medical assistance?'

When the engineer translated this, nearly everyone raised his hand. The pregnant woman was helped to her feet and presented. Her head hung heavily. She was almost too weak to stand.

While the Australian with the manual recited more questions – including some in Indonesian addressed to the crew, who shook their heads dumbly, refusing to answer – his fellow sailors passed to the asylum seekers new life vests, a couple jerrycans of fresh water, some bags of frozen tortillas, bottles of honey and a tub of strawberry jam. 'We're going back to the ship now,' one of them told the engineer. 'You have to turn the engine back on and keep going. We'll be behind you.'

This information was met with disbelief. Once again the pregnant woman was raised up and displayed. 'Can you take her with you at least?' asked the engineer. The sailors exchanged embarrassed looks. Plainly, they wished they could.

We still couldn't see land – and not long after the skiffs left us for the battleship, it, too, was lost from view. The return of the empty and limitless ocean, not to mention the incessantly pounding sun, was incredibly demoralising. To make matters worse, we no longer had any means of communication. When they first glimpsed the plane and ship, all the asylum seekers, following Siya's example, threw their cellphones overboard. For some reason, amid the exultation, the satellite phone and GPS system had also gone into the water.

There was nothing to do but heed the Australian's command and 'keep going'. It was four or five hours after we made contact with the first ship when a second, smaller patrol boat materialised. Two more skiffs of sailors came out to meet us. This time they immediately boarded the boat, moving people aside, herding everyone forward. The officer in charge announced that he was taking control of the vessel.

After the officer spotted Joel's camera, we were both summoned to the stern, at which point we identified ourselves as journalists. While a big Australian with a bushy beard worked the tiller, the officer went through a list of prewritten questions with the crew, each of whom either couldn't read or declined to. (Unless it's their second offence, or someone dies, the Indonesian fishermen who bring asylum boats across are often not prosecuted.) The officer was polite to Joel and me. He said we had been lucky with the weather. If we had left a few days earlier, the boat would have capsized.

*

It inspires a unique kind of joy, that first glimpse of land. The sun was low, and you could almost mistake it for some play of light and shadow. As rousing as it was to see, the presence of a fixed object against which to mark our progress also made you realise just how slowly we had been going. It was late at night by the time we reached Christmas Island. The Australians guided our boat into the shelter of a shallow cove, beneath sheer cliffs draped in vegetation. After tying up on a mooring, the officer revealed that we would stay the night here and disembark tomorrow. When the engineer relayed the complaints of the asylum seekers – who, consolidated in the bow, had even less space now than before – the officer responded: 'Are you safe? Are your lives in danger anymore?' He seemed to be losing patience, and, noticing a wrapper floating by the stern, angrily reproached the Iranians: 'You're in a nice country now.'

It rained fitfully throughout the night. The next day, we were all ferried by a push-barge from the mooring to a jetty around the point. The jetty was swarmed with customs and immigration officials, federal police and employees of a private company that runs the island's detention centres. Joel and I were welcomed to Australia, given water, coffee and a ride to a surprisingly luxurious hotel. Everyone else was interned. Later that afternoon, while walking into town, I saw our little boat being towed out to sea. There, the officer had told me, it would be lit on fire.

The families and minors were taken to a relatively comfortable facility, with access to an outdoor soccer field and recreational area. The single men went to a place resembling a maximum-security prison. None of the asylum seekers would stay at either location for long. While I was on the island, flights full of detainees were leaving almost every night for Papua New Guinea and the Republic of Nauru. By now, most if not all of the people from our boat have been transferred to one of the two island nations. If they were sent to the detention centre on Papua New Guinea, they are probably living in the tent city that was erected there as part of its expansion. If they were sent to the detention centre on Nauru, they are probably living in the tent city that was erected there after rioting asylum seekers in July burned the buildings down.

Because the governments of Nauru and Papua New Guinea lack the capability to process refugee claims – Australian officials are still training them to do so – the asylum seekers have a long wait ahead of them. Some might not be able to hold out: already, dozens of Iranians, after seeing the conditions at the Papua New Guinea facility, have asked to be sent back to their country. Among those who decide to tough it out, it's most likely that few will be found to have valid cases. Moreover, unlike with

Afghanistan and Sri Lanka, no agreement exists between Iran and Australia allowing for the forcible repatriation of asylum seekers whose applications are unsuccessful. This means that the Iranians who are denied asylum by Nauru or Papua New Guinea, and who decline to voluntarily return to Iran, will enter a kind of limbo, in which they can neither be resettled on those islands nor sent to the Australian mainland nor sent home. Absent another solution, these people could be flown back to Christmas Island and detained indefinitely.

*

We reached Australia one day after Tony Abbott was elected prime minister. In keeping with his Operation Sovereign Borders policy, Abbott has since directed the navy to send back to Indonesia, whenever possible, asylum boats intercepted at sea. So far this has happened twice, in late September, when two boatloads of asylum seekers were turned over, offshore, to Indonesian authorities. The second transfer took place the same day that a boat full of Lebanese asylum seekers broke apart less than a hundred yards off the Java coast near Sukabumi, the Indonesian city whose police station Joel and I briefly visited. More than twenty bodies, many of them children, washed ashore, and more remained missing.

According to a Lebanese community leader interviewed by the Australian Broadcasting Corporation, most of the dead came from a small village near the border with Syria. One asylum seeker, who managed to swim to safety, lost his sister-in-law, his brother-in-law, three of their children, his wife and all eight of his children. The community leader said there were many more Lebanese fleeing the Syrian border who had already paid smugglers and were on their way to Indonesia.

When I got back to Afghanistan, I met with several men preparing to go to Australia. One of them, Qais Khan, opened a small auto-parts shop in Kabul in 2005. Qais told me that for years, while Afghans from the provinces came regularly into the city, he did very well. Since 2010, however, the deteriorating security situation in the rural areas adjacent to the capital had stultified commerce and ruined many retailers. Last year, Qais's shop went out of business; now he was struggling to feed his wife and two children.

A couple of months ago, fifteen of Qais's friends paid a smuggler at Sarai Shahzada and left for Indonesia. Among them was Qais's next door neighbor, a driver for a member of parliament, who decided to flee after receiving three letters from the Taliban threatening to kill him. Qais told me he was waiting to hear whether his friends were successful – in which case, he would go as well.

'And if they're not?' I asked. 'If they're sent to Papua New Guinea or the Republic of Nauru?'

Qais thought for a moment and then admitted he would probably go anyway. In fact, he had already taken out the necessary loans to pay the smuggler. 'At least there you have a chance,' he said. 'At least there is a possibility.'

I felt obligated to tell him he was wrong. 'You won't get to Australia,' I said.

Qais didn't seem to hear. The words simply didn't register. 'Australia, Europe, America,' he said. 'They're not like here. You have a chance.'

The New York Times Magazine

A Natural Wonder in Peril

Tim Flannery

Australia's Great Barrier Reef stretches for around 1430 miles along the continent's north-east coast, encompassing an area roughly half the size of Texas. Those who have dived into its pristine reaches know firsthand that it is one of Earth's natural wonders – a coral world of exceptional beauty and diversity. Yet as Iain McCalman's 'passionate history' of the reef makes clear, it is also a stage on which dreams, ambitions, and great human tragedies have been played out. He tells his story by chronicling lives that, either inadvertently or intentionally, have shaped our perception of the coralline labyrinth.

Just who discovered the reef is a matter of conjecture. Certainly Captain James Cook encountered it in 1770 as he charted Australia's east coast in His Majesty's bark *Endeavour*. But did he recognise the formation as a whole? The reef forms a kind of funnel that narrows northward. In its southern reaches it is so wide-mouthed that Cook failed to notice it. Only as he approached the latitude of present-day Cooktown did he realise that he had become ensnared in a coral maze.

Close to midnight on the night of 10 June, *Endeavour* struck bottom, then stuck fast. In the darkness Cook and his crew were about as far from home and help as anyone could be. The great navigator understood that even if the vessel could be hauled free, it would likely sink. He foresaw that sailors would scrabble for seats in the longboat, but believed that those who succeeded could expect a far grislier death at the hands of 'the most rude and uncivilized' people on earth than those who surrendered to the sea.

Still, there was no choice but to risk all. Waiting for a high tide, Cook had the vessel hauled free – and later found that a piece of coral the size of a fist had stuck in the hull, partially stopping the flow of water and allowing the ship to reach the Endeavour River, where it was careened and repaired.

Around six weeks later, after several anxious days threading the labyrinth, the repaired *Endeavour* finally reached the open sea. Then Cook did an astonishing thing – he ordered the vessel turned around, so he could find a way back in and continue his coastal survey. At four a.m. on 16 August, the reef was again making itself known. The sound of a great surf 'foaming to a vast height' filled every ear.

Waves that had gained strength by traveling the breadth of the Pacific were rearing up, then dashing themselves before the serrated coral ramparts. With no ground for an anchor and not a puff of wind, the ship lay helpless as the incoming tide carried it ever closer to what Cook knew was 'the very jaws of distruction'. Amid waves 'mountains high', Joseph Banks, the expedition's gentleman naturalist, later recalled, 'a speedy death was all we had to hope for'.

For two hours in the predawn gloom the desperate crew rowed for their lives as they attempted to tow *Endeavour* clear, but the tide was unrelenting. Then, at first light, a few slight puffs of wind were felt. Cook would live to find his passage and complete his chart. But at what cost in mortal peril?

At the beginning of the nineteenth century Captain Matthew Flinders continued charting where Cook had left off. Remembered as the man who gave both Australia and the Great Barrier Reef their names, he was also the first European to show an appreciation of the reef's beauty. Peering through clear water near the Northumberland Islands, he recorded seeing

> a new creation, as it was to us, but imitative of the old . . . We had wheat sheaves, mushrooms, stag horns, cabbage leaves, and a variety of other forms, glowing under water with vivid tints of every shade betwixt green, purple, brown, and white; equalling

in beauty and excelling in grandeur the most favourite parterre
of the curious florist.

For all the reef's beauty, Flinders 'could not long forget with what
destruction it was pregnant'.

*

The safe passages surveyed by Cook and Flinders had, by the mid-
nineteenth century, become popular shipping routes. Yet every
soul passing though that beauteous landscape surely experienced
moments of terror. The realisation that corals were living organ-
isms 'which lurk and even *grow*' was particularly unsettling.
Shipping channels charted as clear as little as thirty years previously could thus sometimes prove to be bristling with dangers.

The fate awaiting travellers, if the shudder and groan of coral
upon hull ever was heard, was there for all to read in the newspapers and penny dreadfuls of the day. They lingered particularly
upon the fates of those who reached shore, and few held such morbid fascination to the Victorian public as the white women cast
away among cannibals.

When the trading brig *Stirling Castle,* bound from Sydney to Sin-
gapore, struck a reef and sank 200 miles off Australia's north-east
coast in 1836, the captain's wife was among a handful who gained
a seat in the longboat. Eliza Fraser reached shore on Great Sandy
Isle (soon renamed Fraser Island after her), where she lived for six
weeks among the Badtjala Aboriginal people, before being rescued by a convict.

The newspapers of the day could not get enough of her story,
and Fraser herself proved to be an able self-promoter. When she
arrived in London in 1837, she visited a Mr Kelly, the city's lord
mayor, who was also a small-time publisher. Realising that he had
a potential bestseller on his hands, he turned to John Curtis, a
journalist at *The Times*, to write up Fraser's story.

McCalman tells us that 'all early nineteenth-century British
newspapers relied to some degree on income procured by small-
scale bribery or blackmail'. So it was that Kelly paid Curtis to
pen 'a sparkling, real-life newspaper melodrama of cannibal-
ism, imprisonment, murder, torture, and sexual violation'. The
book that followed, *SHIPWRECK of the STIRLING CASTLE . . .*

the Dreadful Sufferings of the Crew . . . THE CRUEL MURDER OF CAPTAIN FRASER BY THE SAVAGES and . . . the Horrible Barbarity of the Cannibals Inflicted upon THE CAPTAIN'S WIDOW Whose Unparalleled Sufferings Are Stated by Herself . . . , set, in a moment, European attitudes toward the native peoples of the Great Barrier Reef region. Much of the tale was wild exaggeration, yet the beliefs it fostered made massacre, displacement, rape and murder of the natives seem more justified.

Just how sensational Curtis's book is becomes evident from reading other shipwreck narratives. When the 313-ton bark *Charles Eaton*, India-bound out of Sydney, was wrecked in 1834 in the Torres Strait, most of the crew were massacred. But two boys, sixteen-year-old John Ireland and three-year-old William D'Oyley, narrowly escaped and were rescued by the people of Boydang Island. The fate of the *Charles Eaton* remained unknown until late 1836, when news arrived in England just in time for John Curtis to include it in his book. But even he found it hard to turn the boys' rescuers into monsters – it was clear from their testimony that the lads were genuinely fond of their adoptive parents.

Ignoring such inconveniences, Curtis took it upon himself to recommend how the Europeans might deal with the reef natives. 'Exterminate the whole of the inhabitants' was one option, though he admitted that he preferred subjugation and conversion to Christianity. Yet driven by Curtis's hyperbole, frequently extermination was the result.

It is a strange fact of Australian history that the most informative of the shipwreck sagas remained all but unknown until the late twentieth century. One of these concerns Barbara Thompson. She was just thirteen in 1844 when she ran away to sea with her lover, William Thompson, captain of the cutter *America*. Shipwrecked on Madjii Reef in the Torres Strait, she was rescued by three Aboriginal boys and adopted when a couple recognised – by certain features of her chin and eyes – that she was their daughter Giom, who had recently drowned. The pale wraith from the sea was thus the returned Giom – *marki naroka*, a ghost maiden.

Giom, who lived among the islands for five years, soon adapted to life there. She forgot her English and much of her past life, and seems to have taken the charismatic young man Boroto as her lover – marriage with *marki naroka* being prohibited among the

Kaurareg people – and it is thought she bore him the child Outsie, meaning 'muddy water'.

What we know about Thompson's life is owed to the unique talents and dedication of Oswald Brierly, the thirty-one-year-old artist aboard HMS *Rattlesnake*, which 'rescued' Thompson. His commitment to learning the local dialects and to living among the Kaurareg during the *Rattlesnake*'s extended stay in the Torres Strait gave him unique insights into the culture. Like Thompson, he too was adopted into a clan.

Brierly's journal and glorious sketches – which unaccountably remained unpublished for over a century – reveal a deep fascination with the Kaurareg and their technology. Again and again he drew and painted the outrigger canoe *Kyee Mareeni* – Big Shadow – owned by the senior man Manu. 'I had,' he writes, 'long admired but never till now seen anything that realized so much the idea of beauty.' And just as he dwelt upon details of the outrigger's construction, so did he dwell on the subtleties of character – including minutely observed details of their physical appearance, personalities, and idiosyncrasies – of his islander friends.

Why did Brierly's masterpiece of ethnography remain unpublished until 1979? It could have done so much to rectify the gross caricature of the peoples of the reef region as cannibals and sadistic murderers. But perhaps that was the point: as told by Brierly, Thompson's story failed to reinforce the stereotype.

Toward the end of the nineteenth century, accounts of shipwreck among native cultures descended from hyperbole into grand farce. Henri Louis Grin (alias Louis de Rougemont) was a Swiss sailor who claims to have been shipwrecked on the Great Barrier Reef and to have lived with the Aborigines for years. His account – serialised in *Wide World Magazine* – became an instant sensation and was followed by a bestselling book. Scandalously, *The Adventures of Louis de Rougemont* and its serialised predecessor were entirely invented. Even the fact that Grin ended his days in a circus sideshow as 'The Greatest Liar on Earth' did little to puncture his fame. Decades before, Samuel Clemens had written, 'Australian history . . . does not read like history, but like the most beautiful lies.' Especially in the case of Grin, these words were prescient.

Grin embroidered his fantasy with two of the most extraordinary shipwreck survival stories ever written. James Morrill was twenty-two when in 1846 the *Peruvian*, a Dundee-based merchantman carrying timber from Sydney to China, foundered near present-day Townsville, while Narcisse Pellettier was just fourteen in 1858 when the French merchantman *Saint-Paul* came to grief off Cape Direction, on Cape York. Both were adopted by Aboriginal clans and integrated easily into tribal life.

Each castaway lived with his adopted family for seventeen years, and both left stories packed with insights into a now vanished way of life. Morrill's adventures were recounted in a brief pamphlet published shortly after his 'rescue', while Pelletier's biography appeared in French in 1876. Yet for McCalman their real significance lies in how, Grin's borrowings aside, they were ignored by the Australian public. It was not until 2006 that Morrill's account was first republished, and then in America, while Pelletier's appeared for the first time in English only in 2009. One possible explanation is that, as it went about dispossessing its native peoples, colonial Australia needed the fiction of tribal barbarism as a balm for its guilt.

*

By the end of the nineteenth century the native tribes of the reef area had been largely subdued or exterminated, and a growing sea snail and pearl shell industry was established. Accordingly, governments sought experts to advise on managing the reef's bounty. The most illustrious of those recruited was William Saville-Kent, today regarded as the founding father of Australian reef science.

Saville-Kent's childhood was not easy. When William was three, his harsh and promiscuous father began siring a second brood with the live-in governess, in the family home. William's mother, ailing and perhaps despairing, died thereafter, leaving William and his siblings isolated and emotionally crushed. William had one ally – his sister Constance, who like him was congenitally syphilitic courtesy of their father. At the ages of eleven and twelve respectively, William and Constance absconded from their unhappy home, but were forcibly returned. The press covered their story, and it seems possible that Charles Dickens adapted it in his last and unfinished work, *The Mystery of Edwin Drood*.

In 1860, a few years after their forced return, the body of William and Constance's three-year-old half-brother Francis was discovered dumped in an outhouse. The child had been savagely stabbed and all but beheaded. Suspicion fell upon the runaways and although Inspector Whicher of Scotland Yard, who led the inquiry, could not obtain a conviction, he was convinced of the children's guilt. He never lost interest in the case, and five years later Constance confessed that she was the sole murderer. William had embarked on a career in science and was due to inherit money from his mother's estate. Only by absolving him and refusing a plea of insanity – which might cast doubts on William's mental state and thus threaten his inheritance – could Constance protect her brother's interests. The cost was heavy indeed – the death sentence for a teenage girl, later commuted to twenty years in prison.

Rendered sterile by his inherited syphilis, and with a difficult and withdrawn personality, William chose life in a remote colonial outpost. In 1888 the Queensland government asked him to join a surveying expedition of Australia's north, and concurred with his suggestion that they appoint him commissioner of North Australian fisheries.

It was not just fisheries but the reef in its entirety that interested William Saville-Kent. A keen amateur photographer, he set about documenting its beauty and diversity. His book *The Great Barrier Reef of Australia: Its Products and Potentialities* was published in 1893. *The Scotsman* hailed it as the 'first authority on its subject', while *Nature* – already on its way to being the world's foremost science journal – commended its photographs, which allowed the public to see for the first time, it said, the wonders of the reef for themselves. At last, admiration began to replace fear of the great coral labyrinth.

In later life Saville-Kent turned to commerce. He claimed to have discovered the secret of culturing spherical pearls, and in 1906 formed a pearl-culturing company. An assistant asserted that he actually succeeded in culturing perfect pearls, but when the pioneering biologist died of a blocked bowel in 1908, his notes on pearl culture proved unintelligible.

If Saville-Kent opened the door to public appreciation of the reef, it was the journalist E.J. Banfield who introduced it to the masses. He was forty-four, disillusioned, and in ill health when he visited Dunk Island, near Townsville, in 1896. Having read Thoreau's *Walden*, he fantasised about living beside the fringing reef with its white sandy beach and rainforest-covered peaks. With the help of a family of Aborigines, who held traditional title to the island, he and his wife Bertha built a house and garden there, and began exploring the wonderland that surrounded them.

Banfield's account of his island paradise, published as *The Confessions of a Beachcomber* in 1908, was an instant hit. It was the perfect panacea for the city-bound office worker, and was followed by two wildly popular sequels. Visitors flocked to the reef and among them were scientists bent on trying to understand the origins of the vast structure.

*

Coral reefs are based on large collections of very small sedentary marine animals that take the form of polyps – they resemble sea anemones, having columnar bodies, with a mouth surrounded by tentacles. Since they can only grow in sunlit waters, how are we to account for the coral atolls rising abruptly from the sunless depths? A crucial insight was provided by Charles Darwin, who launched his scientific career with a paper speculating that coral reefs and atolls were built upon slowly subsiding volcanic foundations. As the coastlines and mountaintops sank, the growth of the coral, with living animals building on skeletons, was sufficient to fill in the space that was opened up, and so the distinctive 'barriers' and O-shaped atolls were formed.

In 1896 Alex Agassiz – son of the renowned Harvard zoologist Louis Agassiz, who was among the most prominent resisters of Darwin's evolutionary theory – embarked on a cruise of the Great Barrier Reef aimed at disproving Darwin's theory of coral reef formation. As a result of a damning review of his father Louis's scientific research by Darwin, Alex bore a deep sense of grievance. He was joined in his anti-Darwinian crusade by many, including the Duke of Argyll and a trio of eloquent English bishops, who believed that if they could refute Darwin's theory of coral reef formation, his ideas on evolution might well vanish too.

Alex Agassiz's expedition was a flop, coming up with nothing conclusive to demolish Darwin's theory. It took the technology of the atomic age to settle the dispute. In the 1950s American scientists prepared to detonate a hydrogen bomb on Eniwetok Atoll. They drilled deep into the reef, penetrating 4629 feet through fossil coral, and finally reached volcanic rock. Darwin's subsidence theory was proved.

A young student of Alex Agassiz, Alfred Mayor, was destined to have greater impact. He discovered that corals were exquisitely sensitive to changes in water temperature, speculating in 1914 that 'those forms which are sensitive to high temperature are correspondingly affected by . . . the influence of CO_2'. Around eighty years later, as climate change began to have an effect, his prescience became clear: he had identified the mechanisms of reef destruction.

The 1920s saw a systematic scientific effort aimed at understanding the Great Barrier Reef, when what became known as the Cambridge expedition settled at the Low Isles in the Torres Strait to conduct its research. In a series of reports published between 1930 and 1968, its scientists slowly unlocked the reef's innermost secrets. Their most important discoveries concerned the extent of cooperation that prevails between species in the coralline mass. From the algae that live in the bodies of the coral polyps to the glass eels that inhabit the anuses of sea cucumbers, it is symbiosis that permits the reef to survive.

This new scientific appreciation did not expunge a more base view. In a study published in 1925, J. Stanley Gardiner, head of Britain's fisheries department, stated that the reef was 'a great nuisance to navigation . . . because it . . . destroys 70,000 to 80,000 square miles of most admirable trawling ground'. This functionalist attitude came to the fore again in 1968. The Queensland premier, Joh Bjelke-Petersen, was – according to McCalman – a man with 'the hide of a rhinoceros and the mind-set of a hyena'. He was determined to mine the reef for fertiliser and drill it for oil and gas. All that stood in his way was a grassroots environmental movement led by a poet, a forester, and an artist. The poet was Judith Wright, one of Australia's most celebrated writers. Nonetheless their task seemed impossible.

The Queensland premier used every opportunity to brand the protesters as 'a lunatic fringe', 'nitwits', 'cranks' and 'rat-bags'. Were it not for the 1967 *Torrey Canyon* disaster, spilling crude oil off the coast of Cornwall, and an oil spill off Santa Barbara in 1969, Bjelke-Petersen might well have had his way. As it was, in 1975, a left-leaning federal government acted to protect the reef by instituting the *Great Barrier Reef Marine Park Act*.

*

Despite such protections, today the reef has never been in greater peril. A vast new coal port is being planned for Abbot Point, on the Queensland coast. It involves dredging 5 million tons of mud, to be dumped within the reef. The coal reserves of Queensland's Galilee Basin will pass through Abbot Point, increasing the global seaborne coal trade by a third. With conservative state and federal governments determined to exploit the mineral, only its low price (currently around US$68 per ton) and a handful of protesters stand in the way.

Despite a ban on drilling for oil, fossil fuels have made a devastating stealth attack on the reef. The first intimations came in the 1970s, when areas of coral turned white, then died. Coral bleaching – as the phenomenon is known – occurs when underwater heat waves act to put stress on the coral polyps, causing them to eject the algae living in their tissues and so turning them white. Without algal partners they cannot grow the bony skeleton that forms the reef, and over weeks the coral polyps slowly starve and die, leaving a white skeleton. Even without bleaching, the rise in ocean acidity caused by CO_2 dissolving into seawater will prevent the corals from laying down their bony skeletons. So it is that heat and acid, derived from burning fossil fuels, kills the reef.

The reef's current champion, Dr Charlie Vernon, saw his first bleached coral – a four-inch-square patch – off Palm Island in the early 1980s. Now, he says, it's 'horrible to see . . . corals that are four, five, six hundred years old . . . die' from the heat. For the reef, Vernon says, catastrophic global warming has already arrived.

William Saville-Kent's photographic record provides a poignant historic benchmark of the reef's decline. Because he was always careful to keep some landmark in the background, the locations of his photographs can still be traced. We see that what a century ago was a delightful coral garden is today a scene of utter devastation. The full extent of damage inflicted on the reef became evident in 2012, when a study revealed that fully half of the Great Barrier Reef has already been killed. Not all the damage has been inflicted by acid and heat, yet as the years go by these emerge as the overwhelming threats.

If the rate at which humanity is currently burning fossil fuels continues, the world will be around 7.2 degrees Fahrenheit warmer by 2100 than it was in 1800. Can the reef adapt? A recent study shows that if the Great Barrier Reef were to keep pace with a 7.2-degree rise in temperature, its complex ecosystems would need to migrate southward at the rate of twenty-four miles per year. Yet corals seem unable to migrate at rates greater than six miles per year. So, it appears, climate change will simply outpace the reef. Even if we slow the rate of change, the damage will be monumental. Scientists foresee that 'the majority of existing coral reef ecosystems are likely to disappear if average global temperature rises much above 1.5°C above the preindustrial values'.

Australians say they love their reef, yet today their actions show that they love easy money more. As an earlier generation struggled to save the coralline wonderland, Judith Wright said of her people:

> We are conquerors and self-poisoners
> more than scorpion or snake
> and dying of the venoms that we make
> even while you die of us.

Today the fate of one of the most magnificent ecosystems of our planet lies in the hands of some of the most technologically advanced and affluent people who have ever existed. We shall soon know whether they value their natural heritage sufficiently to avert a great coral apocalypse.

New York Review of Books

The Island Seen and Felt:
Some Thoughts about Landscape

Tim Winton

I grew up on the world's largest island. This bald fact slips from consciousness so easily I'm obliged to remind myself now and again. But in an age when a culture looks first to politics and ideology to examine itself, perhaps my forgetting something so basic should come as no surprise. After all, our minds are often elsewhere. The material facts of life, the organic and concrete forces that shape us, are overlooked as if they're irrelevant or even mildly embarrassing. Our creaturely existence is registered, measured, discussed and represented in increasingly abstract terms. Perhaps this helps explain how someone like me, who should know better, can forget he's an islander. Australia the place is constantly overshadowed by Australia the national idea, Australia the economic enterprise. Undoubtedly the nation and its projects have shaped my education and my prospects, but the degree to which geography, distance and weather have moulded my sensory palate, my imagination and expectations is substantial and the evidence of this continues to surprise me, even in middle age. The island continent has not simply been background to my life and work. To my life it's been pivotal. To my work it's been a central, vital concern, a source of agitation and inspiration. Landscape has exerted a kind of force upon me that is every bit as geological as family. Like many Australians I feel this tectonic grind most keenly when abroad.

The first time I left the island I was twenty-eight. I say left the island because 'going' abroad doesn't really cut it. Here you can jump in a cab and get a train from King's Cross station and in the time it takes to see a Terrence Malick movie you're abroad. But you may not be quite as overseas as I was. Living in Europe in the 1980s I made the mistake of thinking that what separated me from the natives of this exotic hemisphere was just a matter of language and history, as if I really was the mongrel European transplant of my formal education. Such was the blinkered narrative of my schooling. By the '70s Australians had moved on from being children of empire. We were now, more or less, our own show out there in the Asia-Pacific. And we'd long ago rejected the notion of being branch office Brits. In fact we were militantly un-British. And yet I was still taught by bourgeois Marxists in university English Departments that I was, essentially, whether I liked it or not, a European. Which strikes me as a very sloppy way of reminding a native that he's not an Aborigine. Anyway, the moment I stepped off a plane at Charles de Gaulle I knew I was no European. I was just pink-skinned. Worse, I was of fragmentary pigmentation. The austral sun has, as you can see, confused even my whiteness. Yes, I did happen to speak English. My own brand of English, apparently. And no brand of French anyone had heard in history before or since. But I was *not* English and I was *not* a European.

Until that first mortifying day in Paris, I'd never given my own geography sufficient credit. And neither, of course, had those good folk who taught me. They were educated in the narrow trenches of their own disciplines; they taught only what they knew. Being indoor folk of the inner-city enclave they knew very little about the natural sciences, about ecology, about geography. Theirs was an abstract world before it was a physical, spatial reality. The physical, sensual world was as much a mystery to them as it is to the evangelical fundamentalist.

So there I was in France at twenty-eight. Trying desperately to fit in. Unsettled by gaps of language and history, of course. But even more rattled by my responses to the physical world in this new hemisphere. The cities and villages of the so-called Old World were enchanting. But outside them I felt that all my sensory wiring was scrambled. When I had expected to 'appreciate' the monuments of Europe and 'love' its natural environment, the reality was entirely the reverse. The immense beauty of ancient European buildings and streetscapes had an immediate and visceral impact – I was swooning. And yet in the natural world, where I am generally most comfortable, I was hesitant, diffident, even sniffy. For while I was duly impressed by what I saw of the natural environment, I could never quite connect emotionally. Being from a flat, dry continent I had actually looked forward to the prospect of soaring Alps and thundering rivers, lush valleys and fertile plains, and yet when I actually beheld them I was puzzled by how muted my responses were. A Eurocentric education had prepared me for a sense of recognition that I simply did not feel, and this was bewildering. The paintings and poems about these epic and apparently sublime landscapes still moved me, so I couldn't understand the queer feeling of impatience that crept up when I saw them in real time and space. To someone from an austere, sun-bleached land scape they often looked – how can I say this? – cute. Yes, they were pretty, even saccharine. Like something off a biscuit tin.

In the first instance I struggled with scale. In Europe the dimensions of physical space seemed compressed. The looming vertical presence of mountains cut me off from the distant horizon. This was a kind of spatial curtailment I hadn't lived with before. Think about it, even a city of skyscrapers is more porous than a snow-capped mountain range. You can see through London, even Sao Paulo; they're visually ventilated. But Alps form a solid, visual and conceptual barrier. For a Western Australian, whose default setting is in diametric opposition, and for whom open space is the impinging force, the effect is claustrophobic.

The second form of enclosure that weighed upon me was more obvious. European landscapes were humanised. Even the wildest – looking places were modified, including many of those seemingly implacable mountains, because around every second bend was a tunnel, a funicular, a chairlift or a resort. Above the snowline there was usually a circling helicopter. Down in the valleys and along the impossibly fertile plains, nature was only visible through the overlaid embroidery of the people who'd brought it to heel. In Ireland, France and England it seemed to me that every field and hedge was named, apportioned, owned, subsidised, accounted for. It was a landscape of almost unrelieved captivity and domestication. If they weren't fully inhabited or exploited, most open spaces were modified, so there were no real forests, only woods. Even conservation reserves were more akin to sculpted parks than wilderness. In fact there were few truly wild places left. Even the northern sky felt inhabited. At my lowest moments the European sky looked occluded, like the surface of a ruined eye.

On a bright day in Wales or the Netherlands, the light struck me as blue or slatey. As if someone in the heavens had stopped pedalling. I'd never experienced light deprivation before. I couldn't understand the gruesome moods I was subject to. (But it was a late insight into Ibsen and Kierkegaard. Those grim buggers. You can blame some of it on bad light, the rest on a diet of pork and cabbage.) I woke up one June morning in the Irish Midlands thinking I'd left the bedside light on and realised, after a few seconds' confusion that the sun was tilting in through the narrow stone window, lukewarm and unannounced like an in-law. And it wasn't only light deprivation that left me feeling sapped. I think I was instinctively, unconsciously searching for distances that were unavailable. I was calibrated differently to a European. This difference was not really linguistic or historical. The distinction was geographical; that is, corporeal.

In a seedy cinema on the rue du Temple, watching Disney's *Peter Pan* with my three-year-old son, I found that although we were all gazing at the same screen in the flickering dark, he and I were seeing a different film to the rest of the audience. What seemed fantastical and exotic to those bourgeois Parisian kids and their nannies just looked like home to me. I knew secret coves and hidey holes like those of the Lost Boys. The world of rocky islands, boats and obscuring bush was very much like my own. Only the cold, lonely nursery up in the Darling attic was exotic or fantastical. The wild opportunity of Neverland with its physical openness, lack of enclosure and freedom from adult surveillance was not so far from the ecosystem of my own boyhood. Watching it for perhaps the thirtieth time and seeing it anew, forsaking story altogether and just focusing impulsively, hungrily on the backdrop, I understood what a complete stranger I was in this hemisphere. And yet acknowledging my strangeness made those years abroad easier to digest and enjoy.

When I was born there was about a square kilometre for every person on the island continent. In global terms that's an immense amount of space. In the UK 256 people share that space. In London, 5200. In the half century since I was born Australia's population has doubled, but density is still exceptionally low. Despite a human history of perhaps 60,000 years, Australia is a place with more geography than architecture, where openness trumps enclosure. The continent has not been a lost and silent rock floating in austral seas all that time. It has not been and is not empty. For most of human history it has been walked and sung. It is hatched and laced with story, and yet there has always been more space between these cultural lines than settled perennial inhabitation. Occupation in many regions was either seasonal or notional, held in cultural skeins and webs of ritual. Because of vast distances and scarcity of permanent water, the non-human was always in the ascendant. Country may have been intimately *known* but culture rarely dominated physically, even where land was modified by fire. Culture proceeded from and deferred to country. From sheer necessity. Two centuries after European settlement and its rapid transformations, this is still a place where there is more landscape than culture.

I don't mean to imply that Australia has no culture or that its cultural life is inconsiderable. I seek only to acknowledge the fact that the continent's natural forms remain its most distinguishing features. Most Asian and European countries can be more easily defined in human terms. Mention of India, China, Italy, France or Germany will quickly bring to mind human acts and artefacts, but at first blush Australia connotes something non-human, because no post-invasion achievement, no city, nor towering monument can hold a candle to the grandeur of the land. This is not a romantic notion. Unless you think of mining as a romantic activity. And we have a few prominent citizens who do. Everything we do in our country is still overshadowed and underwritten by the seething tumult of nature. An opera house, an iron bridge, a tinsel-topped tower – these are creative marvels – but as structures they look pretty feeble against the landscape in which they stand. Think of the brooding mass and ever-changing face of Uluru. Will architects ever make stone live like this? I doubt it. Consider the bewildering scale and complexity of Purnululu, like a sculpted secret megacity. Australians are unlikely to ever build anything as beautiful and intricate. Few visitors to our shores arrive seeking the built glories of our culture. Generally they come for wildness, to experience space in a way that's unavailable, and, sadly, sometimes unimaginable in their homelands. I'm not much of a Romantic. Neither am I a self-hating utopian. I am in awe of the genius in humanity, and I love being in the great cities of the world. Some buildings feel like gifts, not impositions, but I am antipodean enough to wonder now and then whether architecture is, in the end, what you console yourself with once wild landscape has been subsumed.

I say this because space was my primary inheritance. I was formed by gaps, nurtured in the long pauses between people, part of a thin and porous human culture through which the land slanted in, seen or felt, at every angle: so, for each mechanical noise, five natural sounds; for every built structure a landform twice as large and twenty times as complex. And over it all, an impossibly open sky, dwarfing every thing, imposing a pitiless correction of human perspective.

On my island the heavens draw you out like a multidimensional horizon. In the south, which boils with gothic clouds, the sky's commotion can render you so feverish your thoughts are closer to music than language. At night in the desert the sky sucks at you, star-by-star, galaxy-by-galaxy. You feel as if you could fall out into it at any moment. It's terrifying, vertiginous. I have literally woken in a panic, digging my hands into the dirt either side of the swag to keep from pitching out into space. In Australia the sky is not the safe enclosing canopy it appears to be elsewhere. Standing alone on the Nullarbor or out on a saltpan the size of a small country, you feel a twinge of terror, even in daylight, because the sky seems to go on forever. It has dramatic depth and oceanic movement. So often the southern sky stops you in your tracks, derails your thoughts, unmoors you from what you were doing before it got you by the collar. No wonder Australian painters still insist on treating it as a worthy subject, despite the pressures to move on to something a little more 'sophisticated'.

Sometimes it feels as if our continent is more about air than matter, more pause than movement, more space than time. The landscape is not yet humanised and this is what distinguishes it.

For the moment Australia is still itself. It imprints itself upon the body, and the mind constantly struggles to catch up and make sense of it. This is why, despite the postmodern and nearly post-physical age we live and work in, Australian writers and painters continue to obsess about landscape. It's not simply that we are laggards. We are in a place where the material facts of life must still be contended with. There is more of it than us. This disparity and the physical details and peculiarities of the continent are strong and distinct enough to continue to amaze, trouble and inspire us. And we're still learning. The meeting of the human and non-human across our thin and ancient topsoil is a drama still in its early and vital stages. Elsewhere in the world this story is very often done and dusted already, with nature in stumbling retreat, but in Australia, where a small population negotiates with a larger, extant and dynamic natural environment, this drama is unresolved. Artists can no more ignore this drama than politicians.

To be a writer or an artist preoccupied with landscape is to accept a weird and constant tension between the indoors and the outdoors, the abstract and the sensual. You work from both mind and body. You need to be thin-skinned. But this has its challenges. I'm particularly thin-skinned about weather. I have a craving for physical sensation, to be in a dynamic, living system. So I seem to spend half my working life fretting and plotting escape like a schoolboy. Sat near a window as a pupil, I was a dead loss. I remain so to this day. Which is why I make myself write indoors. I can't even hang a painting in my workroom, for what else is a painting but a window? My thoughts are sucked outward; I am entranced. So a lot of the time I work in a blank cubicle, my back to the view. Which means I spend quite a bit of the day restless. I'm forever getting up to leave the room, to stand outside in the sunlight for a minute, sniffing the wind, looking at the sky, the birds, listening to the state of the ocean.

Now and then, of course, I just bolt. I pile a few chattels into the LandCruiser and put my foot down. I know many Australian men and women possessed by the same impulse. The wide open road. To drive all day until sunset and then pull over in a different state of mind. There's often no purpose to these excursions beyond the immediate sensation of being in the open, the pleasure of rolling a swag out in a creekbed or in a hollow between dunes, to sit by a fire, to feel the stars come out like gooseflesh in the heavens. I don't think of it as escape. To me it's a homing impulse. Lying under the night sky I feel a sense of return. This feeling of home-coming is not unlike the way I felt as a kid coming in the back door at dusk when the homely smell of the laundry and the slap of the screen door restored me to myself in moments.

These homecomings can be harsh and bewildering. The places dearest to me can be hard to reach. Hence the LandCruiser. They are remote, austere, savage, unpredictable. And like taciturn cous-ins and leery in-laws they're not very forthcoming. They give you the stink-eye at breakfast, do what they can to make your stay uncomfortable. But homecomings are about submitting to the uncomfortably familiar, aren't they? Like a hapless adult child, you go back for more, despite yourself, eternally trying to figure out the puzzle of relationships with parents and siblings, perplex-ities of heritage, dependency, belonging. But you get sustenance from this, from the actual trying, by remaining open to mystery. For if you give up on home, you suspect you'll be left with nothing.

My country leans in on you. It weighs down hard. Like family.

I have spent a lot of time watching Australians do this family dance with the outdoors. Urban and prosperous as they are, living beyond the constraints of weather and nature in a way their fore-bears could never have foreseen, many seek to engage in an almost ritual courtship with the outdoors. We spend billions each year on off-road vehicles, caravans, campers and outdoor recreational equipment. This cultural impulse isn't just a matter of escaping the indoor servitude of working life. There is a palpable commu-nal outward urge, a searching impulse, something embedded in our physical culture, our sensory make-up. To my mind it speaks of an implicit collective understanding that the land is still present at the corner of our eye, still *out there*, awaiting us, but also carried within, like some sense memory. There's such restlessness, such yearning. It's down hard and deep like the tap-root of a half-forgotten tree, and it shows no sign of withering away. For despite how ordered and franchised and air-conditioned contemporary life has become, the land remains a louring presence at the edge of people's minds. We've imbibed it despite ourselves; it's in our bones like a sacramental ache. Waiting for us. If not a felt pres-ence, then a looming absence. I can't count the number of times

I've been standing in a supermarket queue when a complete stranger blurts out, apropos of nothing that I can make out, that one day they're gonna chuck everything, the house, the job, and just go, pack up the Tojo, pull the kids out of school and 'just see what's out there'. If this yearning wasn't real advertisers wouldn't spend their billions exploiting it. Here you can cue the music, open the lens to the rosy light of late afternoon and dub in the breathy voiceover. 'Behold, the glory of Kakadu, the endless beaches of Fraser Island, the blood-red breakaways of Karijini, the dark and primordial mysteries of the Tarkine, the miracle of Lake Eyre in flood.' To sell something disposable and ephemeral you need to set it against something truly substantial, something remarkable and enduring. And in Australia what's more impressive than the land?

Landscape continues to press in, leaning through our windows and insect screens, creeping at the edges of consciousness. No matter how we live, and what we tell ourselves, the sublimated facts of our physical situation constantly resurface; the land continues to make its presence felt. Until climate change began to erode the modern sense of immunity in the northern hemisphere, this felt pressure of nature was almost unique to Australia amongst developed nations. Feeling subject to nature is supposedly the province of the poor in undeveloped places. The recent vulnerability of first-world countries is a sudden reversal in Europe, but in Australia it's been our vivid, steady state. If anything, climate change has only intensified what Australians have always felt – which is, at best, mildly besieged. Nowadays bushfires don't merely threaten the timbered outskirts of small Australian towns; they have infiltrated and ravaged the inner suburbs of capital cities, panicking and paralysing major populations. Similarly, major flood events are no longer just the nightmare of rural riverside communities; in recent years coastal capitals like Brisbane have been calamitously inundated. Others of course, like Perth, are so drought-weakened that without desalination plants they would no longer be viable settlements at all. Clearly, geography and weather have never been less incidental, less likely to remain mere backdrop. You only need to stand on a street corner in the central business district of Perth and watch the desert dust fall like red rain upon the gridlocked traffic to know that. Whatever else we have told ourselves, we are not yet out of nature and nature is not done with us.

Ours has always been a conditional, permeable settlement and it remains so. The land continues to confound, enchant, appal and inspire. It fizzes, groans, creaks and roars at the edge of consciousness. But I think a geographically thin skin is a boon to our culture. We need to guard against growing too thick a hide, in this sense at least. Isn't it good for the spirit, being reminded that there is something bigger to consider than ourselves, something, older, richer and more complex and mysterious than humankind? Despite our immense success, our mobility and adaptability there is still an organic, material reality over which we have little control and for which we can claim no credit.

Humans are a brilliant species, an exception, a privileged minority. And few humans are luckier than Australians. Generations of experience have transformed us. Those who arrived here in antiquity were changed and changed and changed by the continent; the land made them anew. Those of us whose roots are not as deep are startled to learn how different we are from our immigrant forebears, for our island is a place that soon renders people strangers to their own ancestors. It has real, ongoing power to shape people. It influences our thoughts and habits, our language, our sensory register. However stubbornly we resist, it knocks us about, bends us out of shape and moves us on somehow. In my own lifetime Australians have come to use the Aboriginal-English word 'country' to describe what my great-grandparents might have called territory. Slowly, fitfully, geographic ambivalence and diffidence have given way to a new respect. Patriotism has evolved to include a reverence for the land itself, and the passion to defend the natural world as if it were family. This is why we write about the island, the place, the natural physical world. This is why we paint it. From love and wonder, irritation and fear, hope and despair, because like family, it's an enduring puzzle and it refuses to be incidental.

The Weekend Australian Review

Publication Details

Caroline Baum's 'Waltzing the Jaguar' appeared in *My Mother, My Father: On Losing a Parent*, edited by Susan Wyndham, Allen & Unwin, Sydney, 2013.

J.M. Coetzee's 'The Last Instructions of Patrick White' appeared in the *New York Review of Books*, 7 November 2013.

Jessie Cole's 'The Breaking Point' appeared in *Meanjin*, vol. 72, no. 3, Spring 2013.

Peter Conrad's 'A Rolf in Sheep's Clothing' appeared in the *Monthly*, July 2014.

Robyn Davidson's 'Vale Doris Lessing' appeared in the *Monthly*, December 2013–January 2014.

Tim Flannery's 'A Natural Wonder in Peril' appeared in the *New York Review of Books*, 14 August 2014.

Helen Garner's 'Dreams of Her Real Self' appeared in *My Mother, My Father: On Losing a Parent*, edited by Susan Wyndham, Allen & Unwin, Sydney, 2013.

Moreno Giovannoni's 'The Percheron' appeared in *Southerly*, vol. 73, no. 2, 2013. The photograph 'Champlin's horse, Kronprinz' is used with permission of the Ames Historical Society.

Dennis Glover's 'Doveton' appeared in the *Age*, 8 February 2014.

Antonia Hayes's 'Wolf Like Me' appeared in *Meanjin*, vol. 73, no. 1, Autumn 2014.

Karen Hitchcock's regular column 'The Medicine' appears in the *Monthly*. The items reprinted here appeared in the November 2013, December 2013–January 2014, March 2014 and July 2014 issues.

Clive James's 'Poems of a Lifetime' appeared in the *Times Literary Supplement*, 18 May 2014, and in his *Poetry Notebook: 2006–2014* (Picador, 2014); it is used with permission of the publisher. Copyright © Clive James, 2014.

Rozanna Lilley's 'The Little Prince, and Other Vehicles' appeared in *Southerly*, vol. 74, no. 1, 2014.

David Malouf's 'Oh Walt, You're a Leaky Vessel' appeared in *Sydney Review of Books*, 5 July 2014.

David Marr's 'Freedom Abbott' appeared in the *Monthly*, September 2014. The essay grew out of the 2014 John Button Lecture for the Melbourne School of Government, delivered on 23 July 2014.

Luke Mogelson's 'The Dream Boat' appeared in the *New York Times Magazine*, 17 November 2013.

Neil Murray's 'Cry When We're Gone' appeared in *The Best Music Writing Under the Australian Sun*, edited by Christian Ryan, Hardie Grant Books, Melbourne, 2014.

Rachel Nolan's 'Men of a Certain Age' appeared in the *Monthly*, May 2014.

Noel Pearson's 'War of the Worlds' is an excerpt from his *A Rightful Place* (Quarterly Essay 55), Black Inc., Melbourne, 2014.

Nicolas Rothwell's 'The Agony and the Ecstasy' appeared in the *Weekend Australian Review*, 18–19 January 2014.

Guy Rundle's 'Burning Men: An American Triptych' appeared in *Crikey/Daily Review*, 29 January 2014 (on Pete Seeger); 23 May 2014 (on *True Detective*); and 28 May 2014 (on Elliot Rodger).

Christian Ryan's 'The Unremembered Six' appeared in *The Nightwatchman*, Spring 2014.

Luke Ryan's 'Sex and Cancer: A History in Three Parts' appeared in his book *A Funny Thing Happened on the Way to Chemo: A Memoir of Getting Cancer – Twice!*, Affirm Press, Melbourne, 2014.

Carrie Tiffany's 'Reading Geoff Cochrane' appeared in *Griffith Review*, no. 43, January 2014.

Christos Tsiolkas's 'May Day: How the Left Was Lost' appeared in the *Monthly*, May 2014.

Don Watson's 'My Fellow Australians' appeared in *Good Weekend*, 25 January 2014.

Tim Winton's 'The Island Seen and Felt: Some Thoughts about Landscape' appeared in the *Weekend Australian Review*, 14–15 December 2013. It is an edited transcript of his speech to the Royal Academy, London, on 14 November 2013.

Notes on Contributors

Robert Manne was professor of politics at La Trobe University until December 2012. Presently, he is Vice-Chancellor's Fellow at La Trobe and the convenor of its Ideas & Society Program. His books include *Left, Right, Left: Political Essays 1977–2005, W.E.H. Stanner: The Dreaming and Other Essays* (ed.), *Making Trouble: Essays against the New Australian Complacency, Bad News: Murdoch's Australian and the Shaping of the Nation* (Quarterly Essay 43) and *The Words That Made Australia: How a Nation Came to Know Itself* (ed.). In 2012 he was shortlisted for the Melbourne Prize for Literature. *State of the Nation: Essays for Robert Manne* was published by Black Inc. in October 2013.

CONTRIBUTORS

Caroline Baum is the editorial director of Booktopia, Australia's largest online bookseller. She writes for the *Sydney Morning Herald*, Qantas inflight magazine, *Slow Magazine, SBS Feast* and other publications about books, food, travel, the arts and aspects of contemporary life.

J.M. Coetzee was born in South Africa and educated in South Africa and the United States. He has published twelve works of fiction, as well as criticism and translations. He has won the Booker Prize (twice) and, in 2003, the Nobel Prize for Literature. He lives in Adelaide.

Jessie Cole's debut novel *Darkness on the Edge of Town* was short-listed for the 2013 ALS Gold Medal, and her non-fiction work has appeared in the *Big Issue*, *Daily Life*, the *Saturday Paper*, *Meanjin* and the *Guardian*. Her latest novel, *Deeper Water*, was published in August 2014. She lives and works in northern New South Wales.

Peter Conrad lives in London and New York. His latest books are *Verdi and/or Wagner* and *How the World Was Won: The Americanization of Everywhere*, published by Thames & Hudson. He has recently written and presented a BBC Radio 4 series on '21st Century Mythologies', updating Roland Barthes.

Robyn Davidson is an award-winning writer who has travelled and published widely. Her books include *Tracks*, *Desert Places*, *No Fixed Address: Nomads and the Future of the Planet* (Quarterly Essay 24) and, as editor, *The Picador Book of Journeys*. The screen adaptation of *Tracks* was released by Transmission Films in 2014.

Tim Flannery has published over a dozen books, including *The Future Eaters*, *The Eternal Frontier*, *The Weather Makers*, *Now or Never: A Sustainable Future for Australia?* and *Here on Earth*. He was Australian of the Year in 2007.

Helen Garner was born in Geelong in 1942 and lives in Melbourne. Since 1977 she has published eleven books of fiction, essays and long-form non-fiction, including *The First Stone* and *Joe Cinque's Consolation*, as well as screenplays and feature journalism. She won the inaugural Melbourne Prize for Literature in 2006. She is a frequent contributor to the *Monthly*, and her most recent book is *This House of Grief*.

Moreno Giovannoni grew up on a tobacco farm at Buffalo River in north-east Victoria but was born in San Ginese, where he left a large part of himself. He lives in Melbourne, where he works as a freelance translator. He is writing a book, *Tales from San Ginese*.

Dennis Glover is a speechwriter and freelance author. He is the son of factory workers from Doveton and has degrees from Monash and Cambridge universities. He has written speeches for every federal Labor leader since Kim Beazley and is the author of *Orwell's Australia* (Scribe, 2003) and *The Art of Great Speeches* (CUP, 2010).

Antonia Hayes is a writer from Sydney who lives in San Francisco. *Relativity*, her debut novel, will be published in 2015.

Karen Hitchcock is a doctor and writer. She is a regular contributor to the *Monthly*, and the author of a collection of short fiction, *Little White Slips*.

Clive James is the author of more than forty books. As well as his five volumes of autobiography, he has published collections of literary and television criticism, essays, travel writing, verse and novels. In 2003 he was awarded the Philip Hodgins Memorial Medal for Literature, and he is a Fellow of the Royal Society of Literature. His latest book is *Poetry Notebook: 2006–2014* (Picador, 2014).

Rozanna Lilley is a social anthropologist and an author. She has published widely in journals, books and, more recently, literary reviews and magazines. Her current research is on autism and social life. The youngest daughter of writers Dorothy Hewett and Merv Lilley, she is working on a memoir of family eccentricities.

David Malouf is the author of eleven novels, as well as collections of stories, poetry and libretti. He has won the International IMPAC Dublin Literary Award, the Commonwealth Writers' Prize, the Los Angeles Times Book Award, the Prix Femina Étranger and the Australia–Asia Literary Award; he has also been shortlisted for the Booker Prize. He lives in Australia.

David Marr has written for the *Sydney Morning Herald*, the *Age* and the *Monthly*, been editor of the *National Times*, a reporter for *Four Corners*, presenter of ABC TV's *Media Watch* and now writes for the *Guardian*. His books include *Patrick White: A Life*, *The High Price of Heaven*, *Dark Victory* (with Marian Wilkinson) and four Quarterly Essays: *His Master's Voice*, *Power Trip*, *Political Animal* and *The Prince*.

Luke Mogelson is a contributing writer for the *New York Times Magazine*. Based in Kabul, Afghanistan, Mogelson has also worked for *GQ*, *Harper's*, the *Nation* and the *Washington Monthly*. His fiction has appeared in the *Hudson Review, Kenyon Review* and *Missouri Review*.

A founding member of the Warumpi Band, **Neil Murray** has released a dozen solo albums, received an APRA song of the year award, and published stories, lyrics, poems, a play and the auto-biographical novel *Sing for Me, Countryman*.

Rachel Nolan was Transport, then Finance and Arts Minister in Queensland's Bligh Labor Government. Since leaving politics she has travelled extensively; she has just completed an overland journey from Ireland to Australia (excepting warzones). She now writes, owns a café in her hometown of Ipswich, and teaches English to migrants.

Noel Pearson is a lawyer and activist, and chairman of the Cape York Partnership. He has published many essays and newspaper articles. His first book, *Up from the Mission* (2009), is a collection of essays that charts his life and thought from his early days as a native title lawyer to his position today as one of Australia's most influential figures.

Nicolas Rothwell was educated in European schools and was a classical scholar at Magdalen College, Oxford, before becoming a foreign correspondent. He is the author of *Heaven & Earth*, *Wings of the Kite-Hawk*, *Another Country*, *The Red Highway* and *Journeys to the Interior*.

Guy Rundle is the global correspondent-at-large for Crikey. He is the author of *Down to the Crossroads: On the Trail of the 2008 US Presidential Election*, and two Quarterly Essays, *The Opportunist* and *Bipolar Nation*.

Christian Ryan is the author of *Golden Boy, Australia: Story of a Cricket Country* and most recently *Rock Country*, a thirty-three-essay, 160-photo, multi-authored trip into Australian rock music.

His recent essays include 'Five Pictures', 'Gone Crabbing' and 'Jeff Thomson is Annoyed'. He is a former editor of the *Monthly*.

Luke Ryan is a freelance writer, comedian and man about town. He writes short-form non-fiction with a comic edge and has just released his debut book, *A Funny Thing Happened on the Way to Chemo* (Affirm Press), a comedy memoir about having had cancer a couple of times.

Sybille Smith (née Gottwald) was born in Vienna and arrived in Australia with her family in 1939. She studied English and German at Sydney University and then taught German at the University of Tasmania. Her study *Inside Poetry* first appeared in 1985.

Carrie Tiffany was born in West Yorkshire and grew up in Western Australia. She spent her early twenties working as a park ranger in Central Australia and now lives in Melbourne, where she works as an agricultural journalist. Carrie has published two award-winning novels: *Everyman's Rules for Scientific Living* and *Mateship with Birds*.

Christos Tsiolkas is the author of four novels: *Loaded* (filmed as *Head On*), *The Jesus Man* and *Dead Europe*, which won the 2006 *Age* Fiction Prize and the 2006 Melbourne Best Writing Award. *The Slap* won the 2009 Commonwealth Writers' Prize and was shortlisted for the 2009 Miles Franklin Award and the ALS Gold Medal. He is also a playwright, essayist and screenwriter. He lives in Melbourne.

Don Watson's columns, articles and essays have appeared in all major Australian journals and newspapers. His book *American Journeys* (2008) won the *Age* Non-Fiction and Book of the Year awards, the inaugural Indie Award for Non-Fiction, and the Walkley Award for Non-Fiction.

Tim Winton has published twenty-six books for adults and children, and his work has been translated into twenty-eight languages. Since his first novel, *An Open Swimmer*, won the *Australian*

Vogel Award in 1981, he has won the Miles Franklin Award four times (for *Shallows*, *Cloudstreet*, *Dirt Music* and *Breath*), and has twice been shortlisted for the Booker Prize (for *The Riders* and *Dirt Music*). He lives in Western Australia.